Ministry issues
for the Church of England

Also available by Gordon Kuhrt:

An Introduction to Christian Ministry
(Church House Publishing, 2000)

Ministry issues
for the Church of England
mapping the trends

Gordon W. Kuhrt

CHURCH HOUSE
PUBLISHING

Church House Publishing
Church House
Great Smith Street
London SW1P 3NZ

ISBN 0 7151 8122 X

Published 2001 by Church House Publishing

Typeset in Rotis by Vitaset, Paddock Wood, Kent.

Printed by The Cromwell Press Ltd, Trowbridge, Wiltshire

Contents

Contents

Contents

Tables

Diagrams

Contributors

Revd Preb. Dr Paul Avis is Secretary for the Council for Christian Unity and to the House of Bishops' Working Party on the Renewed Diaconate.

Rt Revd Edwin Barnes is Bishop of Richborough and Provincial Episcopal Visitor in the Province of Canterbury.

Revd Canon Lesley Bentley is Vicar of St Philip, Westbrook, Warrington. She is also Dean of Women's Ministries, Diocese of Liverpool, and Chair of the National Association of Diocesan Advisers in Women's Ministry.

Revd Canon Dr Tony Chesterman is Adviser on CME to the Bishop of Derby.

Revd Canon James Clarke is Secretary for Ministry among Deaf People, Ministry Division.

Martin Elengorn is Pastoral Secretary, Church Commissioners.

Revd Ferial Etherington is Ordained Ministry Co-ordinator, Ministry Division.

Revd Neil R. Evans is CME Officer for the Kensington Episcopal Area, Diocese of London.

Shaun Farrell is Financial Secretary to the Archbishops' Council.

Revd Canon John Hall is General Secretary of the Board of Education and the National Society.

Ven. Alan F. Hawker is Archdeacon of Malmesbury (Diocese of Bath) and Chairman of the Working Party that produced *Under Authority* and of the Steering Committee for the legislation.

Dr Mark Hodge is Grants Officer, Ministry Division.

Canon Michael Hodge is Synodical Secretary, Convocation of Canterbury.

Mrs Hilary Ineson was formerly Adviser in Adult Education and Training for the Board of Education.

Margaret Jeffery is Secretary for Deployment, Remuneration and Conditions of Service, Ministry Division.

Ven. David Jenkins is Synodal Secretary, Convocation of York.

Captain Philip Johanson is Chief Secretary of the Church Army.

Ven. Dr Gordon W. Kuhrt is Director of the Ministry Division and was a member of the drafting and Steering Committees for the legislation on Women and ordination to the priesthood.

Revd Charles Lawrence is Chairman of the Vocations Committee, CMEAC.

Revd John Lee is Clergy Appointments Officer.

Revd Giles Legood is the University Chaplain, Diocese of London.

Revd Dr John Mantle is Archbishops' Adviser for Bishops' Ministry.

David Morris is Finance and Administrative Secretary, Ministry Division.

Revd Dr John Muddiman is G.B. Caird Fellow and Tutor in Theology at Mansfield College, Oxford, and Chair of the Theological Education and Training Committee, Ministry Division.

Canon Pat Nappin is Honorary Secretary of the Central Readers' Council, a retired Head Teacher and a Lay Canon of Chelmsford Cathedral.

Revd David Parrott is Team Rector of Rayleigh, Rural Dean of Rochford, author of *Situations Vacant: A Guide to the Appointment Process in the Church of England (1999)* and *Patronage (Benefices) Measure 1986: An Analysis of its Working in Practice* (1999).

Revd Dr Marilyn Parry was formerly National Adviser for Pre-Theological Education, Ministry Division.

Canon Bryan Pettifer is a former staff member, Ministry Division (1994–7).

Ven. Nigel Peyton is Archdeacon of Newark. He was formerly Dual Role Minister, 1991–9, Priest-in-Charge, Lambley, and Diocesan Ministry Development Adviser.

Roger Radford is Secretary of the Church of England Pensions Board.

Mrs Margaret Sentamu is Senior Selection Secretary, Ministry Division.

Patrick Shorrock is Assistant Secretary for Deployment, Remuneration and Conditions of Service, Ministry Division.

Revd Mark Sowerby was formerly Vocations Officer, Ministry Division.

Rt Revd David Stancliffe is Bishop of Salisbury and Chairman of the Liturgical Commission.

Revd Ian Stubbs is Adviser in Adult and Lifelong Learning, Board of Education.

Revd Helen M. Thorp is the Vocations Adviser with responsibility for care of non-recommended candidates, Diocese of Durham. She is also a part-time tutor at Cranmer Hall, Durham and an NSM at St Gabriel, Bishopwearmouth.

Mrs Wendy Thorpe is Honorary National Moderator of Reader Training.

Rt Revd Michael Turnbull is Bishop of Durham and Chairman of the Ministry Division, 1998–2001.

Mrs Hilary Unwin is Diocesan Adviser for Accredited Lay Ministry, Diocese of Oxford.

Dr Alan Wakely is Honorary Deputy Secretary of the Central Readers Council.

Revd Dr David Way is Theological Education Secretary, Ministry Division.

Revd Flora Winfield is Secretary for Local Unity, Council for Christian Unity.

Preface

This report is more like a building site than a completed and decorated monument. It offers a series of pictures and snapshots of ministry issues, many of which are moving and changing. In the Introduction, I have spoken of mapping the terrain – but new footpaths are emerging, and every so often a new motorway is under construction or opened.

This report is not a proposed strategy for aspects of ministry in the tradition of Leslie Paul (1964) and John Tiller (1983). It is more modest in that it seeks to offer aspects of a menu of options for the Archbishops' Council and House of Bishops to consider. It is also far more wide-ranging, and the contributions of many distinguished experts give it some real authority as a survey.

The chapters written by me are the fruit especially of five years of extensive travels and many visits to dioceses, deaneries, parishes, colleges, courses and training institutions of other denominations.

Gordon Kuhrt

Foreword by the Bishop of Guildford

I am delighted to commend the important contribution to our understanding of ministry in the Church, which Gordon Kuhrt has made in the writing of this book. I am sure that it will provide us both with a coherent and comprehensive body of information and perspective on where we are at this present time and also with a map to guide us in making decisions for the future. I hope that people will study this book very carefully and make excellent use of the wealth of information and perspective that it contains.

As Chair of the Ministry Division of the Archbishops' Council, I am enormously grateful to Gordon in the midst of a busy life as Director of the Division for achieving this piece of work and for all that it represents.

✠ John Guildford
Chairman, Ministry Division

Foreword by Professor Derek Portwood

Organizations today are acutely aware of the need to make the most of all types of capital – not solely that of their financial resources and fixed assets but also their social, cultural and intellectual capital, particularly the knowledge capital of their employees, partners, customers and suppliers. In turn, this has made them realize that they must enhance and exploit all kinds of knowledge – contemplative and performative, propositional and procedural.

The intention of Dr Gordon Kuhrt's report is to address these matters, fundamentally and futuristically, for the Church of England, thereby making a definitive contribution to a national strategy for the ministry of the Church of England.

With such an ambition, one asks about the accuracy of the data, the clarity of the analysis and the persuasiveness of the argument. Significantly, for these purposes, Dr Kuhrt undertook his study and research within the demands of an academic doctoral programme. This clearly has ensured that he used relevant literature, appropriate research instruments and the knowledge of authorities in his field. Indeed, a notable feature of his work is how he has solicited and orchestrated specialized contributions while retaining the distinctiveness of his own voice.

However, the ambitions of this report could not be attained by academic means alone. They required professional learning and commitment of the highest order. Dr Kuhrt's well-known passion for the well-being of the Church through an effective ministry supplied them. In consequence, this report will engage the head and heart of anyone concerned with the ministry of the Church of England, and, I suspect, with those of other Christian denominations as well.

What is specially pleasing is that Dr Kuhrt avoids prescription but offers instead comprehensive information and judicious understanding for individuals, groups and agencies to apply to their situation. Consequently the report is both a reference work and a document for action.

As a bonus for us in the academic world, it is an exceptional example of work at professional doctorate level which students and scholars in any professional field would do well to emulate.

Professor Derek Portwood
Middlesex University

Acknowledgements

I am grateful for continual encouragement from the Archbishops of Canterbury and York. The three Chairmen of the Advisory Board of Ministry/Ministry Division have also given unfailing support – they are the Bishops of Hereford (until 1998), of Durham (1998–2000) and now of Guildford. I am grateful too for the encouragement of Philip Mawer, Secretary-General of the Archbishops' Council and General Synod.

Colleagues in the Ministry Division and beyond include both staff and members of committees, working groups, training institutions and dioceses – see Chapter 2 for more detail. I have received kind hospitality throughout the country – and beyond. Over 40 others have contributed material to Chapters 3 and 9–43 (fully acknowledged in the Contents pages and over their sections). The willingness of experts and enthusiasts to be constrained to such modest limits has been impressive and kind. My thanks to each one.

My consultant and supervisor has been Professor Derek Portwood of the University of Middlesex National Centre for Work-Based Learning Partnerships. His enthusiasm, encouragement and advice have been of the highest order. The university seminars were very stimulating, especially the inter-disciplinary dimensions. Last, but by no means least, my assistant/secretary Ros Miskin has been an enthusiastic and meticulous colleague in the recent months of writing and editing.

I have an immense affection for, and indebtedness to, the Church of England. It has been a privilege to live and work in it and for it over the past 40 years as layman, Reader, vicar, archdeacon and now Director of Ministry. If this report brings clarity, encouragement and a stimulus to further appropriate reform and renewal in its ministry and mission I shall be glad.

Abbreviations

ABM	Advisory Board of Ministry
AC	Archbishops' Council
ACCM	Advisory Council for the Church's Ministry
ACCM 22	ACCM Occasional Paper No. 22, *Education for the Church's Ministry*
ACORA	Archbishops' Commission on Rural Areas
ACS	Additional Curates' Society
ACUPA	Archbishop of Canterbury's Commission on Urban Priority Areas
ALM	Accredited Lay Ministry
ALW	Accredited Lay Worker
AOCM	Association of Ordinands and Candidates for Ministry
AP(E)L	Accredited Prior (Experience and) Learning
APM	Assistant Parish (or Pastoral) Minister
ARCIC	Anglican–Roman Catholic International Commission
ASB	Alternative Service Book, 1980
BCM	Bishops' Committee for Ministry
BCP	Book of Common Prayer, 1662
BEM	*Baptism, Eucharist and Ministry*
BFBS	British and Foreign Bible Society
CA	Church Army
CACTM	Central Advisory Council for the Ministry
CATS	Credit Accumulation and Transfer System
CBDTI	Carlisle and Blackburn Diocesan Training Institute
CBF	Central Board of Finance
CC	Church Commissioners
CCHE	Church Colleges of Higher Education
CEN	*Church of England Newspaper*
CFMT	Central Fund for Ministerial Training
CHP	Church House Publishing
CIO	Church Information Office
CME(D)	Continuing Ministerial Education (and Development)
CMEAC	Committee for Minority Ethnic Anglican Concerns

CMDP	Committee for Ministry Among Deaf People
CofE	Church of England
CPAS	Church Pastoral Aid Society
CRC	Central Readers' Council
CSA	Central Stipends Authority
CT	*Church Times*
CTI	Careers and Training International
CTS	Catholic Truth Society
CUF	Church Urban Fund
DBF	Diocesan Board of Finance
DBS	Diocesan Basic Stipend
DDO	Diocesan Director of Ordinands
DLT	Darton, Longman and Todd (Publisher)
DRCSC	Deployment, Remuneration and Conditions of Service Committee
DRM	Dual Role Minister (or Ministry)
EAMTC	East Anglia Ministry Training Course
EJM	Ecclesiastical Jurisdiction Measure
EKI	Edward King Institute for Ministry Development
ELS	Ecclesiastical Law Society
EMMTC	East Midlands Ministry Training Course
EVP	Educational Validation Panel
GROU	*God's Reign and Our Unity,* 1984
GS	General Synod
HMSO	Her Majesty's Stationery Office
IDC	Inter-Diocesan Certificate
IMEC	Initial Ministerial Education Committee
IVP	Inter-Varsity Press
LEA	Local Education Authority
LEP	Local Ecumenical Project
LMA	Lay Ministry Adviser
LNSM	Local Non-Stipendiary Minister
MADP	Ministry Among Deaf People
MDDC	Ministry Development and Deployment Committee
MDP	Ministry Development Programme
MSE	Minister in Secular Employment
MSF	Manufacturing, Science and Finance Union
NADAWM	National Association of Diocesan Advisers for Women's Ministry

NEOC	North East Oecumenical (Ordination) Course
NMS	National Minimum Stipend
NOC	Northern Ordination Course
NS	The National Society (Church of England) for Promoting Religious Education
NSB	National Stipend Benchmark
NSM	Non-Stipendiary Minister
NTMTC	North Thames Ministry Training Course
NVQ	National Vocational Qualification
OLM	Ordained Local Minister (Ministry)
OUP	Oxford University Press
PCC	Parochial Church Council
PDT	Projected Diocesan Total (of stipendiary clergy)
PEV	Provincial Episcopal Visitor
PIM	Partners-in-Mission
POT	Post Ordination Training
PTE	Pre-Theological Education
RC	Roman Catholic
Resolutions A and B	Provisions in Women Priests Measure
RSB	Regional Stipends Benchmark
RSC	Recruitment and Selection Committee
RSCM	Royal School of Church Music
RTP	Readers' Training Panel
SAOMTC	St Albans' and Oxford Ministry Training Course
SCM	Student Christian Movement (Press)
SEITE	South-East Institute for Theological Education
SM	Stipendiary Minister (Ministry)
SPCK	Society for Promoting Christian Knowledge (Publisher)
STETS	Southern Theological Education and Training Scheme
SWMTC	South West Ministry Training Course
TETC	Theological Education and Training Committee
UPA	Urban Priority Area
URC	United Reformed Church
VRSC	Vocation, Recruitment and Selection Committee
WEMTC	West of England Ministry Training Course
WMMTC	West Midlands Ministry Training Course

Part 1

Ministry and strategy

Introduction: the call for this report

When I was appointed in 1996 as Chief Secretary of the (then designated) Advisory Board of Ministry, I was immediately 'invited' (or charged) by the archbishops to prepare a paper on *Issues in Theological Education and Training*. I did this in conjunction with visits to all the theological colleges and courses. In the Foreword to the resulting report, the Bishop of Hereford (who was at that time chairman of the board) wrote:

> There have been some notable developments in this field in recent years, and this paper surveys the recent past, identifies the most significant achievements, and deals clearly and helpfully with current issues of debate. It is particularly valuable in countering the charges which are occasionally heard that the Church of England has no strategy in the field of theological education and training, and has been slow to adapt to rapidly changing circumstances. This paper paints an encouraging picture of the way in which the Church has in fact coped with change, the evolution of new ministry, and of progress in ecumenical co-operation. It contains a remarkable amount of information, which has not previously been gathered together in this way.

The Bishops' Committee for Ministry and the Archbishops' Council itself has, on several occasions in the last two or three years, pressed for a similar document on the whole range of ministry issues. Maps help people find their direction. But maps are of different kinds. If you wish to travel from (say) Newcastle to a particular street in London you may use three maps:

1. the map of main line train services

2. the London Underground map of tube trains

3. a local street map of the district.

Similarly, if you wish to think about the direction(s) of ministry, you may well need to bear in mind maps on different kinds of scale. Most people, quite understandably, have a particular interest in, and concern for, their local district or parish. Here they have neighbours, local shops, schools, GP and church. But that local, relatively small, area is part of a larger unit – in civic terms it may be a borough or county, in Church of England terms it is a diocese with its bishop. Then again, that larger area is part of a national network.

Many ministry issues are worked through at the local *parish* level, e.g. election of churchwardens, and the Parochial Church Council, and the appointment of leaders in children's and youth work, house groups, Alpha and Emmaus groups, etc. Other kinds of ministry are crucially ordained or authorized at the diocesan level by the bishop. These include the ordained ministries of priest/presbyter and deacon, and that of Reader. Finally, there are some ministry issues where a *national* perspective and coherence is currently required, e.g. selection, training and financial support of ordinands, and the deployment and remuneration of clergy.

This brings us to the *purpose* of this report –

1. Most people (even if they are very interested) only know parts of the picture. This report aims to present *a map of the main issues* – the main lines or motorways. Only brief introductions can be offered to these, but travellers will be signposted to where they can find more detailed information on the lines and roads where they have special interest.

2. It is sometimes alleged that ministry policies in the Church of England are essentially pragmatic, ad hoc, finance-led and without vision or coherent strategy. This report will indicate not only *what* is being done but also *why*, i.e. the principles underlying the policies.

3. Ministry issues are many and complex. We will seek to show, in addition, the way in which

   – they interlock and impact on each other
   – they are often moving, and/or under major review at present and/or are subject to external pressures in the short or medium term, pressures which are substantially unpredictable.

4. During times of substantial and fast-moving change (as the ones in which we live) there are understandably hopes and even demands for grand strategy. This report will seek to indicate:

   ● where strategic thinking is in place in certain areas of ministry issues at the national level
   ● how strategic thinking is widespread and coherent in many dioceses across the country
   ● where fresh strategic thinking is actually underway
   ● where other areas need further consideration in the months and years ahead.

We seek to give vital information which may enable the development of grand strategy or may indicate that, in the present circumstances (social, financial and ecclesiastical), such a concept might not be entirely helpful.

The metaphor of maps assisting a journey may well be helpful in many ways. However, like other illustrations, analogies and metaphors it is inadequate to express the rich complexity of dimensions. A two-dimensional linear model is certainly inadequate. I have already indicated the *three* primary dimensions in spatial locality of ministry thinking, decision-making and activity:

the parish and/or benefice

the diocese

the nation.

Many would wish to insert the deanery as well. In addition to these levels, time and history play their part. Repeatedly, we will be looking back to discover evidence highly relevant to concerns today, and also to compare and contrast with aspects of the situations today.

The journey is multi-dimensional with scores of linking pathways, and with rich historical dimensions which may be judged for good or ill but cannot be lightly ignored.

1

The contexts – changes in the last two decades

Before 1980

In the Introduction our present era was described as a time of substantial and fast-moving change. In 1983, one of my distinguished predecessors, John Tiller, published his famous report, *A Strategy for the Church's Ministry*. He followed Bernice Martin (*A Sociology of Contemporary Cultural Change*, 1981) in asserting that 'Britain is presently at a time of significant cultural change: the "counter-culture" has led no-where, but having happened, there can be no return to the old order' (p. 12). The times were described as:

culturally	post-Romantic	leading to 'permissiveness'
economically	post-industrial	leading to information dominance
religiously	post-Christian	leading to pluralism

Martin is quoted: 'In the last few decades the Western world has experienced a transformation in the assumptions and habitual practices which form the cultural bedrock of the daily lives of ordinary people' (p. 1).

Losing faith?

The National Centre for Social Research publishes an annual survey of Britain's changing social values. The latest edition is *British Social Attitudes: Focusing on Diversity* (2000–01 edition, Sage). Chapter 6 is entitled 'Losing Faith: is Britain alone?' Its conclusions are:

Faith and practice

Britain is becoming a less religious country than it used to be and it now has one of the least religious populations in the world. Allegiance to the Church of England has fallen the most in recent years. In 1983, 40 per cent said they 'belonged' to the Church of England and now only 27 per cent do so. In the same period, the proportion of people who say they belong to no religion has grown from 31 per cent to 44 per cent. Even so, over a half of adults in Britain still belong to a religion and nearly a half (48 per cent) say they 'believe in God and always have done' – a proportion that has remained stable for around ten years.

Is Britain alone?

In contrast with Britain, religious adherence in the US is 86 per cent and in Italy 92 per cent. Only the Netherlands (with 42 per cent) comes lower than Britain.

At the same time the recent research by David Hay and Kate Hunt at the Centre for the Study of Human Relations at Nottingham University indicates other significant factors.

> People may be 'very remote indeed from the Christian institutions', or detaching themselves from the mainstream churches at an alarming rate. Nevertheless, a statistical survey under the title *Soul of Britain* shows that just over 76 per cent of the national population are now likely to admit to having had a spiritual or religious experience, compared with 48 per cent in 1987. The percentage increases are across the board, including 'awareness of the presence of God' (increased from 27 per cent to 38 per cent over a 13-year period) and 'awareness of prayer being answered' (a rise from 25 per cent to 37 per cent over the same period). (Quotations from the *Springboard Newsletter*, ed. Martin Cavender, January 2001.)

Church attendance

In 1989 Dr Peter Brierley of the Christian Research Association conducted an English Church Census which was analysed in *Christian England* (1991). This was followed by the 1998 English Church Attendance Survey which was analysed in *The Tide is Running Out* (2000). Its key findings were (pp. 9–10):

- The steep decline in numbers attending church on Sunday in the 1980s has continued at about the same rate in the 1990s.
- The actual decline in the 1990s has been made much worse by the large numbers of churchgoers (about a third) now attending less frequently than they used to.
- Whereas 12 per cent of the English population went to church weekly each Sunday in 1979, and 10 per cent in 1989, this has dropped to 7.5 per cent in 1998.
- A further 2.7 per cent attend once or twice a month, and another 6.0 per cent less frequently.

- Many attend worship services during the week instead of on Sunday, equivalent to a further 0.9 per cent of the population, half in adult services and half at special youth events. A further 2.4 per cent of the population go to mid-week church activities but do not attend church on Sunday.

- Many others are involved in church-like activities but not at church, such as the 1.9 per cent of the population who watch *Songs of Praise* but who do not go to church, or the 0.4 per cent of the population at an Alpha course.

- There is, however, a very serious decline in the number of children (under 15 years of age) attending church. We are currently losing 1,000 a week (net).

- The number of older people, 65 or over, attending church on Sunday, however, is increasing, with 32,000 more in 1998 than in 1989.

- One person in eight going to church is non-white, double the percentage in the general population.

- In the late 1990s far fewer churches were being started than in the early 1990s.

- Evangelicals have declined less than non-evangelicals; the mainstream have grown while broad and charismatic evangelicals have declined.

- The charismatics however have the greatest expectancy of significant growth by 2010, but they account for only 14 per cent of all English churchgoers.

One of the most significant tables is (p. 95):

Table 1: Numbers going to church on Sunday, 1979–98

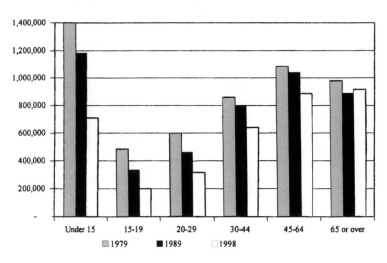

Brierley comments: 'We have therefore a very serious situation – the flight of our youth, the increasing decline of those in "working age", albeit set off slightly by a return of those of grandparent age.'

These findings need to be complemented by the analysis in *Statistics: A Tool for Mission* (2000). This report of the Statistics Review Group argues that the usual Sunday attendance of adults no longer seems appropriate as the sole measure of church attendance. It argues for a new statistic, to be known as the Average Weekly Attendance (AWA). This is defined as the average (over four specified weeks) of the total adult and child weekly attendance (see p. 24).

Shaun Farrell adds:

> There has been much debate in the Church recently about the question of church membership and how it should be measured and recorded. The Archbishops' Council recently received a presentation from Lynda Barley, the Head of Statistics, on the recommendations of the Statistics Review Group chaired by the Bishop of Wakefield. The membership information recently published in Church Statistics 1998 gave a mixed picture with the number of people on electoral rolls rising by 1.7 per cent, Easter Day communicants up 1.8 per cent and baptisms of teenagers and adults up by 2.8 per cent. On the other hand, usual Sunday attendance decreased by 1.5 per cent, Christmas Day communicants by 2.6 per cent and baptisms amongst children and infants by 6 per cent. By any measure it is apparent that the age profile of Church membership is increasing. (GS Misc 627, p. 11, s. 36)

Postmodernism

The last two decades have seen the ever-increasing articulation of 'postmodernism'. There are now countless expositions of this complex phenomenon which indicates a paradigm shift in the perceptions of many. Heather Wraight has proposed five key elements:

- Spirituality without Christianity
- Environment without a Creator
- Words without meaning
- Individuality without belonging
- The present without a future.

(quoted in P. Brierley, *The Tide is Running Out*, p. 16)

Introductions which have proved helpful include:

> Graham Cray, *From Here to Where? The Culture of the Nineties*, Board of Mission, 1992
>
> Graham Cray, *The Gospel and Tomorrow's Culture*, CPAS, 1994
>
> *Tomorrow is Another Country: Education in a Post-Modern World*, Board of Education, CHP, 1996

In a lecture in 1995, Graham Cray (now Bishop of Maidstone) spoke of

> loss of the past — so emphasis on the present
> loss of world-view — so pluralism, relativism, individualism
> loss of depth — so superficiality, indifference.

There has been a shift from emphasis on truth and progress to experience and choice.

Mission contexts

This cannot be the place for an extensive discussion about social change in England. Reference has been made to increasing secularization, declining Sunday congregations in churches and to aspects of postmodernist perceptions. The missiological contexts of ministry in this country have been addressed by a series of publications largely from the Board of Mission. Particular attention is drawn to:

Good News in our Times: The Gospel and Contemporary Cultures, CHP, 1991

John Finney, *Finding Faith Today: How Does It Happen?*, British and Foreign Bible Society, 1992

Breaking New Ground: Church Planting in the Church of England, CHP, 1994

Robert Warren, *Being Human, Being Church: Spirituality and Mission in the Local Church*, Marshall Pickering, 1995

Robert Warren, *Building Missionary Congregations: Towards a Post-Modern Way of Being Church*, CHP, 1995

A Time for Sharing: Collaborative Ministry in Mission, CHP, 1995

The Search for Faith and the Witness of the Church, CHP, 1996

Robert Warren, *Signs of Life: How Goes the Decade of Evangelism?*, CHP, 1996

The Way of Renewal, CHP, 1998

Setting the Agenda: Report of the 1999 Church of England Conference on Evangelism, CHP, 1999

Janice Price, *Telling our Faith Story*, CHP, 1999

Major attention has been given to the urban and rural contexts of mission and ministry in:

Faith in the City, CHP, 1985
Living Faith in the City: A Progress Report, CHP, 1990
Staying in the City: Faith in the City Ten Years On, CHP, 1995
Faith in the Countryside, Churchman Publishing, 1990

The growing awareness of, and concern for, minority ethnic concerns and disability issues will receive special attention in Chapters 10 and 11.

Children and young people

The Church Attendance Survey of 1998 draws particular attention to the very serious decline in the numbers of children and young people attending church. The Church of England's Board of Education has, with others, published various reports analysing aspects of the situation, e.g.:

Children in the Way: New Directions for the Church's Children, National Society and CHP, 1988
All God's Children? Children's Evangelism in Crisis, National Society and CHP, 1991
On the Way: Towards an Integrated Approach to Christian Initiation, CHP, 1995
Youth A Part: Young People and the Church, National Society and CHP, 1996
M. Green and C. Christian, *Accompanying Young People on Their Spiritual Quest*, National Society and CHP, 1998
Taking A Part: Young People's Participation in the Church, National Society and CHP, 2000

Apparently, paradoxically, Church schools are very popular with parents. The recent *Consultation Report* of the Church Schools Review Group (Archbishops' Council, 2000) asserts their dual purpose both of service to the whole community and of nurture for children of Christian families (pp. 10ff). In contrast to the 'entrenched philosophy of relativism' which has 'undermined the basis for any shared system of values', the report says, 'The Church offers a spiritual and moral basis for the development of human wholeness and a sure foundation for personal and social values based on the person and ministry of Christ' (p. 14). The group concludes: 'In all circumstances we would recommend that Church Schools must be distinctively places where the

Christian faith is alive and practised' (p. 33). Similarly, with reference to the Church colleges of higher education, they say 'the great challenge is to sustain and develop their Christian distinctiveness' (p. 55).

Women and ministry

There have been major changes in this area since the 1960s. Most attention has been given to the issue of women priests.

Following the General Synod's decisive vote on the legislation on 11 November 1992 which opened the way for women to be ordained as priest/presbyter and therefore to be incumbents/vicars of parishes, the Church of England has experienced the ministry of 2,000 women priests – many hundreds as vicars or senior chaplains in hospitals or other institutions. The experiencing of women's ministry has had a profound effect on many.

Further information on women priests and related matters will be found later (Chapter 37). However, the changes are of such significance that more must be added at this point. 1 have written elsewhere in *An Introduction to Christian Ministry* (pp. 65–7):

> Through many centuries and across the world women have suffered oppression and injustice from men. It is a tragic and harrowing story – but it is a story little told and little known. Men have controlled the levers of power, men have made the laws, men have written the histories and controlled the publishing houses and the organs of the media. Christianity has made a difference in many countries and in many cultures – but its influence has often been ambivalent, its prophetic stance confused and its reforming programmes unclear. In this respect, the Christian attitude to slavery is often a parallel story. Slowly, gradually, reform has come, but the struggle has been immense, the forces of conservatism massive.[1] But reforms have come.
>
> ### The emancipation of women in society
>
> In Britain, women had very limited rights and opportunities at the beginning of the nineteenth century. The eighteenth-century Enlightenment theory of an individual's natural rights was a powerful factor in the development of feminist thinking. Women's movements in the nineteenth century were often allied to movements for the abolition of slavery, for temperance (the abuse of alcohol has caused untold suffering to women and children) and to moral reform (the treatment of prostitutes and women prisoners is a particularly horrifying story

when so many of them were essentially victims). Gradually, but very slowly in the nineteenth and twentieth centuries, various rights and opportunities have been won – political, legal, educational, economic and employment. But we must never forget the sheer tardiness of the reforms, the entrenched powers of conservative opposition and the sheer ignorance and bigotry of prejudice shown by so many.

The ministry of women in the Church

This has always been evident from the very beginnings of the Church, but often limited and confined. Cultural factors of patriarchy, inadequate biblical translation, and theologies which included fear of sexuality played their various parts in sustaining stereotypes which oppressed women and strictly limited the exercise of their gifts and abilities. For many decades, indeed centuries, women have fulfilled notable ministries of pastoral care and evangelism among other women, among children and to those on the margins of society – the destitute, the ill, the elderly. They have nursed, visited, taught children; they have been in religious orders and in foreign missionary societies – the list is endless. But there have always been strict limits and limitations.

A letter of Florence Nightingale written in 1852 expresses the frustrations of many women. She wrote:

> I would have given the Church my head, my hand, my heart. She would not have them. She did not know what to do with them. She told me to go back and do crochet in my mother's drawing room; or, if I were tired of that, to marry and look well at the head of my husband's table. 'You may go to Sunday School if you like it', she said. But she gave me no training even for that. She gave me neither work to do for her, nor education for it.

But changes have come. The developments of 'shared ministry' between clergy and lay people in public worship, home-groups, church councils and other areas of church life have opened up many opportunities. Many women have become church wardens and lay leaders in the synodical government of the Church. At present, the Chair of the House of Laity of the General Synod is Canon Dr Christina Baxter, Principal of the large St. John's Theological College, Nottingham. Women were admitted as Readers (lay preachers and worship leaders) only in 1969 but there are now over 3,000 of them and their numbers continue to grow rapidly. The lay order of deaconesses was introduced in the 1860s and in the following 120 years hundreds of women were selected, trained and licensed to work in parishes. In the 1980s many hundreds were ordained deacon and then from 1994 ordained priest. They are vicars, priests-in-charge of parishes and senior chaplains in hospitals, prisons, universities and other educational institutions. They are cathedral canons, the Venerable Judith Rose is Archdeacon of Ton-bridge, and the Venerable Dr Joy Tetley is Archdeacon of Worcester. Women have been ordained in the (Presbyterian) Church of Scotland, the Methodist, United Reformed, and Baptist Churches. Also in Lutheran and Reformed churches in Europe. Anglican Provinces in America, Asia, Africa and Australasia have ordained women too.

I am unaware of any church taking this step which has regarded the development as anything other than a blessing and enrichment to church life.

The laity in ministry strategy

Lay people have played significant roles in Church life and ministry throughout the centuries. However, in the major Church traditions these have generally been either exceptional, or missionary (particularly 'foreign missions'), or practical administration, or in an essentially assistant pastoral function (e.g. visitations of homes and children's work).

In the twentieth century there was a quite extraordinary set of developments with regard to the laity.

We must start with theology. However, as with the developments in the ministry of women, social and educational developments were very influential in theological thinking. The most widely influential ecumenical statement on ministry is *Baptism, Eucharist and Ministry* (1982). Its first section is entitled 'The Calling of the Whole People of God'. It is so important that I quote sections 1–5.

---

1. In a broken world God calls the whole of humanity to become God's People. For this purpose God chose Israel and then spoke in a unique and decisive way in Jesus Christ, God's Son. Jesus made his own the nature, condition and cause of the whole human race, giving himself as a sacrifice for all. Jesus' life of service, his death and resurrection, are the foundation of a new community which is built up continually by the good news of the Gospel and the gifts of the sacraments. The Holy Spirit unites in a single body those who follow Jesus Christ and sends them as witnesses into the world. Belonging to the Church means living in communion with God through Jesus Christ in the Holy Spirit.

---

2. The life of the Church is based on Christ's victory over the powers of evil and death, accomplished once for all. Christ offers forgiveness, invites to repentance and delivers from destruction. Through Christ, people are enabled to turn in praise to God and in service to their neighbours. In Christ they find the source of new life in freedom, mutual forgiveness and love. Through Christ their hearts and minds are directed to the consummation of the Kingdom where Christ's victory will become manifest and all things made new. God's purpose is that, in Jesus Christ, all people should share in this fellowship.

3. The Church lives through the liberating and renewing power of the Holy Spirit. That the Holy Spirit was upon Jesus is evidenced in his baptism, and after the resurrection that same Spirit was given to those who believed in the Risen Lord in order to recreate them as the body of Christ. The Spirit calls people to faith, sanctifies them through many gifts, gives them strength to witness to the Gospel, and empowers them to serve in hope and love. The Spirit keeps the Church in the truth and guides it despite the frailty of its members.

4. The Church is called to proclaim and prefigure the Kingdom of God. It accomplishes this by announcing the Gospel to the world and by its very existence as the body of Christ. In Jesus the Kingdom of God came among us. He offered salvation to sinners. He preached good news to the poor, release to the captives, recovery of sight to the blind, liberation to the oppressed (Luke 4:18). Christ established a new access to the Father. Living in this communion with God, all members of the Church are called to confess their faith and to give account of their hope. They are to identify with the joys and the sufferings of all people as they seek to witness in caring love. The members of Christ's body are to struggle with the oppressed towards that freedom and dignity promised with the coming of the Kingdom. This mission needs to be carried out in varying political, social, and cultural contexts. In order to fulfil this mission faithfully, they will seek relevant forms of witness and service in each situation. In so doing they bring to the world a foretaste of the joy and glory of God's Kingdom.

5. The Holy Spirit bestows on the community diverse and complementary gifts. These are for the common good of the whole people and are manifested in acts of service within the community and to the world. They may be gifts of communicating the Gospel in word and deed, gifts of healing, gifts of praying, gifts of teaching and learning, gifts of serving, gifts of guiding and following, gifts of inspiration and vision. All members are called to discover, with the help of the community, the gifts they have received and to use them for the building up of the Church and for the service of the world to which the Church is sent.

Major theological influences include:

1. The understanding of the Church as the Body of Christ – with every part having its task to fulfil (see e.g. Romans 12.4-8).
2. The priesthood of the whole people of God (see e.g. 1 Peter 2.9).
3. Spiritual gifts (charismata) as given to all God's people by the risen Christ through the Holy Spirit and for the building up of God's Church and service to others (see e.g. Romans 12.6; 1 Peter 4.10; 1 Corinthians 12.4-7).
4. Baptism as the sign and seal of God's salvation and of the disciple's life in Christ – often now described as 'the ordination of the laity'.
5. Mission as the inevitable outworking of the life of discipleship and as extensive as the concerns of God himself.

Linked to these theological emphases there have been practical ministerial developments. The remarkable development of Reader ministry is charted in Chapter 16. Further attention is paid to other types of formal lay ministry in Chapter 15 – including pastoral assistants, evangelists and others. Then there are considerable developments in lay ministry in church and parish which do not carry formal accreditation or commissioning. In public worship – reading lessons, leading intercession, administering communion; in pastoral care – baptism, confirmation and marriage preparation, bereavement care and leading home groups; in evangelism and nurture – leadership in Alpha and Emmaus groups, etc.

The development of collaborative ministry and of local ministry teams with strong (usually a majority) lay membership is described in Chapter 35.

Then there were major legal developments during the century. The introduction of parochial church councils in the 1920s, synodical government in 1970 (so that in the General Synod lay people debate and vote on doctrinal, liturgical and ecumenical issues), and the Patronage (Benefices) Measure of 1986 whereby the PCC and its (lay) representatives play critical roles in the appointment of an incumbent (see Chapter 24).

Lay interest in theology, spirituality, ethics and mission is increasing. Their concern for effective ministry and mission is strong. And then, there is the issue of finance – so major and significant that it demands separate attention.

Declining numbers of stipendiary clergy

There was an (almost steady) decline throughout the twentieth century. The number of stipendiary clergy available for parochial and diocesan appointment fell from just under 20,000 to just under 10,000. Full details are given in

Chapter 9 and its statistics. Within the memory of many, numbers fell from 13,660 in 1961 to 9,648 in 1999.

Some of the main consequences are:

1. the ratio of clergy to population moved
   from 1 : 1,570 in 1901
   to   1 : 5,160 in 1999
2. in rural areas many small parishes are grouped
3. in urban/suburban/town parishes assistant stipendiary clergy (whether senior or curates) are increasingly scarce.

Finance – a revolution

During the last 30 years, the Church of England has lived through, coped with (and, many would add, been strengthened by) an extraordinary financial revolution.

Just one generation ago, the lion's share of all stipends, much clergy housing, much new church building and the entirety of clergy pensions were met by the income of the Church Commissioners. In effect, the parochial clergy were office-holders with 'independent means'. Though, even with a right to their fees from weddings and funerals, few were well-off, they felt little financial dependence on their parishioners. All this has radically changed – and, I repeat, within one generation.

Today, the lion's share of the stipend and housing costs, the whole of expenses of office, and the whole of the future pensions liability is raised by parish giving. Instead of the major expense of the PCC being the repair and upkeep of the church building, the ministry costs are now a (if not the) major expense in the annual budget.

The current financial situation is described in Chapter 39.

The national organization of the Church of England

An area of change in the Church which merits attention is its national organization. This has been developing over the decades, not least with respect to ministry issues, but the report of the Archbishops' Commission on the Organization of the Church of England entitled *Working as One Body* and popularly referred to by the name of the Commission's chairman, Bishop Michael Turnbull (1995), was a development of more than ordinary significance.

Twenty years ago 'the various central bodies concerned with the ministry of the Church' included:

1. ACCM, the Advisory Council for the Church's Ministry, responsible for national policy advice on selection and training of ordinands.

2. The Central Readers' Council, advising on all aspects of (lay) Reader ministry.

3. The Church Commissioners, responsible for policy on clergy stipends, fees and housing.

4. The Central Board of Finance, which worked with the dioceses over augmentation of clergy stipends.

5. The Church of England Pensions Board, which supervised clergy pensions and retirement accommodation.

6. Lambeth Palace, where the Archbishop of Canterbury's Lay Assistant had special responsibility for clergy deployment.

We must add:

7. The Standing Committee of the General Synod set up the Clergy Conditions of Service Steering Group.

8. The Church of England Council for the Deaf.

It is no surprise that a Ministry Co-ordinating Group (consisting of Chairmen or vice-chairmen of several of these groups) was deemed appropriate.

Various modest reforms took place over the following years. But it was the Turnbull Report which decisively effected a substantial and radical coherence of most areas of national policy with respect to ministry issues. It proposed what became the Archbishops' Council with new powers to deal with matters of both policy and resources. The council has three major divisions:

- Church and World (which includes Mission, Education, Social Responsibility, Unity, Hospital Chaplains and the Care of Church and Cathedral Buildings);
- Ministry;
- Finance.

In addition, there are 'service' departments of Communications, Human Resources, Central Secretariat, Legal and Central Service (e.g. IT, Publishing, Records and Statistics).

The *Church of England Yearbook 2000* (2000) says (p. 35): 'The provision of a properly trained and supported ministry is critical to the Church's mission. The Council brings together policy on the selection, training, deployment and remuneration of the Church of England's ministry – responsibilities that were formerly scattered at national level between different bodies – thus enabling decisions on ministry policy and strategy to be taken in the round.'

The Ministry Division's work is structured as follows:

MINISTRY DIVISION COMMITTEE STRUCTURE CHART

Bishops' Committee for Ministry
(House of Bishops' Committee)

identical with
THE CO-ORDINATING GROUP

Committee	VOCATION RECRUITMENT & SELECTION	THEOLOGICAL EDUCATION & TRAINING	DEPLOYMENT REMUNERATION & CONDITIONS OF SERVICE	MINISTRY AMONG DEAF PEOPLE
Panel	VOCATIONS	FINANCE	CONTINUING MINISTERIAL EDUCATION	TRAINING
	PRE-THEOLOGICAL EDUCATION	EDUCATIONAL VALIDATION		
	CANDIDATES	RESEARCH DEGREES	CENTRAL READERS' COUNCIL	
		READER TRAINING		

Further detail is included in a free leaflet which the division makes widely available (see p. 20).

The Ministry Division since January 1999 and the Advisory Board of Ministry before that have been both initiating reforms and changes, and responding to external pressures, in an almost unceasing manner in the last six years.

In 1995, the Advisory Board of Ministry worked through *six* main committees:

- Recruitment and Selection Committee (RSC);
- Initial Ministerial Education Committee (IMEC);
- Ministry Development & Deployment Committee (MDDC);
- Committee for Ministry Among Deaf People (CMDP);
- Finance Committee;
- Steering Group on Theological Colleges and Courses.

Each of the first four had one or more sub-committees, or other subordinate bodies. The board had a total of 33 staff.

Table 2: Ministry Division – main functions

	Vocation, Recruitment and Selection	Theological Education and Training		Deployment, Remuneration and Conditions of Service	Ministry Among Deaf People	Readers
		(Education/Training)	(Finance)			
Advising the Church	Develop recruitment policy Selection criteria and procedure Bishops' Regulations for Training Advise bishops on candidates' progress Support for diocesan vocations advisers Support for diocesan directors of ordinands Encourage vocation	Theological issues about ministry Policy about theological colleges, courses, diocesan schemes and alternative forms of training Bishops' Regulations for Training Reader training	Financial support of ordination candidates in training Financial support of theological colleges and courses Financial consideration of all ministry work	Ministry strategy Matters concerning terms and conditions, remuneration, housing, pensions Deployment policy New patterns of ministry Sector and chaplaincy ministers Future ministry needs Support for continuing education officers Review of ministry approval Appraisal	Participation of deaf people in the life of the Church and their pastoral care Support chaplains to the deaf	Contact and central sources of advice for Reader ministry Link with moderators for training and Archbishops' Diploma Stimulate new thinking
Executive functions	Vocation conferences and exhibitions Bishops' selection conferences Train bishops' selectors Monitor candidates' progress Monitor Bishops' Regulations for Training Oversee pre-theological training	Monitor and validate training programmes Appoint and co-ordinate moderators for theological training programmes Encourage provision of future theological educators Coordinate work of diocesan moderators of Reader training	Administer the training budget and grants to candidates in training Department budget, accounts and financial control Approve budgets and fees of theological colleges and courses Administer ministry discretionary funds Develop IT for the department	Recommend changes in stipends, pensions, and parochial fees Monitor clergy conditions of service Monitor standards of continuing ministerial education provision Allocation formulae for stipendiary clergy Deployment of deacons in first post Prepare *Statistics of Licensed Ministers*	Promote deaf awareness Future vocations from deaf congregations Training for chaplains among deaf people Training for deaf lay ministry	Produce magazine and occasional papers Arrange annual meetings, summer conference Administer matters most effectively handled centrally

In 1999, the Ministry Division consisted of *four* main committees:

- Vocation, Recruitment and Selection Committee (VRSC);
- Theological Education and Training Committee (TETC);
- Deployment, Remuneration & Conditions of Service Committee (DRCS);
- Committee for Ministry Among Deaf People (CMDP);

with panels which report to them (see the organization chart on p. 19).

The Ministry Division has at present 34 staff.

Other significant changes that have taken place over the past five years include:

a) Inspectorate work moved to the Secretariat of the House of Bishops in March 1995.

b) 10 per cent budget reduction leads to cuts in Selection/Vocations and Ministry Among Deaf People from January 1996.

c) The Chief Secretary (now Director) and the Theological Education Adviser each used to administer three selection conferences per annum. With the expansion of their areas of work, this arrangement ceased in 1996 and 1998 respectively.

d) Aston Course Closure; introduction of Pre-Theological Education National Adviser (75 per cent) in 1997.

e) Increase in Vocations portfolio from 25 per cent back to 50 per cent in 1997.

f) 50 per cent MDDC Secretary – regraded to principal with addition of remuneration and conditions of service issues as Secretary to DRCS, full-time in 1998.

g) Further integration of Readers' ministry into the Ministry Division.

h) In 1999 two staff from the Church Commissioners join DRCS.

i) Increase in conference secretaries by one from January 1999 because of surge in candidates.

j) Review of Admin/Finance area leads to saving of one support staff post (late 1999).

k) In January 2001 3.8 per cent budget cut leads to

1) A maximum of 54 selection conferences per annum

2) Vocations work reduced from 50 per cent to 25 per cent of an officer

3) Pre-Theological Education work reduced from 75 per cent to 50 per cent of an officer

4) Director takes up CME portfolio (formerly 25 per cent) for a year in the first instance.

Summary

Church of England reports regularly review social change. The mission context is important for Anglican theological thinking on mission and ministry. I have already listed many key documents and analyses in the preceding sections.

John Tiller, *A Strategy for the Church's Ministry* (1983) chose the themes of post-industrialism, permissiveness and pluralism (pp. 11–16).

Criteria for Selection (1993) in its Chapter 8 analysed a new emphasis on mission and evangelism, collaboration with lay people, increasing demands on clergy, stress, ecumenical progress, differing views on women's ministry and the parish system (see further in Chapter 32).

Recovering Confidence (1996) in its Chapter 3 addressed post-industrial uncertainties, difficulties for all voluntary organizations, changing parameters of childhood, adolescence and young adulthood and the development of vague New Age spiritualities as well as sharp-edged fundamentalisms (see further in Chapter 9).

2

The method of research

Three major types of evidence have contributed to the report – documentary, field work and collaboration with colleagues.

Documentary material

This falls into three main categories:

1. *Reports* on ministry issues produced over the last 20 years by the Ministry Division of the Church of England or its predecessors. These are listed in the bibliography and the most important will be referred to in the following pages. They are numerous, wide-ranging and frequently of very high quality. They often combine real vision, strategic thinking and exciting innovation and experiment.

2. *Books* on ministry issues of many kinds. These have been written out of many Christian denominations and include theological, ecumenical, missiological and many other dimensions. They include significant ecumenical convergences – see also Chapter 3.

3. *Diocesan material* on ministry issues. These range from major reports to leaflets, from ministry schemes and strategies to considerations of mission, evangelism, pastoral provision, diocesan structures, staffing and finance. They vary in nature, in size and in many other respects. When an analysis of them was attempted in 1994, the conclusion reported to the Advisory Board of Ministry was that there was no perceived national strategy and no 'underlying or pervasive approach to ministry to be discerned across the dioceses'. However, when another group repeated the exercise in 1997, the report reads quite differently – 'a lively and vibrant picture of fresh ideas and changing practice ... A surprising degree of common analysis and shared commitment' (*Shaping Ministry*, p. iii). See also Chapter 5.

Field work

There is, quite rightly, suspicion of bureaucrats or policy-makers who 'sit at desks in London' and are out of touch with the provinces or the 'grass roots'.

During recent years a programme of visitation throughout the country has sought to pre-empt this criticism.

(i) *Dioceses*

The director has visited:
- 10 diocesan synods
- 2 bishops' councils
- 12 bishops' staff meetings
- 10 boards of ministry or their staff
- 11 cathedrals

Other kinds of diocesan events include:

- 9 vocations events
- 6 Readers' conferences
- 9 clergy conferences

These visits typically involve one or more addresses/lectures/sermons followed by extensive time for questions and discussion.

(ii) *Deaneries*

20 deanery synods
10 deanery clergy chapters

(iii) *Parishes*

c128 visits for Sunday preaching on ministry and vocation. Other parish events include Any Questions, working lunches and seminars. Most services have been followed by informal and/or formal questions and discussions

(iv) *Special groups* of many kinds have invited me to visit them. These visits again typically involve lectures or addresses on ministry strategy generally or on particular aspects followed by extensive questions and discussion. These groups include the Association of Ordinands and Candidates for Ministry (AOCM); groups of ministry specialists, e.g. vocations officers, directors of ordinands, continuing ministry education officers, chaplains to deaf people, ordained local ministry advisers; various Catholic and evangelical groups; religious communities; clergy group of Manufacturing, Science and Finance (MSF) Union; minority ethnic groups; advisers in women's ministry; archdeacons; Church Army; Church Pastoral Aid Society; diocesan secretaries; Ecclesiastical Law Society; Chrism, and others.

(v) *Theological colleges, courses and schemes* I have visited each of the 11 English theological colleges at least twice (and often more) and the 12 regional courses once or twice. Often I have stayed overnight and shared in the corporate life, especially of course residential weekends. It has not been so easy to visit OLM schemes but I have often talked to principals or OLM officers.

(vi) *Church volleges of higher education* I have visited 9 of the 11 colleges to have extensive discussions with principals and senior staff.

(vii) *Ecumenical contacts* are considerable especially in the area of theological training. Some further reference to this will be found later at Chapter 17.

In addition, I have been invited to 12 theological colleges of other denominations or non-denominational to visit and often preach, lecture, debate and advise.

(viii) *International contacts* have included a week in Rome as one of the two ecumenical delegates to the Roman Catholic European Vocations Congress, 1997; giving a paper to the International Conference on Church Leadership in Uppsala, Sweden, 1997; leading seminars in Frankfurt, Germany, for the EKD (Lutheran Church), 1998; visits to St Michael's College, Cardiff (Church in Wales), and discussions with Church of Scotland leaders.

Questions of interest and concern

a) The *range* of visits is significant. Though they are always by invitation of bishop, vicar, principal, chairperson or chief executive of an organization, etc., I have quite deliberately advertised my availability and eagerness to receive such invitations. Many of the visits will have multiple opportunities, and it would be difficult (and tedious) to quantify them all. Perhaps two illustrations will suffice. A typical Sunday visit to a parish may include several of the following – interview about the Ministry Division, sermon/talk about vocation and ministry, Any Questions with all or some of the congregation after the service in a structured way, informal conversations with individuals, a 'working' lunch with church leaders, an afternoon 'seminar' for ordinands or those interested in any form of ministry, evening youth service and/or youth club with talk and discussion. A typical visit to a college or course might include several or all of these – meeting with principal and/or staff, and with students, lecture on an aspect or overview of ministry, Any Questions and debate, preaching and personal interviews.

b) The *purpose* of these visits is at least threefold:

(i) to listen, and to learn. The variety of different situations in dioceses, parishes and institutions is very considerable. There is widespread anxiety (and even cynicism) about national/central structures based in London.

(ii) to share information, and a wider vision. There is frequently considerable interest, but also widespread misunderstanding, and knowledge of only some parts of the overall jigsaw. Where people do not, at the very least, read a national Church newspaper, the levels of misperception can be very serious.

(iii) to answer questions and share in debate. Only on one single occasion has there been anything other than a flood of lively question and comment.

c) The *character* of the dialogue has been such that I cannot precisely analyse or quantify it. I have taken no questionnaire (except in my first series of visits to colleges and courses which led to my writing the report *Issues in Theological Education and Training*, 1997). Nor have I made immediate detailed notes. The nature of the events, their spontaneity and rapid following one upon another meant that such an approach to evidence gathering was inappropriate and would (almost certainly) have been counter-productive. So the rest of this section is inevitably impressionistic from the last five years.

d) *Issues and themes* that have recurred fairly frequently include the following:

(i) *Vocation and selection*

How do we discern God's call?
What is the relation between God's call and the Church's process of selection?
What are the criteria for selection?
What is the relation between the conviction of *local* Church leaders and the assessment of the bishops' selectors?
What can be done to encourage black and minority ethnic leadership?
What about the care of candidates who are not recommended?
Does the Church only want graduates?
Are there 'Access' courses like the former Aston Course?
Does the Church still 'put off' younger applicants?

(ii) *Training*

Does it take sufficient account of prior experience and learning?
Is the balance appropriate between academic study and practical/vocational preparation?
Is it not too expensive?
Are there appropriate facilities for people with disabilities?
Is there not an imbalance between, and lack of integration of, training for ordinands/clergy and lay leaders?

Should lay training schemes and Reader training seek academic credit rating, and then be transferable to different parts of the country, and different dioceses?

Are clergy trained in the management of volunteers?

Are ordinands/clergy trained for collaborative ministry?

Why are college/course inspection reports not made public?

(iii) *Numbers of clergy and their conditions of service*

Why are the numbers of stipendiary clergy falling?

Why are rural communities being grouped into ever-larger clusters?

Why cannot large urban/suburban parishes have more staff?

Why do you turn 'ordinands' away when we need more clergy?

Can we afford more clergy?

Should NSM clergy and Readers be reasonably deployable?

Is clergy freehold still appropriate?

Why is not appraisal and professional development compulsory (as in other professions)?

(iv) *Other issues*

Are Readers used properly?

What are the pros and cons of ordained local ministry?

What are the chaplaincy and sector ministries?

What is the Church Army?

Are women now being treated equally in ministry?

Are women 'refused' by parishes which have not passed Resolutions A or B?

Collaboration with colleagues

In addition to the extensive debates involved in the field work covered in the previous section, I share with many colleagues the regular interaction of discussion and debate (public and private):

- staff of Ministry Division and members of its committees, panels and working parties.

- staff of other divisions of the Archbishops' Council and of the Church Commissioners, Pensions Board, Lambeth Palace and diocesan offices.

- members of the Archbishops' Council, General Synod, the House of Bishops and the Bishops' Committee for Ministry.

Many of these colleagues have contributed material from their specialist perspectives in the pages that follow.

3

Ordained ministry – history and theology

The development of the clergy
(Summarized from a paper given to the Ecclesiastical Law Society on 25 March 2000 by Rt Revd Dr Anthony Russell, Bishop of Ely)

While the Church witnesses to an unchanging God, the Church as a social institution is required to respond to change. The Church of England, and in particular, its organization of its professional ministry, cannot be understood without reference to its history.

The history of the Church of England is often treated as a static entity, and many people invoke the ideal of clergy in every parish. This ideal only came close to realization in Anglican history in the last quarter of the nineteenth century, and in the period following the First World War pastoral reorganization was already part of the Church's life.

A historical understanding helps us to trace the trajectory that the clerical role has followed through the course of Anglican history. There are hints of change and diversity in the many words used to describe a minister of the Church of England – clergyperson, minister, parson, clerk in holy orders, priest, vicar and curate are among the more common. A fundamental distinction exists between those terms that are theologically derived, e.g. *priest*, which comes from New Testament and doctrinal sources, and those derived from occupational roles in society, e.g. *clergyperson*. This chapter is concerned not with the theology of ministry, but with the development of the clergy's role in society.

The clerical role has passed through five identifiable stages:

- the clergy as upper servants;
- the clergy as occupational appendages of gentry status;
- the clergy as professionals;
- the clergy as church managers;
- the clergy as community development officers.

The Reformation provides a point of departure for examining these stages. For, in addition to focusing the growing national self-awareness that effected the break from Rome and Roman control in ecclesiastical affairs, it also brought to a head the tide of anti-clerical feeling that had been increasing through the sixteenth century. In practical terms, the Reformation deprofessionalized an occupational group which had already established a considerable monopoly over its sphere of activity.

The late seventeenth and eighteenth centuries saw a clergy characterized by poverty, rustic manners and lack of learning. Incomes were frequently supplemented from a variety of secular employment. Patronage, plurality and non-residence powerfully affected the nature of the Church in this period. Poverty compelled clergy in Oxford, for instance, to act as school ushers during the week, and to go to parishes outside the city on a Sunday, where they compressed all the offices covered by the term parochial ministry into the space between morning and evening prayer. Not until three Acts of Parliament had been passed in the early nineteenth century were clergy required to live in their parishes.

Three changes in the later eighteenth century greatly altered the position of parochial clergy. First, clerical incomes were derived directly or indirectly from the price of agricultural commodities, and glebe and tithe became much more profitable as grain prices rose in response to national and foreign events. Second, the development of the enclosure movement meant that clergy were able to ensure that, provided all interested parties agreed, a large amount of parish land became glebe land. Third, the necessity of finding employment for the sons of the lesser gentry who could no longer rely on parental support sent a great many younger sons into the Church.

It was not the Ordinal only which defined the role of the clergy at this time, but their role and status in contemporary society. In some places, for instance, a considerable part of all the magistrate's work was conducted by clergy.

The early nineteenth century saw further significant changes as the clergy's role became increasingly modelled on that of the professional. The characteristics of professionalization quickly emerged – expulsion procedures; retirement arrangements; professional organizations; professional journals. In the last quarter of the nineteenth century, clerical dress was almost universally worn, and the diocese became more and more influential in English church life.

With the emergence of new professional roles – *inter alia* the country doctor, the local politician, the Poor Law guardian, the lay magistrate, the sanitary engineer – the clergyman's role contracted to embrace only the elements sanctioned by the Ordinal. New incumbents, trained in recently founded theological colleges, set about transforming the local church to make it conform to new and different standards. Parish clerks and west gallery musicians disappeared, to be replaced by organs bought by local subscription. Worship in the village community ceased to be the offering of a whole community, and become something performed at the front for the onlookers in the congregation. This distancing between the interests of clergy and congregation was part of the price paid for the adoption of a professional model.

The later twentieth century produced reports that drew attention to the need for greater effectiveness and efficiency in the running of the Church. The Paul Report of 1964 was followed by the Morley Report of 1967, the Pastoral Measure of 1968 and the Tiller Report of 1983. Like many organizations, the Church was tending more and more to centralized organization, and a large number of serving clergy, especially in rural areas, felt marginalized. Courses at business schools and management training came to be seen as the appropriate training for clergy, with rural deans, whose role was developing a higher profile, moved into the position of the Church's 'middle management'.

As the total number of stipendiary clergy diminished, clergy took on larger pastoral units and began to feel that their role was that of church manager. The laity responded ambivalently to this trend, feeling that management was not a primary duty of the clergy, and that it could be better accomplished by skilled lay people. At the same time, the growth of non-stipendiary ministry exhibited some of the characteristics observable in sub-professional groups. NSMs were required to meet high entry standards, yet allowed only a limited range of responsibilities.

In the last period, up to the present time, the Church has again responded to significant changes in society. Along with other ancient institutions, it has experienced the processes of de-institutionalization and de-professionalization. Since work and work roles have become the defining core of modern society, religious activity has been redefined as a voluntary leisure pursuit, a non-work activity. This has led, in turn, to a further redefinition of the clergy role. No longer are the clergy regarded as professionals, but as community development workers. On this understanding, the clergy do not need academic skills as a primary requirement. Instead, the clergy are expected to demonstrate gifts of personality to attract, motivate and build the voluntary community; to define its tasks; to resolve its conflicts; and to identify its goals. These are the qualities which parishioners seek when selecting a new priest for a parish.

Voluntary associations are often run by women, who may seem more likely to display the personality characteristics described above. It is no coincidence that the inclusion of women in the Church's leadership role has occurred at a time when the Church has become more like many other voluntary asso-ciational organizations in society.

The problem for the Church today is how to deal with change in the light of continuity. The move into a new era has not meant leaving the old behind. So, for example, the present appointment system remains rooted in the ancient parochial system and the patronage arrangements of Anglo-Saxon England. It is the Church's responsibility to carry into the future those things that are valued from the past, in the context of a changing society.

It is inevitable, in the light of this survey, that the role of the clergy will continue to change, and this must be in the background of any consideration of contemporary ministry.[1]

The theology of ministry and ordination

Introduction

It is often alleged that the Church of England has no agreed understanding or theology of ministry. While it is true to say that there is considerable latitude for interpretation, the allegation is surely exaggerated.

The quarries for the theology include:

---

1 Article 23 of the 39 Articles:

> *Of Ministering in the Congregation*
>
> It is not lawful for any man to take upon him the office of public preaching, or ministering the Sacraments of the Congregation, before he be lawfully called, and sent, to execute the same. And those we ought to judge lawfully called and sent, which be chosen and called to this work by men who have public authority given unto them in the Congregation, to call and send Ministers into the Lord's vineyard.
>
> (cf also Articles 19, 24 and 36)

2. The Ordinals attached to *The Book of Common Prayer* and in *The Alternative Service Book 1980.*

3. The Canons of the Church of England (see Chapter 4).

4. The selection criteria agreed by the House of Bishops (see Chapter 12).

5. Recent official reports on various aspects of ministry (listed later), especially *Eucharistic Presidency* (A theological statement by the House of Bishops of the General Synod), 1997.

6. Sections on ministry in recent reports of ecumenical agreements.

The seriousness with which the issue is regarded is evidenced by the way in which ordination training curricula are now developed and validated. The first question to be addressed by a college, course or scheme during the period 1986–2000 was: What ordained ministry does the Church of England require? (see *Education for the Church's Ministry*, ACCM 22, 1987, Ch. IV), and the institution was asked to provide a statement of the theological understanding underpinning their account. The report *Ordination and the Church's Ministry* (1991), which evaluated the responses to this question, commented that ACCM 22 'set in motion a remarkable development in the Church of England's training of its ordained ministry. It is highly significant that a theological basis is being provided for this training. This is the first time that the Colleges and Courses have ever been asked to articulate a theological rationale for their programme of training' (pp. 3–4).

ACCM 22 has now been developed in *Mission and Ministry: The Churches' Validation Framework for Theological Education* (1999). A new preliminary question has been introduced, so we now have:

Question 1

What is the training institution's understanding of the mission to which the Church of God is called and of the pattern of Church life and order through which the Church of England* responds to that calling?

> * *Institutions are asked to add the names of other denominations for which they prepare candidates, and to change 'pattern' to 'patterns'.*

Question 2

In the light of that understanding, what are the main characteristics of ordained and other public ministries** for which the training institution seeks to prepare its candidates?

> ** *In practice many candidates for ordained and accredited lay ministry will train alongside those studying for other ministries and service. However, the scope of validation remains limited to educational programmes for those sponsored for ordained and accredited lay Ministry.*

This requires a theology of God's mission and of God's Church before moving on to a theology of ministry.

The Archbishops' Council Working Party on the Structure and Funding of Ordination Training is preparing a major theological section for its report which will further address these issues (see Chapter 17).

The following pages include contributions from three crucial perspectives to the theological debates:

1. the theological – from Revd Dr John Muddiman;
2. the ecumenical – from Preb. Dr Paul Avis;
3. the liturgical – from the Bishop of Salisbury.

A theological introduction
John Muddiman

Common prayer has always been, distinctively, the basis of Anglican doctrine: *lex orandi lex credendi* (what is prayed is what is believed). The effect of this doxological approach has been to make Anglicans in general cautious of grand conceptual systems that move too far away from the reality of a praying, worshipping community. Anglicans have also been acutely aware of the historically contingent character of their own polity, and have been reluctant therefore especially in the modern period to define the Church in such a way as to imply that other ways of being church were illegitimate. We are simply content to use the Creed, embedded as it is in the liturgy, and to affirm the substance of the third Article: that the Church is the work and earthly manifestation of the Holy Spirit; it is one, holy, catholic, and apostolic; it is the community of the baptized, who know themselves to be forgiven sinners and who live in hope of resurrection to eternal life.

Within this traditional consensus on the basis of ecclesiology, a variety of theoretical and practical outworkings is to be found within the thought and teaching of the Church of England. For example, opinions differ on the precise form in which *episcope* as an essential element of ordained ministry should be expressed, ranging from a 'high' view of the primatial and collegial character of the universal Anglican episcopate, to a local-bishop-in-synod model, to the 'low' view that pastoral charge of a parish is an integral and not merely derivative expression of the function of oversight. It would be possible to cite other examples of the plurality of views on issues that directly affect ecclesiology, such as the relation between baptismal initiation and adult profession of faith, or between the Church, the State and secular society.

In recognition both of the fundamental importance of ecclesiology in the devising, delivering and assessing of courses of training for ordained ministry and also of the inevitable and enriching plurality of views mentioned in the preceding paragraph, over the last ten years the so-called 'ACCM 22 process' has asked training institutions to provide a coherent and detailed statement of their own distinctive understandings of the Church, against which their proposals for the content of training could fairly be measured. Simultaneous with this 'centrifugal' approach has been a 'centripetal' search for shared theological insights and shared good practice. Already in 1990, the report *Ordination and the Church's Ministry* noted that responses to 'Question One' were converging (p. 17) on the idea that the doctrine of the Trinity might provide the ground for understanding the mission of the Church in continuity with the *Missio Dei* in creation, incarnation and Pentecost, and thus a view of ministry in the service of mission in its fullest sense. Other submissions reached the same conclusion by a different route, for example, by distinguishing between the Church and Jesus' vision of the kingdom of God and seeing the former as a means of realizing the latter. This renewed emphasis on mission is fully reflected in the recent review of the churches' validation framework, entitled *Mission and Ministry*. It marks a new era in the ecclesiological thinking of the Church of England, that begins not so much with its status as established church as with its invitation and prophetic challenge to a largely post-Christian society. All churches in England, of course, are faced with the same situation; this has resulted not only in growing ecumenical co-operation (*Mission and Ministry*, p. 5) but also in a kind of ecclesiological cross-fertilization, through the influence for example of BEM and ARCIC, Meissen and Porvoo, and the Virginia Report. If theological education in the 1960s and 1970s may be said to have discovered a new sociological and managerial realism, perhaps we have seen in the last decade or so the recovery of a new theological realism about the mission and ministry of the Church of England.[2]

Ministry: ecumenical aspects
Paul Avis

Royal priesthood and representative ministry

In setting out a theology of representative ministry, ecumenical ecclesiology tends to begin from the calling of the people of God into existence through faith and baptism. 1 Peter 2 uses cumulative imagery from the Old Testament to show the high calling of all Christians. The argument moves from corner-stone to temple, from temple to priesthood and from priesthood to sacrifice. 'Come to him, a living stone, though rejected by mortals yet chosen and precious in God's sight, and like living stones, let yourselves be built into a spiritual house, to be a holy priesthood, to offer spiritual sacrifices acceptable to God through Jesus Christ.' Sharing in Christ's messianic identity as our great Prophet, Priest and King, Christians are incorporated into God's purpose for Israel.

Invoking the imagery of baptism, as a passage from darkness to light (as well as from death to life), 1 Peter affirms that baptized believers belong to the corporate priesthood of the Church that is both kingly and prophetic: 'you are a chosen race, a royal priesthood, a holy nation, God's own people, in order that you may proclaim the mighty acts of him who called you out of darkness into his marvellous light' (1 Peter 2.9f). As a royal house, Christians play their part in the governance of Christ's kingdom. As a priestly nation, they offer spiritual sacrifices to God through Christ, above all the offering of their very selves (Romans 12.1). As a prophetic people, they make known the saving work of God in Christ. The *laos* comprises the whole people of God collectively, and is theologically prior to the distinction between 'laity' and 'clergy'. As *Eucharistic Presidency* insists, ordination does not take anyone out of the *laos* (3.21).

There is wide agreement that all Christians, through faith and baptism, through witness and daily discipleship, represent Christ to their neighbour (see *Bishops in Communion*). For the dedicated Christian, all that he or she does is done in the name of Christ and consecrated to the glory of God (Colossians 3.17; Ephesians 5.20). Christians are Christ-bearers. The whole Church is sent by Christ into the world and is therefore said to be apostolic (from the Greek verb to send). The idea of representation therefore applies to all Christians, not simply to the ordained (though it does apply in a particular way to them).

There is an ecumenical consensus that a ministry recognized by the Church is not by any means confined to the ordained. All Christians have received a spiritual gift or charism through baptism (1 Corinthians 12.4-7,13). Every single limb or organ of the Body of Christ has a vital role for the sake of the well-being of the whole body (1 Corinthians 12.12-27). All are called to minister in one way or another. When that ministry is called forth by the community, recognized and owned by the community, in tacit and implicit as well as explicit and formal ways, individuals are seen to act in the name of Christ and his Church. However, this is not a matter of individual whim, or staking a personal claim, but is subject to the sovereign call of the Holy Spirit, which the Church is called and equipped to discern. Ministry is something more than Christian discipleship. It is a form of service that is representative of Christ and the Church in a way that is publicly acknowledged, either explicitly or tacitly.

Ordained ministry

Building on the representative nature of all public ministry in the Church, whether lay or ordained, there is broad ecumenical agreement that there is a need for ministries that are given authority to speak and act in a public, representative way that goes beyond what lay people are authorized to do. All recognized ministry, whether lay or ordained, is the ministry of Christ. The ordained, however, minister in the name of Christ and with his authority in a publicly representative way. Ordained ministers are called, trained, commissioned, licensed and accountable to higher authority in a particular way. They are set apart for diaconal, presbyteral or episcopal ministry for life. Their ministry – the ministry of the word, the administration of the sacraments and the exercise of pastoral care and oversight in the Church – is carried out in ways that are laid down in the law of the Church and overseen through the government of the Church, that is to say, by means of structures of synodical conciliarity and episcopal collegiality. In the exercise of their office, the ordained represent, stand for and typify the ministry of Christ through his Body the Church.

To represent Christ and his Church through a ministry of word, sacrament and pastoral care requires authorization (the giving or sharing of authority) from those one represents. This authority is given in ordination when a person is commissioned and empowered in the name of God. In licensing, the authorization is channelled to a particular portion of the people of God. In these respects the bishop has a particular role in oversight. The Canons of the Church of England describe the bishop as 'the chief pastor of all that are within his diocese, as well laity as clergy, and their father in God' (Canon C18). The bishop shares his ministry of oversight, with its responsibility for the ministry of the word and the administration of the sacraments, with the parish priest in a cure (or care) of souls that is 'both yours and mine'. Both bishop and presbyter are assisted by the deacon as a representative minister of word, sacrament and pastoral care. The authority and the gifts for public ministry come not simply from the community but from the Lord as head of the Church. The head cannot be separated from the members of the Body. Together, as St Augustine of Hippo says, they comprise the whole Christ (*totus Christus*). In ordination and oversight the bishop speaks for Christ and for his people.

Ecumenical agreements

Ecumenical agreed texts have affirmed this broad understanding of the particular representative calling of the ordained within the overall under-standing of the calling and ministry of the *laos* or people of God. They affirm an apostolic ministry as well as an apostolic community.

Baptism, Eucharist and Ministry (the multilateral Lima Report of 1982) states: 'In order to fulfil its mission, the Church needs persons who are publicly and continually responsible for pointing to its fundamental dependence on Jesus Christ, and thereby provide, within a multiplicity of gifts, a focus of its unity.' BEM adds: 'The ministry of such persons, who since very early times have been ordained, is constitutive for the life and witness of the Church' (BEM M8). On this point, Anglicans, Orthodox and Roman Catholics, Lutherans, Reformed and Methodists are agreed.

The report of the Anglican–Reformed international dialogue *God's Reign and*

Alongside these debates and conversations, three significant pieces of work are in progress. There is a working party on the renewed diaconate, chaired by the Bishop of Bristol, which hopes to report by the end of this year (see Chapter 36); there are the reports of the Inter-Anglican Liturgical Consultations in 1997, 1999 and (finally) in August 2001, which give an indication of where the rest of the Communion is in their revision of ordination rites and in the practice of ordination; and there is a working party on the future of theological education for ministers, chaired by the Bishop of Chichester, which will be pertinent (see Chapter 17).

Against this background a number of strands have already emerged in the House's thinking, with which the new commission will be working:

- First, a recognition that ordination to the distinctive ministry of the deacon, priest or bishop must be set in the context of the baptismal call of the whole people of God.

- Second, a conviction that we should be conservative in the creation of the performative texts, in view of their ecumenical genesis and the continuing ecumenical significance of ordination rites.

- Third, a shift in the theology of vocation from the overwheming priority of a personal sense of call towards the church calling those in whom it discerns the gifts.

- Fourth, a recognition of the significance of ordinations in the mission of the church.

- Fifth, the hope that we might achieve much of what we need by attending to the re-ordering of the rite and its rubrics, and to questions of presentation.

The commission hopes to bring the first drafts of revised rites to the House of Bishops in 2002, hoping that they may be introduced to Synod no later than July 2003 to begin the process of reception and revision before final approval.

4

Ministry policy

There are three significant groups of policy statements. These are not sufficiently known and appreciated.

The Canons of the Church of England

The Canon Law was substantially revised in the period following the Second World War and has been further revised in recent years by the General Synod.

Because they are rarely read (let alone studied) by ordinands, clergy or lay leaders, I have included key quotations which are of particular interest and relevance to the issues considered in this report.

C 1   Of holy orders in the Church of England

1. The Church of England holds and teaches that from the apostles' time there have been these orders in Christ's Church: bishops, priests, and deacons; and no man shall be accounted or taken to be a lawful bishop, priest, or deacon in the Church of England, or suffered to execute any of the said offices, except he be called, tried, examined, and admitted thereunto according to the Ordinal or any form of service alternative thereto approved by the General Synod under Canon B 2, authorized by the Archbishops of Canterbury and York under Canon C 4A or has had formerly episcopal consecration or ordination in some Church whose orders are recognized and accepted by the Church of England.

C 4   Of the quality of such as are to be ordained deacons or priests

1. Every bishop shall take care that he admit no person into holy orders but such as he knows either by himself, or by sufficient testimony, to have been baptized and confirmed, to be sufficiently instructed in Holy Scripture and in the doctrine, discipline, and worship of the Church of England, and to be of virtuous conversation and good repute and such as to be a wholesome example and pattern to the flock of Christ.

C 18 Of diocesan bishops

1. Every bishop shall be faithful in admitting persons into holy orders and in celebrating the rite of confirmation as often and in as many places as shall be convenient, and shall provide, as much as in him lies, that in every place within his diocese there shall be sufficient priests to minister the word and sacraments to the people that are therein.

C 22 Of archdeacons

4. Every archdeacon shall within his archdeaconry carry out his duties under the bishop and shall assist the bishop in his pastoral care and office, and particularly he shall see that all such as hold any ecclesiastical office within the same perform their duties with diligence, and shall bring to the bishop's attention what calls for correction or merits praise.

C 23 Of rural deans

1. Every rural dean shall report to the bishop any matter in any parish within the deanery which it may be necessary or useful for the bishop to know, particularly any case of serious illness or other form of distress amongst the clergy, the vacancy of any cure of souls and the measures taken by the sequestrators to secure the ministration of the word and sacraments and other rites of the Church during the said vacancy, and any case of a minister from another diocese officiating in any place otherwise than as provided in Canon C 8.

C 24 Of priests having a cure of souls

1. Every priest having a cure of souls shall provide that, in the absence of reasonable hindrance, Morning and Evening Prayer daily and on appointed days the Litany shall be said in the church, or one of the churches, of which he is the minister.

2. Every priest having a cure of souls shall, except for some reasonable cause approved by the bishop of the diocese, celebrate, or cause to be celebrated, the Holy Communion on all Sundays and other greater Feast Days and on Ash Wednesday, and shall diligently administer the sacraments and other rites of the Church.

3. Every priest having a cure of souls shall, except for some reasonable cause approved by the bishop of the diocese, preach, or cause to be preached, a sermon in the church or churches of which he is the minister at least once each Sunday.

4. He shall instruct the parishioners of the benefice, or cause them to be instructed, in the Christian faith; and shall use such opportunities of teaching or visiting in the schools within his cure as are open to him.

5. He shall carefully prepare, or cause to be prepared, all such as desire to be confirmed and, if satisfied of their fitness, shall present them to the bishop for confirmation.

6. He shall be diligent in visiting the parishioners of the benefice, particularly those who are sick and infirm; and he shall provide opportunities whereby any of such parishioners may resort unto him for spiritual counsel and advice.

7. He and the parochial church council shall consult together on matters of general concern and importance to the parish.

8. If at any time he shall be unable to discharge his duties whether from non-residence or some other cause, he shall provide for his cure to be supplied by a priest licensed or otherwise approved by the bishop of the diocese.

C 25 Of the residence of priests on their benefices

1. Every beneficed priest shall keep residence on his benefice, or on one of them if he shall hold two or more in plurality, and in the house of residence (if any) belonging thereto.

4. In the case of any benefice in which there is no house, or no fit house of residence, the priest holding that benefice may be licensed by the bishop of the diocese to reside in some fit and convenient house, although not belonging to that benefice: Provided that such house be within three miles of the church or chapel of the benefice, or, if the same be in any city or borough town or market town, within two miles of such church or chapel.

C 26 Of the manner of life of ministers

1. Every bishop, priest and deacon is under obligation, not being let by sickness or some other urgent cause, to say daily the Morning and Evening Prayer, either privately or openly; and to celebrate the Holy Communion, or be present thereat, on all Sundays and other principal Feast Days. He is also to be diligent in daily prayer and intercession, in examination of his conscience, and in the study of the Holy Scriptures and such other studies as pertain to his ministerial duties.

2. A minister shall not give himself to such occupations, habits, or recreations as do not befit his sacred calling, or may be detrimental to the performance of the duties of his office, or tend to be a just cause of offence to others; and at all times he shall be diligent to frame and fashion his life and that of his family according to the doctrine of Christ, and to make himself and them, as much as in him lies, wholesome examples and patterns to the flock of Christ.

C 27 Of the dress of ministers

The apparel of a bishop, priest, or deacon shall be suitable to his office; and, save for purposes of recreation and other justifiable reasons, shall be such as to be a sign and mark of his holy calling and ministry as well as to others as to those committed to his spiritual charge.

E 1 Of churchwardens

4. The churchwardens when admitted are officers of the Ordinary. They shall discharge such duties as are by law and custom assigned to them; they shall be foremost in representing the laity and in co-operating with the incumbent; they shall use their best endeavours by example and precept to encourage the parishioners in the practice of true religion and to promote unity and peace among them. They shall also maintain order and decency in the church and churchyard, especially during the time of divine service.

E 2 Of sidesmen or assistants to the churchwardens

2. It shall be the duty of the sidesmen to promote the cause of true religion in the parish and to assist the churchwardens in the discharge of their duties in maintaining order and decency in the church and churchyard, especially during the time of divine service.

These Canons will repay careful study and reflection. The original creation of them and the various revisions occupied considerable time and care. This is not the place for detailed exposition, but attention is drawn to four themes which are of particular relevance to aspects of this report and the situation in the Church today:

1. *holiness of life* in church leaders. C 4 requires bishops to look for this in their ordinands. C 26 expands the theme for all ordained ministers. Further-more E 1 urges churchwardens who are 'foremost in representing the laity' to 'use their best endeavours by example and precept to encourage the

parishioners in the practice of true religion and to promote unity and peace among them' – similarly E 2 for sidesmen/women. This ties in with later considerations of discipline (see Chapter 28) and a code of professional practice (see Chapter 27).

2. *'sufficient priests* to minister the word and sacraments' – C 18 looks to diocesan bishops to be at the forefront of vocations work and the development of ministry strategy.

3. *professional competence* in the clergy in the performance of their duties. C 22 requires archdeacons to have a special care in this regard. This too ties in with concerns on discipline and professional practice mentioned above.

4. *children and young people.* It is interesting to note C 24.4 with its reference to 'teaching or visiting in schools'. The Board of Education and others have recently pressed the question upon colleges and courses as to whether ordinands are effectively trained for these particular opportunities.

Ministry regulations and guidelines

I quote the Foreword to the loose-leaf binder of papers which has the title *Ministry Guidelines*:

> The House of Bishops has, over the years, approved many regulations and guidelines with respect to different aspects of ordained and lay ministries. These are often to be found in various Reports of the Ministry Division (or its predecessors). This book is a Guide to these many documents.
>
> At its meeting in March 1998, the Bishops' Committee for Ministry warmly endorsed the proposal from the staff to produce such a Guide.
>
> I warmly recommend the Guide to you and hope that you will find it a useful tool in your episcopal ministry.
>
> Suggestions for improvement and amendment will be welcomed by the Ministry Division. The Division will endeavour to revise and update sections as necessary.
>
> ✠ Michael Dunelm
> Chairman
> Ministry Division   12.1.2000

Bishops' statements

In the last 23 years, the House of Bishops has given much detailed attention to ministry issues. Many of their policy decisions (usually based on recommendations from the Ministry Division or its predecessors, or major working parties) are detailed in other parts of this report, e.g. on selection, training, deployment. However, there are three particular statements from the House on matters of broader ministry policy that ought to be more widely known – dating from 1978, 1992 and 1994.

The statements are set out almost in full because of their intrinsic importance, their historical significance and their continuing relevance. At the end I offer a comparative analysis which will indicate both continuity and development.

1978

The future of the ministry

Report by the House of Bishops

At its meeting on 22nd February 1978, the House carried the following motions:

1. 'That this House considers that the time has come for the Church of England to establish publicly certain clear guidelines of policy for the future of the Church's ministry.'

2. 'That this House welcomes the opportunities for more effective pastoral care and for mission offered by the development of a variety of ministries ordained and lay, stipendiary and voluntary, and believes that every diocese should be considering its responsibility for recruiting, training and developing the forms of ministry which the Church will need in the next 25 years.'

3. 'That this House considers that, within a developing pattern of ministries ordained and lay, there will continue to be need for a full-time ordained stipendiary ministry sufficient to maintain a nationwide parochial ministry and to allow for the maintenance and, where appropriate, the further extension of non-parochial ministries.'

4. That this House, believing that in recent years uncertainty about the Church's future need of full-time stipendiary ministers and about its ability to support those ministers financially and otherwise may have discouraged some candidates from offering themselves, asks the General Synod to affirm publicly

---

(i) its recognition of the continued need for a full-time stipendiary ministry of at least the present size and

(ii) the Church's willingness to provide the resources required to train that ministry, and to ensure that clergy, deaconesses and full-time lay workers are adequately paid, housed and pensioned.

5. 'That this House

(i) gives general endorsement to the proposals of the Policy Sub-Committee for more effective liaison between the various central bodies concerned with recruitment and selection, with deployment and with the provision of stipends, housing and pensions of the clergy, deaconesses and full-time lay workers, and commends them to the Standing Committee of the General Synod, to ACCM, and to the Church Commissioners, for further consideration

(ii) welcomes the proposal that a co-ordinating group should be established under the chairmanship of a member of the House of Bishops, working in close consultation with the Committee of ACCM Bishops, with a special responsibility for establishing the number of ordained and lay persons required for full-time ministry, and

(iii) asks that the House should have the opportunity to consider reports from the co-ordinating committee before these are debated by the General Synod, so that the view of the House can be adequately expressed in the Synod's debates.'

6. 'That this House

(i) believes that the encouragement and fostering of vocations to the ministry must at all times have a high priority for bishops, clergy and lay people in prayer and action, and most especially in the years immediately ahead;

(ii) welcomes the recent increase in the number of candidates recommended for training for the full-time ordained ministry, and expresses the hope that, while there will be no lowering of standards, the numbers recommended will increase to the range of 400/450 suggested as a target by the Policy Sub-Committee.'

Paras 7–12 are now summarized:

para. 7 expresses support for the theological colleges
para. 8 recommends a period of stability
para. 9 proposes financial provisions to enable that stability
para. 10 proposes stronger links between the colleges and General Synod
para. 11 is about the development of regional courses
para. 12 is about deaconesses and licensed lay workers
para. 13 concerns future publicity and debate of these 13 resolutions.

Originally in *The Future of the Ministry*, GS 374, 1978.
The resolutions will also be found in *The Church's Ministry: A Survey, November 1980*, GS 459, Annex 1, pp. 46–9; and in *The Ordained Ministry: Numbers, Cost and Deployment*, GS 858, 1988, Annex 1, pp. 29–31.

January 1992

'THIS HOUSE', conscious of the financial and other pressures affecting dioceses, affirms

(i) The parochial system as a basis for mission to offer every person and every community in the land:

    a) the proclamation of the Gospel in worship, word, sacrament and service;

    b) the pastoral ministry of the Church;

    c) access to public worship.

(ii) The need, within this parochial system, to develop the ministry of the whole people of God, and to continue to give radical consideration to developing and using imaginative and varied patterns of lay and ordained ministry.

(iii) The commitment to the principle of the Sheffield and women's formulae for the distribution of stipendiary clergy.

(iv) The commitment to support the training and ordination of all whose call to ordained and accredited ministry has been successfully tested and to provide sufficient Title posts for those who satisfactorily complete training for ordination.

(v) The principles of Christian Stewardship in the use of the Human and financial resources available to dioceses and in Providing for the support of the necessary ministry by way of Increased giving, and calls on the dioceses to meet the Challenge of improved stewardship presented by the report 'Receiving and Giving' (1990).[1]

January 1994

Ministry
A pastoral letter from the House of Bishops

At our meeting in Manchester we have prayed and reflected on the tasks for the ministry and mission of the Church of England in the light of the debate on ministry at the November 1993 meeting of the General Synod. We have been mindful also of the financial difficulties now facing dioceses, and we have heard a report on the latest financial prospects of the Church Commissioners.

Six principles

2. During the General Synod debate there was a strong call for a new strategy to be developed for ministry which would take account of, but not be driven by, the changed circumstances now confronting the Church. We believe that the details of such a strategy need to be worked out in each diocese, where local opportunities, needs and resources can best be assessed, and that it is important to develop a strategy for the whole Church of England based on certain common principles which we believe should undergird every diocese's approach:

(i)   Our Commission – Our commission from God is to proclaim the Gospel of God's saving power to everyone. In responding to its financial problems, the Church must not become introverted or focused on survival. Mission and active evangelism – bringing more people to know and respond to the love of God – must be at the heart of our approach.

(ii)   Our commitment – the Church of England has a continuing responsibility to serve all the nation. We affirm our responsibility to offer, with our ecumenical partners, to every person and every community in England:

- the proclamation of the Gospel in worship, word, sacrament and service;
- pastoral ministry;
- access to public worship;
- witness to Christian truth at every level of public life.

We acknowledge also the challenge of the new Europe and the part the Church of England has to play in it.

(iii) Imaginative and flexible patterns of ministry – how this is best done must be judged locally. In considering it, all the resources of ministry available – lay as well as ordained – need to be drawn upon. New ways of providing ministry, looking at resources across as well as within diocesan, deanery and parochial units, will need to be further developed by dioceses in the months and years ahead. This will often involve the creation of viable pastoral units larger than or different from existing parishes, building on the strengths and opportunities of identification with the local community. It will involve developing clergy conditions of service appropriate to current needs, and calling into question practices of long standing, such as the ecclesiastical freehold. A new willingness to adapt to changing patterns of ministry and deployment will be required in clergy (whether stipendiary or non-stipendiary), readers and other lay people.

(iv) The Ordained Ministry: a Priority – within the resources available for ministry, the ordained clergy have a vital role, not least as enablers and leaders of wider ministry teams. As we amplify later, care will need to be taken to ensure that, within the available resources, the number and morale of the stipendiary clergy is given high priority. In particular, continuing support must be given to the encouragement of vocations among those younger men and women who will provide the basis of tomorrow's ordained ministry.

(v) Partnership – in responding to this challenge, the Church must act together, with mutual consultation and open discussion. Unilateral action by individual bodies (be they dioceses, parishes, Boards of Finance or those at national level) without reference to the wider Church and its needs is unacceptable.

(vi) Mutual Support – in particular, we call on all concerned to recognise as they discuss these matters – whether at national, diocesan or parochial level – that they remain members one of another, with a responsibility to bear one another's burdens and to offer mutual support and encouragement, whether in identifying opportunities or facing difficulties. A narrow insistence on self-sufficiency is not enough: we must look beyond this to a genuine sharing of resources which will ensure that the needs of mission and of the less well-off among us continue to be met. To do otherwise would be a breach of Christian duty.

We pledge ourselves to work in the spirit of these principles.

The stipendiary ministry

3. As bishops, we have a particular care and responsibility for those who have accepted the call – often sacrificially for themselves and their families – to full-time stipendiary service in the ordained ministry. We wish to pay tribute to the faithful and inspiring work being undertaken by the clergy. We are also acutely aware of the anxiety the present uncertainty is causing to those already in, training for, or considering entering that ministry. They need to know where they stand. We, therefore, intend:

  (i) To do all in our power together to employ the number of clergy in the 'Sheffield' allocation until a replacement for that system has been agreed.

  (ii) To ask the Advisory Board of Ministry urgently to review the 'Sheffield' allocation system and bring forward specific proposals to sustain or modify it, taking account of the financial situation and the need for national fairness and consistency.

  (iii) To do all in our power to offer stipendiary places to those currently in training for stipendiary ordained ministry, and all who begin training in 1994.

  (iv) To ask the Advisory Board of Ministry in consultation with the Church Commissioners and all dioceses, to bring to us as soon as possible an analysis of the number of stipendiary clergy the Church appears likely to need and can afford, if possible up to the year 2000. ABM will identify any consequences it believes this analysis has for numbers to be admitted to training for stipendiary ministry. Once this information is to hand, we shall aim to take rapid and clear decisions on these matters so that all concerned (notably theological colleges and courses and potential ordinands) know where they stand.

4. In the present situation we have particular concern for those whose call is to the stipendiary diaconate, Church Army or to full-time accredited lay ministry. We recognise that it is likely to be increasingly difficult for them to obtain suitable appointments.

Responsible stewardship

5. There is a danger that, conscious of the reduced resources available to us from the Church Commissioners, we will forget the many other resources – of people, buildings, church schools and church colleges as well as money – which continue to be at our disposal. The responsible stewardship of all our resources is at the heart of the response we are called upon to make.

A call to generous and committed giving

6. In formulating their new plans for ministry, dioceses will also be considering how resources can be increased by a fresh call to generous, proportionate and committed giving by church and community members. We have discussed with the Chairman of the Stewardship Committee of the Central Board of Finance how dioceses can be helped in this. We believe that all those who have the Church's welfare at heart must ask themselves not merely 'what does the Church need in the circumstances now facing it?' but 'what am I called upon to give gladly out of the bounty God has given me?', and should test their response against the standards already established of the tithe (10 per cent of take home pay to charitable purposes) and that set by the Synod of not less than 5 per cent of net income to the Church.

Facing the challenge

7. The shape of the Church's response to its altering financial circumstances can only emerge over time, as the practical consequences for dioceses of reduced Commissioners' allocations are explored and the opportunities for meeting shortfalls by enhanced giving and more flexible patterns of ministry are addressed. We invite dioceses and parishes to have in mind the approach we have set out in this note as they discuss the way forward. We ask them to see the situation facing them not only as a challenge but as an opportunity to tackle deep-seated issues – of inflexible ministry, of inadequate giving – so that from it the mission and ministry of the Church may emerge renewed and reinvigorated. We have asked the Advisory Board of Ministry to monitor the responses of dioceses and we shall keep the closest eye on developments in the months ahead, reporting to our people through General Synod and Diocesan Synods as necessary.

8. The context in which the discussion throughout the Church will take place is the Decade of Evangelism. As other provinces in the Anglican Communion have found, the commitment to share our life and faith with others can transform present difficulties into a positive incentive for growth. Led by the God whom we worship, we shall together endeavour to fulfil our ministry to all the nation.

On behalf of the House:

George Cantuar   John Ebor
12 January 1994

Analysis

I believe six major themes emerge from these important statements:

Theme	1978	1992	1994
1. encouragement of *variety* in ministries	para 2	para ii	para 2(iii)
2. *diocesan* responsibility	para 2	(implicit in paras i and ii)	para 2 intro
3. national *parochial* ministry and mission	para 3	para i	para 2(i) and (ii)
4. the particular role of full-time *stipendiary clergy*	para 3	(implicit in para iii)	para 2 (iv) cf. para 3(i), (ii)
5. commitment to and appeal for *financial* provision	para 4	para v	para 5–6
6. encouraging *vocations*	para 6	para iv	para 2(iv), 3(iii)

There is very significant continuity of purpose and commitment over these 16 years in spite of the many turbulent issues facing the Church during that period. The six themes will each be the subject of review in later parts of this report along with many other issues which are important contexts for their further discussion and strategic development.

A significant new feature in 1994 is the request for 'an analysis of the number of stipendiary clergy the Church *appears likely to need and can afford*' (para 3(iv), my italics). This issue will be addressed further at Chapters 5, 6 and 21.

5

Ministry strategy – its development since 1960

Synopsis of major reports/events

1964   Paul Report

1967   Fenton Morley, *Partners in Ministry*

1969   The Pastoral Measure
        Designation of Areas of Ecumenical Experiment
        Sharing of Church Buildings Act

1974   The Clergy Appointments Adviser
        The 'Sheffield' Report on Clergy Deployment
        Melinsky, *Patterns of Ministry*

1978   *The Future of the Ministry* – 13 resolutions from the House of
        Bishops

1980   *The Church's Ministry: A Survey*

1981   The Partners in Mission Report

1983   Tiller Report

1985   *Faith in the City* (ACUPA)

1988   *The Ordained Ministry: Numbers, Cost and Deployment* –
        discussion paper

1989   *Call to Order*

1990   *Faith in the Countryside* (ACORA)

1992   *The Ordained Ministry: Numbers, Cost, Recruitment and
        Deployment*
        Resolution from the House of Bishops

1993   *Order in Diversity*

1994   *Pastoral Letters* from the House of Bishops
        Survey of Diocesan Ministerial Strategies
        National Consultation on Local Ministry

1998   *Shaping Ministry for a Missionary Church* (a review of diocesan
        ministry strategy)

The Paul Report (1964)

Are there too few clergy in the Church of England? How well off are they? Are they in the right places? In 1960 the National Assembly of the Church of England instructed the Central Advisory Council for the Ministry (CACTM) 'to consider, in the light of changing circumstances, the system of payment and deployment of the clergy, and to make recommendations'. Dr Leslie Paul was asked by CACTM to undertake a full survey. In 1964 was published his report, *The Deployment and Payment of the Clergy.*

Paul gave detailed attention to social changes, especially of population and community. He highlighted the issue of clergy isolation, and asserted that 'the new role of the laity ... constitutes the religious revolution of the 20th century' (p. 92). He recommended:

1. Major recruitment drive and direction of curates in first five years to areas of need.
2. Replacement of freehold by leasehold of ten years which would be renewable.
3. Development of major parishes with team ministries where the traditional parish system has broken down in both rural and downtown areas.
4. Development of diocesan powers of pastoral reorganization linked with pastoral care of, and career structures for, clergy who would be salaried employees. Patronage would be by a system of staff appointment boards.

Though the proposals had strong supporters, there was widespread opposition to direction of curates, abolition of freehold and patronage, and the concept of clergy as employees.

The Paul Report led to the establishing of the *Ministry Co-Ordinating Group* (see p. 18 above) and other initiatives listed below.

Partners in Ministry (1967)

This was a substantial report by the Commission on Deployment and Payment of the Clergy which had been set up in 1965 following the debates on the Paul Report. Its chairman was Canon Fenton Morley. Its recommendations were unanimous from its 20 members and (they claimed) 'constitute an organic whole'. They recommended:

1. abolition of benefice, patronage and freehold.
2. clergy security through ordination and being 'on the strength of the diocese' which is the basic unit.

3. all patronage and appointments through a Diocesan Ministry Commission.
4. appointment for a term renewable with consent, or without a term and subject to review.
5. a Provincial Board of Referees for appeal if disagreement cannot be resolved.
6. centralization of glebe to the Church Commissioners, and of parsonages to the dioceses.
7. Central Ministry Commission to oversee national policy and register of clergy.
8. clergy pay should be simpler and fairer, with the Church Commissioners as the central payment authority.

The Pastoral Measure (1969)

In 1967 the then National Assembly of the Church of England passed the final stages of the *Pastoral Measure*. This complex legal package consolidated many earlier Acts and Measures under which pastoral reorganization had been effected. It became law in 1969. It enabled major changes to parishes, properties, ministry and appointments. A major review of the Pastoral Measure and associated law is explained in Chapter 40.

Terms of Ministry Committee

A third consequence of the Paul Report and subsequent debates was the setting up of the Terms of Ministry Committee which reported in 1972 (GS 87). They recommended the appointment ... of a Clergy Appointments Adviser (see Chapter 24) and the formulation of a deployment plan which emerged as

The 'Sheffield' Report (1974)

Deployment of the Clergy: The Report of the House of Bishops' Working Group (GS 205, 1974), chaired by the Bishop of Sheffield. The fundamental issue was the inequitable distribution of clergy – more particularly, the clergy were too heavily in the southern Province. The proposed formula had four criteria, weighted as:

Population	8
Area	1
Electoral Roll	3
Places of Worship	3

The recommendations were accepted and have been very effective over the years.

Patterns of Ministry (1974)

Canon Hugh Melinsky (Chief Secretary of ACCM) prepared this discussion paper. Its aim was to draw out principal themes from key reports of the period 1968–74 and describe the progress of proposals. In Chapter 1, 'Where are we now?', he described pressures of manpower, 'the most serious decline in the number of men ordained in this century apart from the periods of the two world wars' (p. 1), pressure on livings, pressure of money and theological pressures about the nature of faith and ministry.

The chapter on 'Present Developments' touched briefly on lay training, groups and teams, specialists, NSM, bishops, women, deacons and lay ministry. The chapter 'Indicators for the Future' suggested God may not be calling as many men 'as we think desirable' and raised the spectre of clergy unemployment. The final chapter, 'Training', addressed the issue of the rationalization of colleges and the need for improved further training post-ordination.

Maintaining the Ministry (1978)

This was an unpublished report by the Policy Sub-Committee emphasizing the 'serious crisis in staffing to be expected within the next decade'. The material was used in *The Future of the Ministry* (1978), which was a report by the House of Bishops containing and explaining 13 Resolutions (GS 374). Because of their importance, they are recorded in full in Chapter 4.
Key elements included:

- the need for 'clear guidelines of policy';
- the encouragement to dioceses to develop a variety of ministries, ordained and lay, stipendiary and voluntary;
- the continuing need for full-time stipendiaries (a) to maintain nation-wide parochial ministry, and (b) at the present size.

The Church's Ministry: A Survey (1980)

The Ministry Co-Ordinating Group produced this report. This group had been set up two years earlier (see above) at the request of the House of Bishops to implement the 13 Resolutions mentioned above which had been approved by the General Synod. The survey described the present shape of ministry – lay and ordained, NSM and deaconess, etc. (see Chapter 2). The chapter on deployment described the reforms since the Paul Report (1964). Chapters 4 and 5 addressed training (rising costs), stipends (catching up after decline, and increasingly met by parishes rather than the Church Commissioners), housing, expenses and retirement provision.

The final chapter raised questions for the formulation of strategy. These included:

- the nature of ministry and mission;
- nationwide responsibility and the parochial system;
- deployment and possible implications of clergy shortage;
- mission, lay ministry and shared leadership;
- flexibility, ecumenical progress and signs of renewal.

Partners in Mission Consultation (1981)

Of this John Tiller reported (p. 4):

> This was an exercise in which Christians from other traditions and from other Anglican provinces were invited to help members of the Church of England formulate its priorities for mission for the next few years. The Consultation highlighted the need for a much greater emphasis on 'shared ministry' so that the energies and gifts of the laity, too often stifled or discouraged by clerical domination, could be released for both the planning and the practice of ministry. The Standing Committee of the General Synod, in considering how best to follow up the PIM Report, asked ACCM to make 'shared ministry' an important dimension of the forthcoming strategy document.[1]

The Tiller Report (1983)

Canon John Tiller (Chief Secretary of ACCM) was asked to produce a report 'which would have the unity of one person's view' and also take into account previous discussions (see Foreword). The report was published in 1983 entitled *A Strategy for the Church's Ministry*.

Tiller argued that a dynamic conservatism would be quite inadequate. He proposed a radical alternative with these features:

- every basic Christian community should provide its own essential ministry in a team of ordained and lay;

- the bishops' role is to ensure that this happens;
- a team of diocesan clergy would be available for specialist ministries and mission.

Along the way, Tiller expounded the (sixfold) weaknesses of the parochial system, and proposed abolition of the benefice (with its incumbent), of patronage and of the freehold (see pp. 135ff and 155ff).

Though welcomed by many, there was strong concern to maintain a stipendiary priest in (most) parishes, and anxiety about the diocesan task force clergy not being rooted in local situations. There was *theological* anxiety about local non-stipendiary clergy being primarily *pastoral* with the (often stipendiary) diocesan clergy specializing in *mission* and *teaching*. Finally, there was again strong opposition to the abolition of patronage and freehold (as previously with Paul and Fenton Morley).

Faith in the City (1985)

This was the report of the Archbishop of Canterbury's Commission on Urban Priority Areas (ACUPA). The report encouraged further attention to the development of local ministry and the undertaking of mission audits. The development of the Church Urban Fund led to many projects and schemes.

Faith in the Countryside (1990)

This was the report of the Archbishops' Commission on Rural Areas (ACORA). It argued that reduction of clergy numbers should be integrated with:

- re-training of rural clergy;
- development of lay leadership;
- re-examination of clergy freehold.

The Ordained Ministry: Numbers, Cost, Recruitment and Deployment (1992)

This (ABM Ministry Paper No. 2) was an analysis of the responses of the dioceses to a series of questions on these issues which arose from the report of the Ministry Co-Ordinating Group, *The Ordained Ministry: Numbers, Cost and Deployment*, GS Misc 858, 1988, and *Call to Order*, ACCM, 1989.

The Chairman's Preface includes the text of the Resolution from the House of Bishops in January 1992 (see Chapter 4). After sketching the background and updating the figures for ordinands, the report summarizes diocesan responses. Some of the main issues are that, in general, the dioceses:

33. i   affirm the parochial system as a nationwide basis for the mission of the Church recognising that the way in which this is expressed needs constant development and often some radical reappraisal.

     ii   recognize that the number of stipendiary clergy is as low as can reasonably be acceptable and that a modest increase would benefit the mission of the Church.

     iii see the development of the whole people of God in a variety of ministries as being essential.

40. i   (mostly) were confident that their commitment to fund a modest increase in parochial clergy would be supported by increased income.

60. i   affirm the commitment to train and support all those whose vocation to ordained or accredited ministry has been successfully tested.

     ii   have shown by the appointment of diocesan vocations advisers that they accept responsibility to encourage vocations to Christian service within the parishes and churches of the diocese.

69. i   accept that there should be greater sense of accountability for the clergy.

     ii   welcome moves to develop appropriate methods of clergy appraisal which should be directed towards ministry development.

     iii accepted the need for a caring method of helping clergy whose ministry is no longer adequate.

Order in Diversity (1993)

This (ABM Ministry Paper No. 5, GS Misc 1084) mapped some features concerning the variety, numbers and issues for the ordained ministry. There is valuable information about varieties of ministry and clergy deployment. However, the financial recession in the country and the reduction of the Church Commissioners' allocations to the dioceses for stipend support had led to some evidence that there were the earliest signs of clergy unemployment (in spite of reducing numbers of stipendiary clergy). In 1992 and 1993 a few ordinands found it difficult to obtain title posts for their curacy. The problem quickly disappeared – but the repeated references in the report to financial pressures and lack of posts had a dispiriting effect on some bishops, directors of ordinands and vocation advisers and the morale of ordinands. Numbers of ordinands fell significantly.

Ministry: A Pastoral Letter from the House of Bishops (1994)

This important statement is given in full in Chapter 4. It arose out of the debates in General Synod and the House of Bishops on the report *Order in Diversity*.

Survey of Diocesan Ministerial Strategies (1994)

The report of a working group. The small group was commissioned by ABM to undertake this survey following the debates on *Order in Diversity* where there was repeated appeal for strategic leadership. The report of ten pages was never published. It assessed evidence received from 31 dioceses. The report itself is unclear at many points, but argues that there is no evidence of clear and coherent trends in the dioceses that might reveal a national strategy, explicit or implicit (7.1). It said of 'the tension between national decisions by the House of Bishops and activities in their dioceses' that 'there seems to be minimal coherence here' (8.5). Note the very different analysis reported just four years later, in 1998 (described below).

Local Ministry: A Key Element in the Church's Strategy for Mission (1994)

This is the report of a National Consultation on the Development of Local Ministry held over three days at High Leigh and attended by representatives of more than 30 dioceses. The consultation was sponsored by the Edward King Institute for Ministry Development. This concept is so significant and clearly creating such energy among both clergy and lay people that the report is included at Appendix 10. The Conclusions and Recommendations will also be found in *Formal Lay Ministry* (1999). Further attention is given to this issue in Chapter 35.

Clergy Conditions of Service (1994)

A consultative paper was widely debated throughout the Church. This paper, the responses and consequences are dealt with in Chapter 23. It is noted here because of major strategic implications in the area of the ecclesiastical freehold.

Shaping Ministry for a Missionary Church (1998)

A review of diocesan ministry strategy documents 1997 (ABM Ministry Paper No. 18, published October 1998). The report of the working party (chaired by the Ven. Dr John Marsh, Archdeacon of Blackburn) is strikingly different in style, analysis and conclusions from its predecessor four years earlier. The Bishop of Gloucester (in the Preface) described the task as:

- to review what was going on in practice
- to analyse the practice and draw out the theory and theology on which strategies were based, and
- to ask where the Church was and should be going, recognizing that this might vary from context to context.

He remarked: 'This report presents a lively and vibrant picture of fresh ideas and changing practice in the ministry of the Church of England.' He concluded: 'The picture that emerges is complex and varied but overwhelmingly forward-looking. It reveals what many might find as *a surprising degree of common analysis and shared commitment*' (my italics) (p. iii).

The report indicates that 'dioceses are increasingly aware of the changing social context'. Two important factors have acted as catalysts to the serious re-thinking:

1. the changing financial position as dioceses take increasingly the major responsibility for ministry finances;
2. the reducing number of stipendiary clergy available for deployment.

However, these issues are not the primary ones. Behind many documents 'there were signs of both vision and spirituality'. Theological grounding of strategies uses theology of the Trinity, incarnation, mission and baptism. Three ministerial themes appear repeatedly:

1. partnership in the whole people of God;
2. every-member ministry – in the world and in the Church;
3. the changed role of stipendiary ministers (see further at Chapter 7).

In almost every document this led to talking about *teams*. These might be teams of (largely) 'ordained ministers in formal Group or Team Ministries or in Local Ecumenical Partnerships. However, in addition to these, or sometimes in combination with them, there was a much newer emphasis upon teams of clergy and lay ministers, especially in dioceses which had an Ordained Local Ministry scheme. Indeed what seems to be emerging in many dioceses is a concept of team which is predominantly lay but which also includes some who are ordained stipendiary and/or non-stipendiary' (p. 8).

There are a variety of basic pastoral units, e.g. multi-parish benefice (in rural areas), single parish, minster model, cluster of parishes. The strategic developments of NSM, Reader and diocesan authorized lay ministries (e.g. pastoral assistants, evangelists, etc.) are noted.

The conclusions are immensely significant, and are quoted in full:

Out of this detail a number of points can be pulled out as provisional general conclusions about the evolving ministry strategy of the Church of England at diocesan level.

(i) The Church of England is emphatically not retreating from its commitment to offer ministry to the whole community. Dioceses are addressing a diversity of context in very different ways, but none of their approaches remotely suggests a shift into congregationalism.

(ii) There does seem to be a broad consensus about the theological approach to be followed in thinking about ministry. Paragraphs 2.5–2.10 have outlined this.

(iii) There is a massive emphasis on 'teams'. However, that word means very different things in different places. There are different types of teams, teams working in different units, different methods of diocesan authorization of teams, and different ministers and ministries being included in teams.

(iv) There is a strong emphasis on the changing role of the (reducing number of) stipendiary clergy.

(v) A striking conclusion is that nearly all the plans which refer to clergy numbers accept the 'Forecast Sheffield' allocations as a basis for planning. People have been suggesting that Sheffield is dead. Reading these documents suggests that this is not true.

(vi) There is a trend towards larger structural units – often through the clustering of parishes. In some dioceses, deaneries are becoming more powerful in pastoral reorganization.

(vii) As well as the issue of stipendiary/non-stipendiary there is an emerging question about deployability. Dioceses are seeking to make at least some Non-Stipendiary Ministers and Readers more deployable, in contrast to local ministers, retired clergy, and even some stipendiary clergy.

The final section of the report poses some searching questions, as follows:

Questions to the dioceses

a) How far do the proposals reflect the theology?
b) What about the eschatological dimension of the kingdom?
c) Areas of mission that need more than local attention, e.g. among deaf people?
d) The changed use of Sunday and irregular attendance?
e) Coping with change – help for both clergy and congregations?
f) Implications of changing role of clergy for training posts, i.e. experience of team work?
g) Implications for diocesan senior staff and oversight?
h) Winning consensus and ownership of new strategies?
i) Changes in Reader ministry, and growth in numbers?

Questions to the Church at national level

a) Clergy and Readers are nationally regulated but there is an emerging plethora of lay ministries at diocesan level. Is this right?
b) implications of 'episcopal' team leaders for training, CME, and adult education?
c) implications for theology of ordination to the priesthood – are we now selecting for incumbency? Should there be a differentiation of criteria?
d) do the Pastoral Measure and the Teams and Groups Measure need radical revision – to provide the flexibility required?

Questions to all levels

There were very few references to

a) the ecumenical dimension;
b) the diaconate;
c) ministry in secular employment.

Why is this?

The Postscript includes this important paragraph:

> A significant feature of this review is that there is clearly emerging an underlying common pattern: a central core of ordained stipendiary ministers deployed appropriately in each diocese and enriched by a variety of other ministers, ordained and lay. This pattern is welcomed and affirmed: it provides a model which is thoroughly flexible and able to be shaped and reshaped in each local situation in response to the ever-changing missionary task.

6

Uncertainties and issues under review

The call for a coherent ministry strategy was made many times during the twentieth century. Real efforts were made to provide such a strategy or, at least, major elements towards one. Major contributions and developments have been reviewed earlier (see Chapter 5). The names of Paul, Fenton Morley and Tiller, the Pastoral Measure and the Sheffield Report are landmarks. Then there are the three major Statements from the House of Bishops – 1978, 1992 and 1994.

However, a responsible consideration of national ministry strategy today needs to pay careful attention to:

a) areas of uncertainty, and how they might impact on such strategy, and

b) issues that are under substantial review at the moment, and the time-frame for proposals.

Areas of uncertainty include:

The financial situation

This was introduced earlier, in Chapter 1, and will be explained in more detail later, in Chapter 39. At the time of writing this section (February 2000) we are awaiting the Actuarial Reviews in a few weeks' time of both the Church Commissioners' distributions and the Pensions Board commitments. The results of the former will affect the amount the Commissioners can make available for stipend support, and the results of the latter will affect both that and the level of contribution levied on parishes/dioceses to secure future pension funding.

The financial overview of the Church of England seems to indicate that diocesan finances are under severe pressures while many parishes are in a significantly better position. The implications of these factors are very difficult to judge at this moment.

The Employment Act

The possible implications of this Act with reference to the parochial clergy are explained in Chapter 23. However, the full consequences, structurally and pastorally, of the clergy either becoming employees, or having comparable protections (and obligations) as if they were employees, are very difficult to predict. Relationships between clergy and bishops, and between clergy and the laity, could change in very significant ways.

The Data Protection Act

The rights of access by the subject to written material becomes operative in October 2001. This will have major consequences for:

(i) the selection systems. Sponsorship forms, references and the selectors' reports will become, in principle, open documents to the one about whom they are written.

(ii) the appointments procedures. References, bishops' files and notes on the results of interviews will again become, in principle, open documents to the one about whom they are written.

This Act is about truthfulness, integrity and justice and so should be welcomed. However, many will need to learn a new kind of honesty over references, and openness over appointments. It will be interesting to observe how this will work out.

Numbers of clergy

The numbers of retirements can be predicted with substantial accuracy, but the number of ordinands is really impossible to predict. Statistics for past years will be found in Chapters 9 and 12. Numbers have varied considerably. The setting of optimistic targets has had a depressing history.

The capping of numbers (when the total is reducing significantly) has been steadily resisted.

Work on long-term projections of stipendiary clergy numbers was done in 1999:

1. The first assumed that current numbers of ordinands will remain static at 338 for the next 20 years. This projection indicated that by 2020 there could be approximately 1,300 fewer stipendiary clergy than the Church has at present.

2. The second suggested that, in order to maintain the number of stipendiary clergy at roughly its present level, recruitment would have to rise roughly to 470 over the next five years.

3. It is assumed that the age structure of new entrants would remain the same over the 20-year period and that patterns of retirement would also remain constant.

4. We must bear in mind that the numbers of Non-Stipendiary Ministers, Ordained Local Ministers and Readers continue to rise. In 1999 there were 1,771 Non-Stipendiary Ministers, 274 Ordained Local Ministers and 8,557 licensed Readers (plus about 1,500 active Readers over 70 with permission to officiate).

5. Dioceses have responded to the declining numbers of stipendiary clergy thus far by developing different strategies for ministry. See *Shaping Ministry for a Missionary Church* (ABM Policy Paper No. 18). These strategies have included:

- a new emphasis on evangelism and building missionary communities;
- pastoral re-organization schemes;
- deanery agreements about reducing full-time clergy posts;
- the development of various ministry models such as 'clusters' and 'minsters';
- house for duty arrangements;
- the expansion of dual-role ministries;
- local ecumenical partnerships;
- the development of collaborative ministry, local or total ministry teams of various kinds;
- the development of ordained local ministry;
- the growth in numbers of parish or deanery-based youth officers, pastoral assistants and evangelists.

The questions of how many stipendiary clergy the Church of England (a) wishes to have and (b) can afford are very difficult to answer in a way that is widely acceptable.

Answers are affected by views on finance (see above), and on other forms of ministry, e.g. NSM, OLM, Readers and others.

Churches worldwide have lived and thrived (and still do) with amazing varieties of ministry resource, e.g. African dioceses with few stipendiary clergy.

The question is asked whether the Church should and/or can attempt/operate workforce planning like other organizations? Some reply that this is inappropriate because of a theology of vocation, the financial base being essentially voluntary and the existence of a substantial voluntary workforce (ordained and lay). Others object that these arguments are not compelling, and that workforce planning within certain parameters would be a salutary exercise. The Working Party on Ordination Training is planning to address these issues.

The strategic use of non-stipendiary clergy, Reader and other lay ministers

As will be seen, dioceses differ over the adoption of ordained local ministry and the development of formal local ministry schemes (see Chapter 35). Some dioceses without OLM will use NSM clergy and/or Readers in their strategic planning. These are significant resources. Some dioceses have developed major schemes of pastoral assistants, evangelists, etc. Any national strategy must take careful note of these developments.

Issues that are under substantial review include:

The Clergy Stipends Review

This includes the entire remuneration package (see Chapter 22), i.e. training, stipend, fees, expenses, housing and pension. This group has carried out a major survey of all stipendiary clergy. They are planning to report to the Archbishops' Council in 2001. There will be some far-reaching recommendations. Terms of reference and membership are at Appendix 5.

The structure and funding of ordination training

This working party has a wide remit to ask searching questions. The theology of ministry and ordination and the issue of appropriate numbers of ordinands are being addressed along the way. The group is to report to the Archbishops' Council in 2002/3. Terms of reference and membership are at Appendix 3. See also Chapters 17–20.

The renewed distinctive diaconate

A working party of the House of Bishops is planning to report to them in 2001. See Chapter 36.

The Pastoral Measure

This (and associated legislation) is being reviewed. The issues are very far-reaching – see Chapter 40. The review group will probably take at least two years from its start in February 2001.

7

The changing role of the stipendiary clergy

Introduction

This issue has been repeatedly mentioned in ministry reports in recent decades. The main lines of argument include the following:

1. sociological – the status of the clergy as a profession has declined.

2. theological – the great emphasis in recent decades has been on the theology and ministry of the laity, the whole people of God.

3. professional – the financial shift of power means that clergy now receive the large proportion of their stipends not from the Church Commissioners (which gave them a feeling of gentlemanly independence) but from their congregations (which encourages the development of local accountability).

4. missiological – the increasingly secular context, and marginalization, of Church and ministry.

5. numerical – the decline in the numbers of stipendiary clergy throughout the twentieth century.

The report *Ministry Strategy for a Missionary Church* found this a major theme in diocesan analysis and strategies. It declared:

> 2.15 Thirdly there is *a changed role for stipendiary ministers. Any notion of dependency upon this stipendiary ministry, as in the past, must be avoided. It exists to help each Christian realize their own vocation, discern their own gifts and develop their own ministry* (Oxford). *The role of the stipendiary minister in this situation changes from being the person who does everything to the person who enables and equips others to do almost everything* (Sheffield). *The specific role of the clergy in this type of shared priesthood is to do, at a local level, what the Bishop does at a diocesan level. That is, to exercise a servant leadership of caring oversight that will enable the priesthood of the*

baptised. For the laity to become more 'priestly' it is therefore necessary for the clergy to become more 'episcopal' (Derby). The model is of a reduced number of stipendiary clergy having a strong focus in leading/enabling/resourcing/overseeing a range of others engaged in ministry – laity (some of them paid), Readers, Non-Stipendiary Ministers, Ordained Local Ministers, and various new forms of diocesan-authorized lay ministry.

Discussions of this subject can become unhelpfully polarized in various ways. I have shared in many dozens of such debates over the years and have concluded that people need wider perspectives on the issues. We need to understand the five issues outlined above, but this analysis will also be influenced by:

- historical perspectives;
- theological and missiological understandings;
- realism over finance and clergy numbers;
- morale – and relationships with bishops/archdeacons on the one hand, and with lay leaders in the parish on the other hand.

The Ordinals

Amid the many changes of the last half-century, the fundamental charter elements of diaconal and priestly/presbyteral ministry have been expressed in, and defined by, the Ordinals. The primary elements of ministry of word and sacrament, pastoral care and of godly example are clear in both the Ordinal attached to the Book of Common Prayer, and that in the Alternative Service Book. So the changing role must not be exaggerated. Surely it is more about the *how* of these aspects of ministry rather than about the *what* (i.e. the style and method rather than the substance).

The history

The changing roles of the clergy of the Church of England through history have been charted by Anthony Russell (now Bishop of Ely) in his famous book *The Clerical Profession* and in very summary form earlier in this report (see Chapter 3). Even when allowances are made for the generalizations and possible exaggeration of the proposed categories, the fundamental thesis is surely compelling. Ours is not the first generation to face profound change at many levels in both society and in church life.

The interpretation

Intertwining with Russell's essentially sociological interpretation are other dimensions of theology, spirituality and churchmanship. The great historical movements in the Church of England were commonly oversimplified into 'high', 'middle' and 'low'. However, the theology and spirituality of these movements are of great significance to the practice of ministry:

- the Reformation divines, the eighteenth- and nineteenth-century evangelical revivals and the evangelical renewal of the later twentieth century;
- the seventeenth-century High Church Caroline divines and nineteenth-century Oxford Movement and Anglo-Catholic revival;
- the Broad Church tradition and liberal and modernist traditions with biblical criticism, engagement with modern scientific disciplines, and issues of justice and social structures;
- the Pietist and mystical traditions, monastic and religious communities, the Pentecostal and renewal movements of the 1960s onwards.

All these – and others – have led to clergy emphasizing different aspects of their ordained ministry, and mixing these aspects in countless and complex permutations:

- pastor/teacher;
- priest/mystic/religious representative;
- community worker/counsellor/healer/chaplain/prophet;
- missionary/evangelist/church planter;
- enabler/manager/leader.

It is all too easy to stereotype others, and to oversimplify the nature and forms of their church life and ministry. I have omitted to mention above the ecumenical and liturgical movements which, again, cut across all (or most) traditions.

The 'episcopal'

I quote again from the Diocese of Derby ministry strategy document (cited earlier in this chapter): 'it is therefore necessary for the clergy to become more "episcopal"'. This development has two main causes – firstly, the theology of the laity as the priestly community of God's people called and baptized to the mission of God, and secondly, the reducing numbers of stipendiary clergy. So, it is agreed, the role of clergy becomes increasingly 'at local level what the bishop does at a diocesan level' (see again the quotations from Oxford, Sheffield and Derby documents, above).

The Bishops' Criteria for selection of ordinands were revised in the early 1990s to reflect this development. Criterion G says:

> Candidates should show ability to offer leadership in the Church community and to some extent in the wider community. This ability includes a capacity to offer an example of faith and discipleship, to collaborate effectively with others, as well as to guide and shape the life of the Church community in its mission to the world.

The 'missionary'

The recognition of an increasingly secularized context has been noted for many decades with regard to the conurbations and especially inner-city areas. The extent and depth of the analysis developed significantly in the last two decades of the twentieth century and through the responses of dioceses and parishes to the 'Decade of Evangelism'. Some of the literature is cited earlier (see p. 10).

For most of the centuries until the middle of the twentieth, the clergy were primarily in 'pastoral' rather than 'mission' mode, although there are many more exceptions to this oft-quoted generalization than are commonly recognized. However, the need for leaders in mission is now more and more widely recognized. It is reflected in the Bishops' Criterion G (quoted above) 'to guide and shape the life of the church community in its mission to the world', and in C – candidates 'should demonstrate personal commitment to Christ and *a capacity to communicate the Gospel*'.

The 'manager'

Bishop Russell's fourth identifiable stage in the development of the clerical role is the church manager (see Chapter 3). He refers to the laity's ambivalence about this trend, but it raises very strong and polarized feelings among clergy too.

Allegations of a 'managerialist' and 'centralist' culture have been fuelled by:

1. careful developments in diocesan and national selection systems;

2. the growing use of university accreditation for training courses;

3. the very widespread use of diocesan schemes of appraisal/ministry review and associated setting of objectives;

4. the growing use of advertisement, job descriptions, short-listing and competitive interviews;

5. the seven-year 'leasehold' agreements in team ministries with review;

6. debate on 'employment' rights and obligations, deployment, remuneration and conditions of service issues;

7. the Turnbull Report and establishing of the Archbishops' Council;

8. diocesan strategic planning of ministry, pastoral reorganization and financial budgeting;

9. the Data Protection Act, the Child Protection Act, etc.

Older clergy are heard to murmur 'this is not the Church I was ordained into'. Canon Ian Bunting examined the development of *Models of Ministry* in a Grove Booklet with that title and the sub-title *Managing the Church Today* (1993, revised 1996). He appreciates the theological suspicion attached to the concept in this context, but argues that the model has undergone a transformation to an imaginative leader, a practical theologian – a *pathfinder*! Perhaps anxiety in this area might be helped by further reflection on:

- the Ordinal, and the primacy of the spiritual and vocational;

- the bishops' selection criteria (see Chapter 12);

- the concept of *episcope* (oversight, superintendence);

- the role of equity and justice in issues of selection and appointments;

- the significance of 'effectiveness' and its appropriateness or otherwise in different areas of ministry, including selection, training, and oversight.

Clergy stress

There is a growing library on this subject. It is important to distinguish factors which have been part of clergy life for many generations and those of more recent origin.

The traditional causes of clergy stress are:

- being 'on call' 24 hours a day;

- living 'over the shop';

- living 'in a goldfish bowl'.

However, clergy spouses and families find these factors less acceptable than a generation ago. These sources of stress can be substantially reduced by a setting of appropriate boundaries:

- of time, with a judicious use of an answer-phone during mealtimes, etc., proper days off and holidays;

- of place, with most of the vicarage being essentially a private home.

Relatively more recent causes of stress include:

- the reducing number of stipendiary clergy;

- changing roles, especially in relation to the laity;

- reduced status in society with loss of deference;

- increased incidence of personal assault and burglary;

- the introduction of Child Protection measures;

- marriage and family breakdown.

These issues of stress can be addressed and helped by:

- annual review, with associated professional training and development;

- development of ministry teams with close mutual support at local level;

- theological and practical explorations of the 'episcopal', the 'missionary' and the 'manager/pathfinder' roles;

- sensible precautions and training.

The morale of the clergy is a complex phenomenon. Many today are exhilarated and envisioned by the issues and changes of recent decades while others are perplexed and disheartened.

While it is in no way a simple or sole answer to these issues, the establishing of diocesan HR (Human Resources) advisers or consultants will be of increasing significance. Some dioceses have already made such appointments and more will surely follow. I quote from a (sadly) anonymous letter to the *Church Times* (dated 29 December 2000): 'Professionally trained and qualified ... They would oversee recruitment and retention of clergy, their terms and conditions of service, stipends, accommodation, resignations, preparation for retirement, in-service training, disciplinary proceedings, and the termination of employment' and oversee appointments procedures – profiles, applications, interviews, etc. Now some of these elements will need the closest collaboration with the bishops and some of their other senior staff, but as another letter the following week from David Fulljames said tellingly: 'The Church expects to buy in professional expertise from architects and accountants to assist in looking after the buildings and its money. So it should expect to buy in human-relations expertise for its most precious resource, its staff' (*Church Times*, 5 January 2001).

Implications

The implications of these changes are much debated and lead to some controversy. Many of the issues will be developed in the following pages. Some are introduced briefly now:

1. Should the selection procedures be varied between those who are to be incumbents and those who are not – because of the 'episcopal' element?

2. Is there sufficient scope for the missionary strategist and church-planter in present patterns?

3. Is there sufficient attention given to the 'episcopal' and 'missionary' dimensions in both initial and continuing training and professional development?

4. What are the implications for the ministry of bishops, archdeacons and bishops' advisers in training, and in mission?

5. Are there implications for lines of accountability, remuneration and conditions of service?

8

Conclusions: ways ahead in ministry strategy

What sort of Church?

When the Archbishops' Council was giving preliminary attention to issues of ministry strategy, the prior consideration of the nature of the Church inevitably required addressing. This is not, of course, the place for any extended treatment of ecclesiology. However, here is a revised edition of the introductory paper 1 produced at the council's request.

What might the Church of England look like in 10 or 20 years' time, and what is our vision for it?

1. It will continue to be an *episcopal* Church. However, the exercise of episcopal ministry will continue to develop in the light of reducing numbers of stipendiary clergy, the increasing roles of lay people, the continuing financial revolution, ecumenical arrangements, the debates about women in the episcopate, reconsideration of freehold and the mission dimension.

2. The *laity* will play an ever-increasing part in ministry strategy – both its consideration and its execution. The context has been introduced in Chapter 1. Ministry teams with strong (and often predominantly) lay participation will continue to develop. The financial changes will lead to lay pressure for further ecumenical and pastoral re-organization. Laity will expect high-quality preparation for their ministry in the *world*.

3. *Missionary flexibility* will be required at all levels, but it will continue to be closely linked to the traditional pastoral concerns. There will be increasing flexibility re worship (mid-week, youth, etc.), re buildings, re venues (including homes, pubs and warehouses), re mission (with varieties of networks, ways of being church and approaches to children and young people).

4. The *local* dimension will be increasingly important for mission, ministry and finance. With episcopal oversight and encouragement, local ministry schemes (of various kinds) will flourish. The precise interpretation and extent of 'local' will vary widely. It will be understood as parish, benefice,

cluster, team, group, deanery and sometimes diocese. The financial and mission forces will be major factors. The parish system will remain generally in place – but with increasing modifications, and the development of wider 'mission areas' where the parochial system is patently not working. Ecumenical pressures will be more significant from the local contexts rather than from national schemes.

5. The Church of England will continue to be a *national* Church whatever happens on the establishment or ecumenical fronts. The national cohesion will be placed under a series of great pressures – financial, staffing and theological. However, the vast majority will value commitment to:

   - biblical foundations;
   - credal orthodoxies;
   - common worship;
   - national mission and ministry;
   - reformed catholicity with charismatic renewal.

   In practical terms, bishops along with their dioceses and synods will consider the values of having (and dangers of losing):

   - bishops' regulations for selection, training and financing of ordinands;
   - national stipendiary clergy apportionment formula;
   - national systems of stipends, fees, and pensions and guidance on housing and other conditions of service;
   - mutual support systems.

6. The church will wish to be *prophetic and inclusive* – speaking to the issues of the day at every level, and committed to justice for groups who have been 'marginalized' through gender, ethnicity, disability and other forms of exclusion.

7. A *three-dimensional* church, i.e. working at three main levels – the local (often but not always parish), the diocesan, and the national (see Introduction). The deanery will remain significant in some parts of the country. The province is significant for the north, but the southern is far too large for practical purposes.

A crucial issue will be a continuing reassessment of what matters are best addressed at which level. Some analysts believe that the Turnbull reforms and establishing of the Archbishops' Council is evidence of growing centralization. On the contrary, I believe that the macro-trends in finance and ministry strategy indicate substantial shifts of power to the dioceses and parishes. The Turnbull reforms are about *coherence* of the national Church institutions. However, they will only (and should only) do what the dioceses agree (and fund) as appropriately and best done at the national level.

Major planks of strategy

The considerable and growing consensus is revealed in the continuity of the six major themes from the Statements of the House of Bishops in 1978, 1992 and 1994 (see Chapter 4 and its concluding analysis) and the Conclusions of the review of diocesan strategy documents 1997 (see Chapter 5). Of the latter, I repeat the words of the Bishop of Gloucester in his Preface to the report *Shaping Ministry for a Missionary Church*: 'The picture ... reveals what many might find as *a surprising degree of common analysis and shared commitment*' (my italics, p. iii). In the following paragraphs I cite my analysis of the Bishops' Statements as BS, and the Conclusions of the report on diocesan strategies as DS (see pp. 52, 62).

1. A *shared theological approach*. See DS (ii). In spite of the financial pressures and the reducing numbers of stipendiary clergy these issues are not the primary ones. Behind many documents 'there were signs of both vision and spirituality'. Theological grounding of strategies uses theology of the Trinity, incarnation, mission and baptism. Three ministerial themes appear repeatedly:
   - partnership in the whole people of God;
   - every-member ministry – in the world and in the Church;
   - the changed role of stipendiary ministers (see Chapter 7).

2. The encouragement of *variety in ministries*. See BS 1 where the references show that all of the Bishops' Statements emphasize this point. Typical is this from 1992: 'continue to give *radical* consideration to developing and using *imaginative* and *varied* patterns of lay and ordained ministry' (emphasis mine).

3. The need for *diocesan strategy*. See BS 2 for references. In 1978 the bishops said: 'every diocese should be considering its responsibility for recruiting, training and developing the forms of ministry which the Church will need in the next 25 years'. In 1994 they said: 'We believe that the details of such a strategy need to be worked out in each diocese, where local opportunities, needs and resources can best be assessed.'

4. A commitment to a *national ministry* to the whole community. See BS 3 and DS (i). In 1978 and 1992 the bishops endorsed the nationwide '*parochial* system as a basis for mission' to all, and in 1994 reaffirmed the national commitment 'with our ecumenical partners'. Of the diocesan strategies 'none of their approaches remotely suggests a shift into congregationalism'.

5. There is a *particular role for stipendiary clergy* and so a need for continuing emphasis on this *vocation*. The role is *changing significantly*. See BS 4 and 6 and DS (iv). The bishops say in 1994: 'the number and morale of the stipendiary clergy is given high priority ... continuing support

must be given to the encouragement of vocations'. The diocesan papers emphasize the changing role.

6. A call to *generous and committed giving*. See BS 5. The bishops have called for this regularly, and in 1994 urged church members to ask 'what am I called upon to give gladly out of the bounty God has given me?' and 'should test their response against the standards already established of the tithe (10 per cent of take-home pay to charitable purposes) and that set by the Synod of not less than 5 per cent of net income to the Church'.

7. The development of *teams*, DS (iii). It is a 'massive emphasis' in diocesan documents. There are different types, and they work in different units. There is also a trend towards *larger structural units* (DS (vi)), by clustering of parishes or by deanery. See also the 1994 Statement BS 2 (iii).

8. The *clergy allocation formula* (formerly known as the 'Sheffield' formula) is generally accepted as the basis for planning clergy deployment (DS (v)). This is contrary to widespread suggestions that 'Sheffield is dead'. In actual fact the House of Bishops reaffirmed their commitment to the principle in both their 1992 and 1994 Statements.

Further strategic issues

Introduction

Some of these have been introduced earlier in the report, e.g.

the theology of ministry	– see Chapter 3
the Ordinal	– see Chapter 3
national ministry policy	– see the Canons, Bishops' Regulations and Statements, Chapter 4 and the previous section
diocesan strategies	– see Chapter 5
ecumenical strategy	– see Chapters 3 and 43

Others are introduced in the many contributions in Part 2. In many of these areas good policy is in place (and has been subject to major review in recent years). There are also areas of significant uncertainty and others where major reviews are underway at present – see Chapter 6.

Areas of uncertainty include:

- the financial situation;
- the Employment Act;
- the Data Protection Act;
- numbers of (stipendiary) clergy;

- the strategic use of non-stipendiary clergy, Readers and other lay ministers.

Issues under substantial review include:

- clergy remuneration;
- the structure and funding of ordination training;
- a renewed distinctive diaconate;
- the Pastoral Measure.

An example of the *complexity* of some of these is the issue of:

The ecclesiastical freehold of the clergy

The Paul (1964), Fenton Morley (1967) and Tiller (1983) reports each argued strongly for the abolition of the freehold. On each occasion, the Church's government at the time declined to approve the proposals.

I am sure that the matter needs careful reconsideration some time in the next three or four years. The contexts are becoming very different in significant ways. The fundamental prerequisite is a just and reasonable alternative form of protection for those thousands of clergy who have, at present, no freehold and no protection under employment legislation either (see Chapter 6).

The following diagram indicates the complex interrelationship of issues:

Diagram 1: Freehold

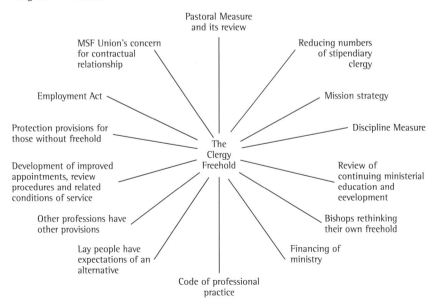

Some questions and issues for the future are mentioned in Part 2, but here I note a further six areas, also considered in Part 2, that might well call for review in the next few years.

Selection of ordinands

Does the Church wish to continue the present system of nationally organized bishops' selection conferences? It is a major part of the Ministry Division's work (and budget), and the dioceses are becoming increasingly thorough in their own selection procedures. On the other hand, there is, at present, a major national resource for advice, training of selectors, high-quality residential procedures and moderation to give national consistency.

Should there be fresh consideration to varying the bishops' selection criteria for different categories of ordained and accredited lay worker ministries? The question is increasingly asked 'Are we selecting for incumbency, rather than for priesthood, diaconate, etc?' See also Chapter 12.

Clergy 'employment' status and conditions of service

This will be a major issue in the coming months. Either clergy will be brought within the realm of employment legislation and the Church's bishops and institutions will have to observe it, or the Church will have to develop such demonstrable good practice as to gain some kind of exemption. However, the underlying issue is that whatever the presence or absence of legal constraint, the Church needs to have the highest standards of concern for its staff, and the moral, spiritual and pastoral dimensions should not be of less rigour than the legal (see also Chapters 7 and 23).

Women in ministry

Our two contributors (see Chapter 37) exemplify the tensions that exist in the Church of England over the existing provisions. Some believe that the Act of Synod provisions are demeaning and unjust, and should be repealed as soon as possible, while others believe that the provisions should be, if anything, strengthened. The Working Party on Women in the Episcopate starts its work in 2001. See also Chapter 38.

Continuing ministerial education and development

The new and substantial report *Mind the Gap*, along with ministerial review systems, takes this area into a new dimension. The issue that is linked to ecclesiastical freehold and the 'employment' status of the clergy, as described above, is how such education and development can become a vital part of every minister's life when they are either office-holders without contract, or volunteers. To put it bluntly – 'how can the proposals be made to stick?' There are two main possibilities. Firstly, parochial clergy could have contracts like those working in sector and chaplaincy ministries, or they could subscribe to some kind of 'covenant' with the bishop on the one hand and/or their church council on the other hand. This contract or covenant would (as for teachers, lawyers and many other professional groups) lay down certain requirements in this area.

A related matter is that of induction training on appointment to a new post. It is, at present, erratic or non-existent. I would recommend urgent consideration be given to finding ways to make appropriate induction a prerequisite to appointments at every level of Church life. See also Chapter 26.

Code of professional conduct, disciplinary and grievance provisions

These provisions are linked to employment and continuing education and development. The issues in the three sections constitute a package of measures which would be regarded as standard good practice in many other areas of life. Although there are significant theological, legal and pastoral issues involved, they need to be addressed with some urgency (see Chapters 27 and 28).

The parish system and the Pastoral Measure

The parish system can be interpreted in rather different ways. Fundamentally, it involves a commitment by the Church (in the words of the Bishops' Statement of 1992) 'to offer every person and every community in the land

a) the proclamation of the gospel in worship, word, sacrament and service;

b) the pastoral ministry of the Church;

c) access to public worship'.

Now this commitment does not require a precise number of clergy (let alone stipendiary clergy) per thousand people. The high-quality involvement of lay people in baptism, confirmation, marriage, bereavement and other pastoral ministries and the excellent funeral ministry of many Readers is evidence of the flexibility of parochial ministry provision. Nevertheless, as the Bishop of Durham argues, there is good reason to revisit aspects of the parochial system and explore other models in certain circumstances. This leads to the reconsideration of the Pastoral Measure and related legislation which has recently started. See also Chapters 32 and 40.

Recommendations

This report demonstrates substantial coherence, confidence and vision in the areas of ministry strategy.

My recommendations to the Archbishops' Council, the House of Bishops, the General Synod and to the dioceses are in the nature of *continuing* the programme of reform. Though they could be construed as evolutionary rather than revolutionary, the *sum total* of reforms described from the recent past, under present consideration and recommended here, do indeed add up to a considerable revolution over a single generation.

Immediate recommendations are to:

1. *Affirm the eight major planks of strategy* itemized above. These express the consensus revealed in the Statements of the House of Bishops and the review of diocesan strategy documents. I hope these could be widely affirmed with confidence and communicated with clarity.

2. *Clarify* (or seek clarification in) as far as is reasonably possible the *areas of uncertainty* listed above and explained in Chapter 6. These are not to be seen as matters of embarrassment – they arise from fast-moving contexts (religious, social, financial, legal and missiological).

3. *Note the areas under present review.* They are also listed above on p. 79 and explained in Chapter 6. I hope the two where the work is substantially completed and the reports that are expected in 2001 will be considered in the light of the overall picture. I trust the other working parties with a longer timescale will find this report a valuable source of background material.

4. *Reflect on the seven issues* listed above – agree which are of crucial importance, prioritize and allocate appropriate resources.

5. *Address the following* specific areas:
   - continue systematically to review the *eight planks of strategy* at the various appropriate levels;
   - seek (or encourage the Ministry Division urgently to propose) a reasonable form of *employment protection* for those clergy who are without the 'freehold';
   - seek to employ (and ask the Ministry Division to make recommendations about) *fairer procedures for appointments*, review of appointments, associated conditions of service and in situations of grievance;
   - develop (and perhaps ask the Ministry Division for guidelines on) *induction training* as a prerequisite for appointments, and *continuing education and development* as a covenanted (if not contractual) part of every appointment.

The Collect for Vocations from *Common Worship* (p. 105)[1]:

> Almighty God,
> you have entrusted to your Church
> a share in the ministry of your Son our great high priest:
> inspire by your Holy Spirit the hearts of many
> to offer themselves for the ministry of your Church,
> that strengthened by his power,
> they may work for the increase of your kingdom
> and set forward the eternal praise of your name;
> through Jesus Christ your Son our Lord.

Part 2

Mapping the areas of ministry

Introduction

I refer the reader back to the Introduction to Part 1 for an explanation of the purpose of this section. Ministry strategy is frequently debated and developed with an inadequate grasp of the range of relevant areas and issues.

I am indebted to about 40 colleagues for being willing to give a very brief survey of areas where they are expert. They have agreed to very tight word limits so that the report does not grow into unhelpful proportions. Each contributor is an officer in the Ministry Division responsible for the area and/or someone clearly authoritative in the field.

I have had extensive discussions with most of them, read their publications, and often proposed editorial revisions to their contributions. It is a survey of unprecedented range and authority.

9

Vocation

Mark Sowerby

Call to Order was published in 1989 (with a short, attractive study guide). The chairman of the working party was Peter Baelz (the retired Dean of Durham). It was circulated alongside the report *The Ordained Ministry: Numbers, Cost and Deployment* (GS Misc 858). The report provided important theological exposition of vocation and ministry, and particularly emphasized the church context and corporate dimension of vocation over and against the personal sense of call direct from God.

Our Common Calling was a 16-page consultation paper published in 1995 by the Vocations Strategy Working Party. It concluded that where every-member ministry and the use of God's gifts are developed, vocations to ordained ministry will emerge.

The Ministry Division seeks to hold a broad and inclusive understanding of Christian vocation. It holds in tension the need, on the one hand, to see ordained ministry as but one path of discipleship and, on the other hand, the responsibility for recruiting and selecting people to serve specifically as clergy in the Church of England. Building upon the work of *Our Common Calling* and *Call to Order*, *Recovering Confidence* has been, since 1996, the guiding document for vocational work by the Ministry Division and diocesan officers concerned with vocation. A primary assertion of this report is that the pressure to produce more ordinands, especially now for stipendiary ministry, should not lead to a reduction in their quality. That report also recognized that recruitment was not a matter of maintenance or reconstruction but rather that it was to resource an ordained ministry with a changed role in a changing Church and society (Para. 18 and Ch. 4). The mobilization of much lay ministry raises the importance of oversight (episcopé) in priestly ministry. It was noted in *Recovering Confidence* that the manner in which some lay ministry had developed led to a confusion of role and a lack of clarity about ordained ministry which may affect recruitment (Paras 36–8 and 50).

Particular importance is given, in *Recovering Confidence*, to the recruitment of young ordination candidates who have particular gifts of energy and enthusiasm, grasp of contemporary intellectual structures, innovative and experimental qualities and the flexibility to be formed (Paras 47 and 52). Recognition was given that the recruitment of young candidates requires much more of the Church in terms of nurture, discernment, encouragement and formation. Since the publication of that report, there appears to have been a rise of approximately 50 per cent in the number of diocesan vocations advisers, though these appointments are still not evenly spread and only a very few attract a part-stipend (e.g. Blackburn, Salisbury). Constraints upon financial resources at national as well as diocesan levels lead to a concentration upon the reactive work of assessment and selection rather than the proactive stimulation of vocations to ordained ministry, a point noted in *A Climate of Encouragement* and evident in Ministry Division staffing in the early 1990s and from 2001. The support of proactive vocational work in the dioceses continues to be a priority of the Ministry Division and specifically through its Vocations Officer, who is responsible for the production of several booklets and leaflets. These include *Professional Ministry* (a guide to vocation, recruitment and selection), *Steps on the Road to Ministry, What on Earth am I Here For?* and regularly updated materials such as *Opportunities for Service Overseas and at Home*, and an annual list of vocations events run by the Ministry Division and other bodies. The Director of the Ministry Division and the Vocations Officer seek to attend, support and resource diocesan and other vocational events whenever possible.

Recovering Confidence recognized the theological difficulties and counter-productive tendencies of stop/go recruitment campaigning and sought to resist any setting of targets, which leads to lower morale when such targets are not met (Paras 18 and 53). The report sought to foster a culture of vocation so that the initial identification and development of individuals' vocations is a responsibility shared by local ecclesial communities be they in parishes or chaplaincies. As leaders of such communities in their liturgy and ministry, clergy have a particular role and responsibility within the Church's vocational culture. This culture of vocation gave a name to the forthcoming report, *A Climate of Encouragement.*

A Climate of Encouragement found some good practice around the dioceses and was able to make positive recommendations about how parishes should share ministry in order to offer experience and confidence in Christian ministry and teaching. This experience of Christian ministry and leadership can be seminal and developmental in terms of individual vocations. Such experience is not equally easy to grant in all expressions of Anglicanism and particular thought may be needed where sacramental liturgy dominates public worship and specifically sacramental aspects dominate the ministry of the parish priest. While role model continues to be important, it appears to be less significant than the encouragement and affirmation gained by experience. Patterns of ordained ministry that tend towards the training and supervision of laity in mission and ministry may reduce the number of people with whom the clergy have direct pastoral contact such that there is less opportunity for a distinctive role model to be effective. By whatever means clergy actually encourage vocations, their effectiveness is dependent upon their own confidence in their role (*Recovering Confidence*, Para. 76) and upon their morale (*A Climate of Encouragement*). Inequality of enthusiasm for the ways in which the Church is responding to the changes in its own circumstances and the changes in society does not lead to an even climate of encouragement or contribute helpfully to a broad culture of vocation.

A concern noted in *A Climate of Encouragement* is the tendency of contemporary society to see itself in progressive rather than cyclical terms. Individuals inclined to seek progression from one kind of ministry to another in a quest for ever more experiences do not fit comfortably into the parochial ministry of the Church of England, which can offer only so much variety as the parishes and their people afford. Where parish ministry (which engages approximately 90 per cent of clergy in stipendiary/paid ministry) does not offer the necessary stimulation, affirmation, nurture and satisfaction to retain its priests, there will be difficulty in recruiting to it. *A Climate of Encouragement* therefore made particular recommendations to bishops with regard to the morale of clergy.

While there is consistency of approach in the recent documents of the Ministry Division and its immediate predecessors, the same consistency is not always apparent in the dioceses of the Church of England, where variable efforts and resources are put into the proactive stimulation of vocations, and the patchy morale of clergy detracts from their effectiveness. Both *Recovering Confidence* and *A Climate of Encouragement* make links between ecclesiology and the nature of ordained ministry. Post Vatican II ecumenical theology recognizes a variety of models of the Church and that these imply a variety of models for its priesthood. Differing models of priesthood respond to change within the Church and within society in differing ways, and it is not straightforward to unite them in a common vision or strategy for the Church of England.

Further reading

Recovering Confidence, ABM, 1996
A Climate of Encouragement, Ministry Division, forthcoming

See also booklets and leaflets mentioned above.

In 1999 the following posters were produced by the Communications Department and used widely in parishes and cathedrals.

Clerical collars make good moustaches

They also symbolise a life of challenge, service and deep fulfilment.

In the last five years, the number of ordinands in training has almost doubled. More and more Church of England priests are back in the community.

Urban, rural, chaplaincy, the opportunities for clergy in the Church of England are many and varied. Once selected, training can be full or part-time. After ordination, serving, too, can be full or part-time.

If someone you know would make a fine priest (or indeed, Reader or lay member of a ministry team), actively encourage them! Speak to your priest, e-mail mark.sowerby@mindiv.c-of-e.org.uk or visit www.cofe.anglican.org.

Sponsored by Ecclesiastical Insurance, the number one provider of insurance and financial services to church and clergy – 0800 33 66 22

This man doesn't have a job. He has a life.

In the last five years, the number of ordinands in training has almost doubled and you will see more and more Church of England priests in our communities. This Petertide some four hundred will become deacons whilst a similar number will become priests. Please pray for them and the challenging, rewarding ministry they face.

If someone you know would make a fine priest (or indeed, Reader or lay member of a ministry team), actively encourage them! Speak to your priest, e-mail mark.sowerby@mindiv.c-of-e.org.uk or visit www.cofe.anglican.org.

The selection for ordination takes a little time. Those who go forward can train full or part-time. And once ordained they can serve full-time or keep the day job.

Miss Sarah Evans, Statistics Officer of the Ministry Division, provides these statistics and commentary:

Diagram 2: Stipendiary ordinations, 1879–1999

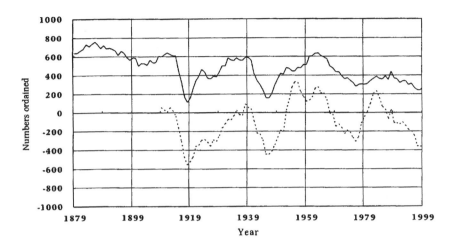

——— Numbers ordained each year
------ Numbers ordained each year less numbers ordained 37 years previously

The graph above shows the pattern of stipendiary ordinations over the last 120 years. It also shows, in a fairly crude form, whether these ordinations were 'replacing' those clergy who were likely to be retiring in that year. The graph shows that stipendiary ordinations have, over this period, fluctuated significantly, with large decreases in the 1910s, 1940s, 1970s and early 1990s, relative stability in the 1930s and 1980s and increases in the 1920s, 1950s and early 1960s. 'The pattern is partly explained by the two world wars, which clearly led to losses in the late 1910s and the 1940s. Broader social and cultural factors might account, for instance, for the steep decline in the later 1960s and the 1970s. It is also possible that some correlation would be revealed by matching the ordination figures against indicators of national economic performance, such as unemployment figures' (further details in *Recovering Confidence*).

The graph also shows that, except for a period in the 1950s/60s and 1980s the number of ordinations has not been high enough to replace those retiring. Indeed even those periods of 'gain' were to a great extent caused by the impact of the two world wars 37 years before. The result of this has been a steady decline in the number of active stipendiary clergy since the beginning of the century from a peak reached after late nineteenth-century expansion, as the following table shows.

Table 3: Clergy numbers, 1851–1999

Census year	Total	Clergy (active and retired)	
		Below 65	Over 65
1851	16,194	14,714	1,480
1861	17,966	16,055	1,911
1871	19,411	17,525	1,886
1881	20,341	17,272	3,069
1891	22,753	(19,044)*	(3,709)*
1901	23,670	19,520	4,150
1911	23,193	18,939	4,254
1921	22,570	17,643	4,936
1931	21,579	(16,046)*	(5,263)*
1951	18,196	12,666	5,530
1959	18,148	12,796	5,352
1963	19,185	14,345	4,840

	Full-time stipendiary clergy within the diocesan structure
1956	13,144
1961	13,660
1966	13,724
1971	13,182
1976	12,056
1981	10,882
1986	10,649
1991	11,076
1996	10,004
1999	9,762

*separate figures not available; interpolated estimate

This shows a temporary recovery in numbers in the early 1960s which is followed by a steep decline particularly in the early 1970s and 1990s and a much slower decline in the 1980s.

Since the early 1970s there has been an expansion in different types of ministry, starting with non-stipendiary ministry in the early 1970s and the expansion of ordained local ministry in the late 1990s. The following graph shows the impact this has had on the numbers ordained. For the last 20 years on average 100 national NSM ministers have been ordained per annum and since 1998 around 90 OLMs.

Diagram 3: Ordinations, 1970–2000

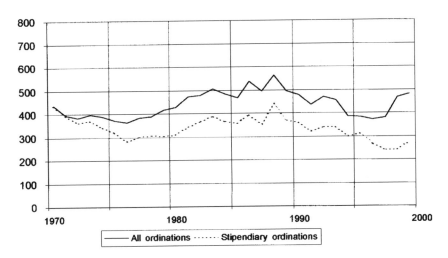

The graph below shows the breakdown of ordinations for 1993–9:

Diagram 4: Ordinations, 1993–9

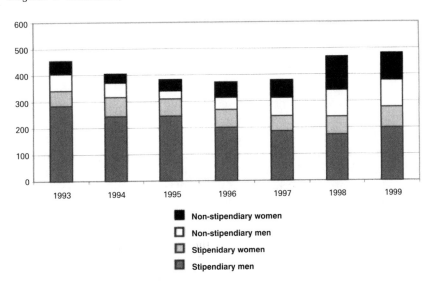

10

Minority ethnic concerns

Charles Lawrence

In 1987, arising out of the publication of the Archbishop of Canterbury's report *Faith in the City: A Call for Action by Church and Nation* in 1985 and the subsequent debate in the General Synod, the Committee for Black Anglican Concerns (CBAC) was established. It was directly responsible to the Standing Committee of the General Synod. Subsequently CBAC was renamed in 1996 the Committee for Minority Ethnic Anglican Concerns, and CMEAC is now directly responsible to the Archbishops' Council.

The mandate of CMEAC is *to monitor issues which arise or ought to arise in the context of the work of the Archbishops' Council, boards and councils of the General Synod, and the Synod itself, as far as they have policy implications for minority ethnic groups within the Church and the wider society.*

Faith in the City and subsequent research made it clear that minority ethnic Anglicans had been and continued to be marginalized within the life of the Church. Their particular gifts and abilities were therefore not being used by the Church to the greater good of the whole. Many people spoke of cold-to-hostile reception when coming to an Anglican church for the first time. Responses from 'Your church is down the road' to 'Please don't come again – you're upsetting people' were depressingly frequent from laity and clergy alike.

Important terminology

The Stephen Lawrence Inquiry report, presented to Parliament on 24 February 1999, offered the following definitions of racism and institutional racism:

RACISM: *Racism in general terms consists of conduct or words or practices which disadvantage or advantage people because of their colour, culture or ethnic origin. In its more subtle form it is as damaging as in its overt form.*[1]

INSTITUTIONAL RACISM: The collective failure of an organization to provide an appropriate and professional service to people because of their colour, culture or ethnic origin. It can be seen or detected in processes, attitudes and behaviour which amount to discrimination through unwitting prejudices, ignorance, thoughtlessness and racist stereotyping which disadvantage minority ethnic people.[2]

While racism and institutional racism may be concepts which some members of the white community find difficult to accept, they are not just terms but the living reality many minority ethnic people experience on a daily basis. The Church of England appears no less likely than any other large institution to have conscious or unconscious levels of racism.

Part of the work CMEAC has done in response to its terms of reference is undertaking an audit of each diocese in the Church of England. Thirty-five of the 43 dioceses have already been visited to date (February 2001). This has revealed substantial areas of good practice but it has clearly underlined that we have a great deal further to go before minority ethnic Anglicans are a fully accepted part of the Church.

Vocations sub-committee of CMEAC

However, it remains true that there are greater numbers of black and Asian Christians in Anglican churches than in almost any other Church in England. Research has shown that more minority ethnic children attend Sunday worship with their families than children from the majority ethnic community.[3] Church of England schools where there are significant numbers of black and Asian children play an important role in encouraging them into the church family. This is particularly evident in London, Southwark and Blackburn Dioceses. It is a cause of some concern that the number of clergy from a minority ethnic background is very different and particularly that the number of English-born minority ethnic clergy is tiny.

Realizing the significance of this, and particularly in response to Section VI of CMEAC's terms of reference: *seeking the development and empowerment of minority ethnic Anglicans and in particular fostering and encouraging vocations within the Church*, CMEAC established a Vocations sub-committee in June 1997. With the Youth Issues sub-committee of CMEAC, it has planned and run two national vocations conferences in 1998 and 1999. While looking at vocation under the specific headings of ordained ministry, Reader, Church Army and religious, emphasis was placed on the vocation of all Christian people in the service of God and his kingdom. The age group targeted by these conferences is 20–40. Those who have attended have been enormously gifted people, many of them professionally qualified. Many have not been encouraged to pursue their vocation by their congregation, their clergy or diocesan director of ordinands. Although information about the conferences was distributed to parish clergy, only a handful were directly approached by their vicar to attend. It seems fair to infer that the attendees are the tip of an iceberg and there are considerably more minority ethnic Anglicans with vocations to all forms of ministry just below the surface. CMEAC hoped that their vocations conferences would be pump-primers.

How can vocations be fostered?

Many would say that they became aware of their vocation or had it confirmed by the support and encouragement of their local parish priest. This role of encouragement is crucial to the fostering of vocations among minority ethnic Anglicans.

Yet apparently very few clergy are able to discern such vocations and support them, and anecdotal evidence suggests that far too many clergy find it very difficult to see black and Asian people in leadership roles. For this and for many other reasons the presence of role models is vital. Current trends in the age profile of ordinands, as well as the tiny number from the minority ethnic community, mean that it is highly unlikely for anyone to see a young black or Asian clergy person at their altar or in their pulpit.

Although it might be hoped that this imbalance will be corrected by the passage of time and the grace of God, it is right to consider a deliberate strategy that will ensure the end result we seek. There are two main issues which need to be addressed:

1. racism and institutionalized racism within the Church of England;

2. vocations work targeting black and Asian Anglicans.

Both of these are broad-brush strokes and some work has already been undertaken in these areas. Specific recommendations will be found at the end of this section.

Areas of concern

The following points are offered for information and/or as areas of concern:

- Out of over 12,000 serving clergy, there are just over 200 black and Asian clergy, the vast majority of whom were born outside the UK.

- Until the mid-1990s there were only three English-born minority ethnic priests in the Church of England.

- Stories are still heard that parishes are resistant to having a black or Asian incumbent.

- It is often wrongly assumed that black and Asian clergy can and should only minister in inner cities and conurbations.

- There are significantly fewer minority ethnic Anglicans on electoral rolls than regularly attend church on Sundays.

- The percentage of minority ethnic young people attending church is on the whole higher than their percentage representation in the community at large.

- There seems to be a leadership glass ceiling set at the level of PCC member/churchwarden beyond which very few minority ethnic Anglicans can progress.

- For those ordained, there is a similar glass ceiling at incumbency level.

- There is still a great deal of misinformation and general ignorance within the Church about issues relating to both racism and minority ethnic Anglicans.

- The importance of role models cannot be over-emphasized.

The presence of significant numbers of minority ethnic people in Anglican churches throughout the country should be a clear enough indication that not all black and Asian people are naturally drawn to black-led and/or Pentecostal churches. Is it too late to bring disaffected Anglicans back and to maximize the gifts of those still within our churches? Peter Brierley in his book *The Tide is Running Out* (2000) states that the number of black Anglicans has doubled, from 27,200 in 1992 to 58,200.

Serving God in Church and Community makes important recommendations to diocesan bishops, diocesan directors of ordinands and vocations advisers, parish clergy and education chaplains on pages 33, 34 and 35. In brief these are:

1. that diocesan bishops show clear support for minority ethnic Anglicans' vocations to accredited ministries and those already exercising these ministries;

2. that as more than 40 per cent of minority ethnic people in the Church of England are British born, every effort should be made to recruit and support them in their ministry;

3. that diocesan directors of ordinands acknowledge and value cultural diversity and not seek to impose a cultural norm, and that they should undertake training in racism awareness and cultural diversity;

4. that parish clergy seek to raise their own understanding of these issues and seek out minority ethnic Anglicans, particularly the young, and explore their vocation with them;

5. that parish clergy and education chaplains should affirm God's call not to one particular group but to all his people.

A great resource

The Black Celebration at York in 1994 was a resounding confirmation of the presence of gifted black and Asian people within the Church and a revelatory and informative experience to the white participants. A fascinating strand that has come out of all of this work is that, while some issues are particularly focused in relation to minority ethnic communities, they are by no means peculiar to them, so work on inclusion, young people, vocations, etc. among minority ethnic Anglicans will often give significant pointers to similar work among the wider community.

It is also important to state clearly that the *raison d'être* for this work is not merely to redress imbalance and to increase the number of active Christians within our churches, but a direct response to the gospel as revealed in Jesus Christ, who taught us to pray 'Your kingdom come, your will be done on earth as in heaven'. St Paul rightly notes that 'In Christ Jesus there is no such thing as Jew and Greek, slave and freeman, male and female, but all are one' (Galatians 3.28). God's kingdom is one of justice and peace where all are able to achieve their potential and be who they are, beloved children of God. Our Church is striving to reflect that reality in a broken world.

Further reading

Called to Lead: A Challenge to Include Minority Ethnic People (GS Misc 625), 2000

Serving God in Church and Community (GS Misc 606), Church House Publishing, 2000

Simply Value Us (GS Misc 601), Church House Publishing, 2000

The Passing Winter (GS 1220), Church House Publishing, 1996

How We Stand: A Report on Black Anglican Membership of the Church of England, 1994

11

Deaf people and disability issues

James Clarke

Until the 1960s, most services for deaf people (welfare, interpreting, social and religious) were supplied by voluntary organizations which had long connections with the Church of England. Since then the dioceses have gradually, and to varying degrees, made provision for ministry among deaf people. Sometimes this has remained in voluntary organizations, but they are declining, and Christian worship with deaf people is more often found in parish churches, albeit at separate times from the parish's own worship.

The present situation is very patchy, some dioceses being fully committed to this ministry, and placing deaf people firmly in the central life of the diocese, others standing back from it, as if it were a luxury to be supported when the 'going is good'. If we take chaplaincy as a criterion, then we see that there are:

Full-time chaplains	17
Half-time (or more)	13
NSM	8
Honorary	16

At the time of writing there is one full-time vacancy, and one half-time. Birmingham has made no appointment to replace a full-time chaplain for 18 months, and is now talking of a possible half-time appointment. Services are maintained by a deaf ordinand and an NSM from a neighbouring diocese. York has not replaced a half-time chaplain who retired some years ago; services in York are maintained by a leader of a Fellowship Church Community. Ely, Liverpool and Truro rely entirely on NSMs, with diocesan allocation to expenses, although Ely's contribution was under threat in the 2001 budget. Peterborough made a part-time chaplain redundant this year.

These figures are such, despite the fact that General Synod in York 1998 received the report *The Church among Deaf People* with acclaim. This report urged that dioceses should accept responsibility for providing adequate and well-resourced chaplaincies, based on a figure of one full-time chaplain per million of the population.

However, this survey does not give a true reflection of the situation. While ministry was based in the deaf centres, the theological quality of the ministry varied widely, but in every case it was delivered by someone with strong deaf skills and high-quality communication with deaf people, based in the social and communal life of deaf people in the area. Around these 'Missioners' congregations were built up which resembled mini parish congregations, and were thought to be Church of England, in that ministers were licensed, or even ordained by the diocesan bishop, who was often the president of the organization. Technically, these congregations were not franchised within the dioceses, and tended to be very separate from the life of the diocese. In many cases, the present chaplains are simply maintaining the rumps left by these congregations, which are diminishing in size, ageing, and showing little sign of attracting younger deaf people to join them.

Chaplains today are often not part of any deaf communal life, since such communities are less evident than before, and since part-time ministry does not allow time to be involved to the extent necessary to acquire good relationships, and to develop the personal and communication skills essential to being accepted into such groups. Today's generation of deaf people expect a high standard of access, and that people who work among them should have communication skills at a very high level, similar to the linguistic level of staff working among people in different countries. For a chaplain to acquire these skills requires at least four years of study and practice, and constant interaction with deaf people. This is extremely difficult for part-time chaplains to do, and has led to a further isolation from the people among whom they are appointed to work.

'The Church of England has abrogated its responsibilities to deaf people', and 'The C of E is saying to deaf people, "we don't want you"'. These are views that have been expressed forcibly in recent months, based on the overlong delays in appointing chaplains, the reduction in the deaf content of some chaplains' work, and the reduction in commitment manifested in redundancy and threats to budgets. At the same time, the Jehovah's Witnesses are actively resourcing visitors to gain communications skills, and the Mormons are holding missions in many towns where vast sums are expended on literature, and high-quality reproductions of photographs of sign language, etc.

Consequently, many chaplains feel they are fighting against the tide, without the full and convinced backing of their own Church behind them. This feeling conveys itself to deaf people, and the diminishing numbers of elderly people in congregations does little to raise morale. A recent letter from a deaf lay leader sets this out all too clearly:

I could not feel that much of what we did was relevant to the spiritual needs and understanding of the deaf people in the diocese, most of whom seemed to be putting up with the chaplain and me, and a church service simply because it has always been done that way in ages past. Very, very few of them seemed to be actively involved in any church activities, or felt that the church had anything to offer them.

Many feel that there is little point in inviting younger deaf people to be part of the present church set-up, and some radical thinking is going on in the chaplaincies at the moment. The feeling that these old models of ministry are utterly inappropriate is very strong, yet no-one is quite sure what should replace them. Secular society is facing similar radical reappraisals of its attitude to all disability, and learning to recognize the need to respect people as they are, and to enable integration to take place. This is statutorily enacted in the Disability Discrimination Act, and is part of a major societal attitude shift. Modern educational and technological provision also means that many deaf people are reaching high standards of education and employment, and do not want the old 'ghettoized' approach. What this means is that a much more flexible attitude and provision is needed, with much less separation, yet provided by people with excellent and recognized skills in deafness and communication. Some will want to belong to hearing congregations, others will want to be attached to them in deaf groups, and some will want uniquely deaf provision.

The house church movement, and some free churches, particularly the Baptists, are recognizing this much more quickly than the C of E, and are actively welcoming deaf people to their fellowship, using interpreters and communicators to enable access to the full worshipping life of the community. Indeed, 'Christian Deaf Link', which has grown out of a deaf fellowship movement, is strong and vibrant, and especially in London, welcomes many young people to its activities. It would be much more appropriate to direct a young deaf person to their activities than to most C of E events at this time. It is not too much to claim that the Church among deaf people is at a 'turning point' or 'moment' in its story, and that there is a serious risk of the Church of England being seen in the same light as the old-fashioned dominating and patronizing welfare organizations that led to the reforms of the 1960s. A recent visitor to this country, a Methodist minister from Sri Lanka, here to study deaf issues at the University of Bristol, found that he had to defend the Church from such charges within the confines of that university setting – where many leading deaf people meet and influence the views of others.

The report GS1427 highlighted the need for the Church to recognize the gifts and qualities of deaf people, both in that they remain people on the margins of society, who have much to say to us, and that as visual rather than aural people, they bring back to us insights into the drama and grace of liturgy. More than this:

> The problem comes not in deafness, but in fallen humanity's alienation from the intentions of our loving God. Such belief liberates deaf people to be ourselves trusting that our gifts have a vital role to play in the world. Indeed, the community of good creation is not complete without us. Nor is the community of God's children complete without the participation of any of the so-called minorities. (*op. cit.*, p. 58, quoted from Weir, 1996)

In other words, a Church that neglects deaf people and makes them feel unwelcome cannot call itself complete, and is not enabling all people to be part of the whole Body.

In these circumstances, what is the role and function of the Committee for Ministry among Deaf People?

1. to hold and ensure a pool of expert knowledge at the centre of the C of E;
2. to represent the interests of deaf people to the Church and vice versa;
3. to set standards for the life and work of the Church among deaf people, especially in the chaplaincies;
4. to train and support chaplains and deaf Church leaders, and to encourage and develop ministerial vocations among deaf people;
5. to give guidance to dioceses concerning deaf people and the Church;
6. to ensure the Church is aware and reacting appropriately to current thinking on deafness and other disability groups.

As a vision for the future, it is only necessary to go back to Mary Weir's call for a different understanding of disability, and work to implement it. CMDP has a kind of vision statement, which can be expressed in two ways, firstly, to enable deaf people to be the church in their community, and secondly, to give all deaf people access to the Church's life and ministry, as givers *as well as* receivers. All that is done should be in pursuit of these aims.

In practice, we see a flexible approach to ministry among deaf people. Because of the current situation in the 'deaf world', it is very likely that a variety of approaches will continue to be necessary:

1. Individuals and groups will want to be part of a worshipping community of their local church or chapel;
2. Groups of deaf people who use British Sign Language (BSL) will want to meet as such, and express their faith in liturgy and community life in BSL;

3. House churches or small groups built around families, especially as an evangelistic tool;

4. Among other things, the majority of ministry offered directly to deaf people will need to be in the hands of other deaf people, so the role of the 'hearing' chaplain will be to act as mentor and trainer of the deaf Church leaders;

5. An imaginative approach to liturgy is arising as the deaf churches have to adjust to the introduction of *Common Worship*, and the freedom given to use BSL in liturgical activity.

Unfortunately, most of this will be a waste of time and resource unless something is done to halt the slide in membership, and to overcome the huge credibility gap with three generations of deaf people. The absence of anything that actually touches and moves deaf people in Christian terms is very worrying, as is the lack of opportunity to mingle with and share the lives of deaf people today. This is why the role of the deaf priest in the future will be vital. CMDP has acted in this matter by establishing an Evangelism Working Party to report at the end of 2002.

General disability issues

In terms of general disability, the vision could be repeated almost exactly, although in practice it is to enable people with disabilities to have access to the mainstream life of the Church, and the role of CMDP is to provide guidance and encouragement to the Church at all levels to allow this to be. It also seeks to persuade the Church at parish and diocesan level that the provisions of the Disability Discrimination Act (DDA) do apply to them, and to take them seriously on theological, moral and legal grounds.

The DDA partly responds to a change in attitudes in society, and partly leads to other change. Initially the language used becomes very significant, and the difference between *impairment, disability* and *handicap* understood. For the purposes of the Act, the following definition has been devised:

A physical or mental impairment which has substantial and long-term adverse effect on a person's ability to carry out normal day-to-day activities.

From October 2000, the Church, as a service provider, has to take all reasonable steps to ensure that a person with any disability can take part in its activities on no less favourable terms than a non-disabled person. It is important to realize that this is not merely a matter of physical access, but of *access to its activities* for those who may have sensory losses like deafness or visual impairments. This means that certain aids and equipment should automatically be provided, and texts in large print, braille or other appropriate format made available, in every church or worship centre. It is not a matter of waiting for a person with a disability to request them – they should be there so that there is no barrier to access!

From 2004, there will be further requirements on access to premises, and it will be necessary to have considered well before then what reasonable steps should be taken to allow access for all.

At present, the amount of time allowed for this work in the Ministry Division means that only an advisory role can be effectively fulfilled, on such matters as Awareness and Good Practice Training for staff, building modifications, equipment and alarms, and compiling a dossier of information from dioceses on implementation of the Act.

Finally, in all cases of disability, we see that the essential core of Christian theology is built around Christ's own interactions with many people on the margins of society. People with disabilities are all too often on the margins of society today. It could be that we are missing important messages from these margins, and should be more open to hear them. This surely is an appropriate call to the Church to act as prophet and advocate in this cause, and to set an example to the rest of society, rather than lagging behind, waiting for legislation to enforce change.

Further reading

The Church among Deaf People (GS 1247), 1998

The Place of Deaf People in the Church, IEWG, 1996, ed. Visible Communications

Constructing Deafness (OU set book)

J.M. Hull, *Touching the Rock: An Experience of Blindness*, SPCK, 1990

R. Chubb, *Lifting Holy Hands: A Dictionary of Signs Used in Church Services* (ABM Paper 7), 1994

C. Bourne, *The Discrimination Acts Explained*, HMSO, 2000

12

Selection

Margaret Sentamu

The major report on *Criteria* (1993) was produced by a working party chaired by the (then) Revd David Conner (later Bishop of Lynn, Dean of Windsor and Chairman of VRSC). The revision built on the highly regarded *Criteria* from 1983 but developed the sections on Leadership and Collaboration and on the missionary aspect of ministry. This was then a basis for the report on *Procedures* (1995), a far-reaching review. It included among its many detailed recommendations:

- that central selection should continue as a key focus;
- the revised categories (which are set out later);
- improved training of bishops' selectors;
- the Ministry Division Conference Secretary would not be a selector but rather a moderator;
- the report to be written at the conference by the bishops' selectors;
- the report remains confidential advice to the bishop.

The booklet *The Care of Candidates – Before and After Selection Conferences* sets out rules of good practice concerning all candidates, but concentrates particularly on better care of those not recommended for training. It clarifies different roles, and commends a written résumé of reasons for the bishop's decision (see Chapter 13).

Each year the Ministry Division organizes on behalf of the House of Bishops over 50 selection conferences where candidates who have been sponsored by their dioceses come to test their vocation for professional ministry in the Church of England.

The conferences of up to 16 candidates take place over two and a half days at diocesan retreat and conference houses around the country. Each conference has six selectors, working in two groups of three, drawn from a panel chosen by the bishops. The conference secretary is a member of the Ministry Division staff.

Diocesan procedure

The assessment and preparation of candidates within the diocese prior to sponsorship to a selection conference is the concern of the bishop and those appointed by him to share this particular responsibility. After a bishop has sponsored a candidate to attend a selection conference it is the responsibility of the diocesan director of ordinands (DDO) to prepare the candidate for this. The DDO Handbook explains the criteria and selection procedures.

The diocese assembles a picture of the candidate based on diocesan forms, references and personal interviews. This information forms a major part of the sponsorship papers. The main areas include:

1. The candidate's personal history and family background;
2. Educational history, qualifications;
3. Occupational history;
4. State of general health;
5. Pilgrimage of faith and commitment, including maturity in Anglicanism;
6. Understanding of Christian faith;
7. Spirituality;
8. Sense of call and its working out in mission and ministry;
9. Responsibility and sense of vocation in secular areas;
10. Experience of sharing in mission and ministry in a local church;
11. Interests;
12. Personal maturity and ability in relationships;
13. Marriage and family commitments;
14. Financial situation.

Categories of sponsorship

The diocesan sponsoring papers indicate the category for which the candidate is being sponsored, and selectors are encouraged to apply the criteria universally but intelligently in a way which enhances the development of mission and ministry in the Church. The decision about category of sponsorship lies with the sponsoring bishop, the diocese and the candidate. The categories are as follows:

1. Ordained local ministry (OLM)
   This category normally refers to those sponsored in a diocese where there is a scheme recognized by the House of Bishops (see Chapter 35).

2. Ordained ministry (permanent NSM)
   This category includes a variety of non-stipendiary ministry, e.g. parish- or deanery-focused ministry, ministry in secular employment (MSE) and post-retirement ministry (see Chapter 34).

3. Ordained ministry (SM and NSM)
   This category includes those who perceive their ministry as full-time and stipendiary as well as those who, whether for vocational or practical reasons, see themselves moving between stipendiary and non-stipendiary posts.

In all the above categories, the diocese specifies whether a person is being sponsored for the priesthood or the diaconate.

4. Accredited lay ministry
   Candidates can be sponsored as either stipendiary or non-stipendiary. There are accredited lay workers currently serving in pastoral ministry in parishes, in church administration or in social and community work. To assist both selectors and candidates it is particularly important that the sponsoring papers should set out the nature of the proposed ministry with an indication of how the accredited lay worker will be deployed (see Chapter 33).

The candidate's paperwork

On receipt of sponsorship details the Senior Selection Secretary will allocate a candidate to a particular selection conference. The conference secretary for that conference will write to the candidate inviting him or her to attend, and a copy of the letter is sent to the DDO. Candidates are asked to fill in a registration form, an ethnic monitoring form, a disclosure of criminal record form, a list of referees and a medical form.

The Ministry Division carries out a Department of Health Protection of Children Act List Search (POCALS). If a candidate is divorced and has remarried s/he must obtain a Canon C 4 Faculty (i.e. a permission from the archbishop) before coming to a conference.

Copies of the registration form, references and sponsoring papers are sent to selectors about three weeks before the selection conference. A final invitation letter and conference programme are sent to the candidate about a fortnight before the conference.

The candidate receives two booklets, *Going to a Selection Conference and Preparing for a Selection Conference*. The former booklet talks about the conference in general terms, the latter helps the candidate prepare specifically for two tests (Verbal Organization and Deductive Reasoning) which they will undertake at the conference.

Assessment tools at the conference

1. Three 50-minute interviews with a senior selector (who will look at vocation, spirituality and ministry within the Church of England), an educational selector (faith, quality of mind) and a pastoral selector (personality and character, relationships, leadership and collaboration).

2. Candidates spend 40 minutes completing a personal inventory. This comprises three sections of open-ended questions of interest to particular selectors who may use the responses as a basis for some questions in interview.

3. Candidates take two half-hour tests (one in Verbal Organization, the other in Deductive Reasoning) to give some objective information about capacity for training and flexibility of thought. The conference secretary is trained to administer and mark these tests.

4. Candidates are asked to do a written exercise which is aimed at assessing their ability to understand and respond to a complex human situation, show an appropriate pastoral response and their ability to communicate in writing in terms appropriate to the task.

5. There is a two-and-a-quarter-hour group exercise aimed at assessing the candidate's capacity to chair and facilitate a discussion and his or her performance as a member on a ministry-related task or topic.

The selectors stay for an extra day after the candidates have gone, making their assessments, recommendations about each candidate and writing their reports to the sponsoring bishop. The conference secretary moderates this discussion and offers advice.

The conference secretary will process the selectors' reports and convey the decision to the sponsoring bishops. Although individual differences of emphasis are quite likely, the overall recommendation must be unanimous. These reports are sent out as promptly as possible to the bishops, who then communicate their decisions to the candidate, whether they should enter training or not.

Further reading

Criteria for Selection for Ministry in the Church of England (ABM Policy Paper No. 3A), October 1993

A Review of Selection Procedures in the Church of England (ABM Policy
Paper No. 6), September 1995

Regulations for Non-Stipendiary Ministry (ABM Policy Paper No. 5), 1994

Stranger in the Wings: A Report on Local Non-Stipendiary Ministry (ABM
Policy Paper No. 8), 1998

The Care of Candidates before and after Selection Conferences (ABM Ministry
Paper No. 16) 1997

Miss Sarah Evans, Statistics Officer of the Ministry Division, has provided the
following statistics and commentary.

The diagram below shows the number of candidates recommended for
ordination training since 1950.

Diagram 5: Selection conference results, 1950–2000

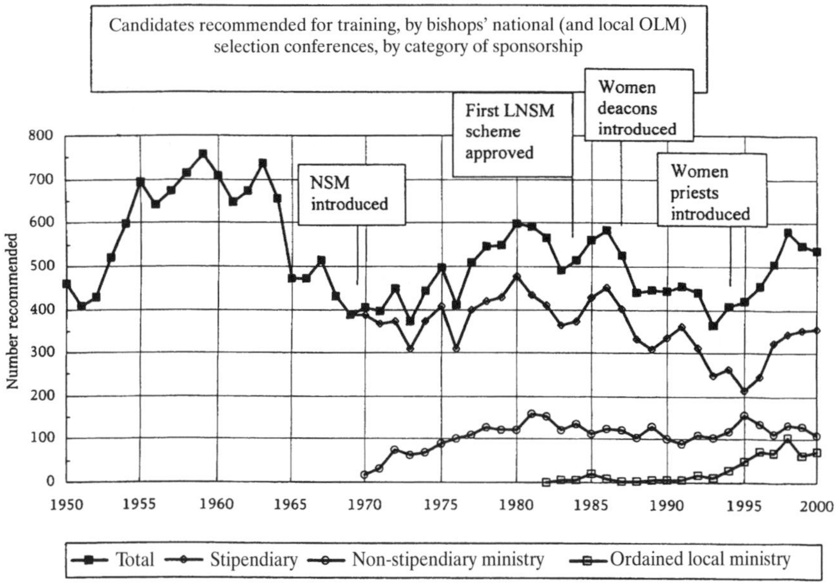

Candidates recommended for training, by bishops' national (and local OLM)
selection conferences, by category of sponsorship

The graph shows that, as with ordinations, there was a sharp fall in recommended candidates during the late 1960s and in the early 1990s. (This reflects
the 'time-lapse' of three to four years between selection and ordination.) The
graph also underlines the increasing diversity of ordained ministry. The chart
on page 114 shows even more graphically the change in the make-up of
ordination candidates in the last 50 years.

A summary of the criteria for selection for ministry

A Ministry within the Church of England

Candidates should be familiar with the tradition and practice of the Church of England and be ready to work within them.

B Vocation

Candidates should be able to speak of their sense of vocation to ministry and mission, referring both to their own conviction and to the extent to which others have confirmed it. Their sense of vocation should be obedient, realistic and informed.

C Faith

Candidates should show an understanding of the Christian faith and a desire to deepen their understanding. They should demonstrate personal commitment to Christ and a capacity to communicate the gospel.

D Spirituality

Candidates should show evidence of a commitment to a spiritual discipline, involving individual and corporate prayer and worship. Their spiritual practice should be such as to sustain and energize them in their daily lives.

E Personality and character

Candidates should be sufficiently mature and stable to show that they are able to sustain the demanding role of a minister and to face change and pressure in a flexible and balanced way. They should be seen to be people of integrity.

F Relationships

Candidates should demonstrate self-awareness and self-acceptance as a basis for developing open and healthy professional, personal and pastoral relationships as ministers. They should respect the will of the Church on matters of sexual morality.

G Leadership and collaboration

Candidates should show ability to offer leadership in the Church community and to some extent in the wider community. This ability includes the capacity to offer an example of faith and discipleship, to collaborate effectively with others, as well as to guide and shape the life of the Church community in its mission to the world.

H Quality of mind

Candidates should have the necessary intellectual capacity and quality of mind to undertake satisfactorily a course of theological study and ministerial preparation and to cope with the intellectual demands of ministry.

Each year the Ministry Division organizes, on behalf of the House of Bishops, about 50 selection conferences, where candidates, who have been sponsored by their bishops come to test their vocation for professional ministry in the Church of England. The House of Bishops has agreed these selection criteria that are firmly rooted in the Anglican tradition, recognizing that vocation depends not simply on personal faith but on the call of the Church and the grace of God. As such they provide a continuing solid base for the work of bishops' selectors.

✠ John Guildford
Chairman
Ministry Division
February 2001

Authorized publications on the criteria for selection are as follows:

The Report of a Working Party on Criteria for Selection for Ministry in the Church of England (ABM Policy Paper No. 3A) Price £3.00

Criteria for Selection: Excerpted from the Report of a Working Party on Criteria for Selection for Ministry in the Church of England (ABM Policy Paper No. 3B) Price £1.75

Leaflet entitled *A Summary of the Criteria for Selection for Ministry in the Church of England*. Price £2.00 for 20.

Diagram 6: Categories of recommended candidates, 1950 and 2000

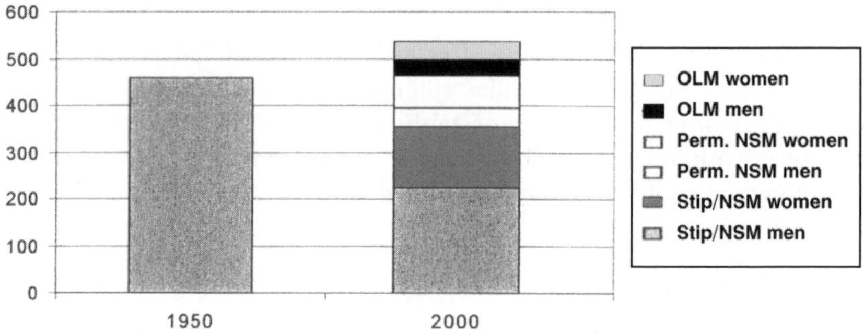

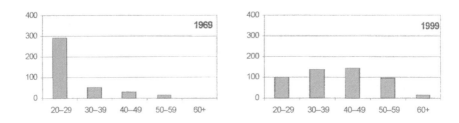

As well as changes in the type of ministry for which candidates are now coming forward, there has over recent years been a significant change in the age profile of candidates.

Diagram 7: Age profile of candidates, 1969 and 1999

In 1969 75 per cent of recommended candidates were under 30 years of age. By 1999 the number under 30 was only 20 per cent. Two contributory factors to this change are that NSM and OLM candidates are older than stipendiary candidates, and also that women candidates in all categories tend to be older than their male counterparts.

The marriage profile of candidates has also changed over the last 40 years. The figures below show the percentage of candidates in training who were married.

1965	1975	1985	1995
39%	49%	61%	69%

The following table sets out in detail the outcome of bishops' selection conferences in the last five years:

Table 4: Outcome of national and local bishops' selection conferences, 1996–2000

	1996	1997	1998	1999	2000
STIPENDIARY/NSM MEN#					
Recommended	178	227	212	212	225
Not recommended	74	67	95	79	78
TOTAL	252	294	307	291	303
PERMANENT NSM MEN#					
Recommended	63	40	61	58	41
Recommended OLM	42	32	50	40	31
Not recommended	56	48	29	41	23
Not recommended OLM	15	7	13	7	10
TOTAL	176	127	153	146	105
STIPENDIARY/NSM WOMEN#					
Recommended	66	95	130	141	130
Not recommended	41	47	56	53	49
TOTAL	107	142	186	194	179
PERMANENT NSM WOMEN#					
Recommended	72	72	74	73	68
Recommended OLM	30	36	54	24	42
Not recommended	58	59	33	35	35
Not recommended OLM	7	8	14	8	7
TOTAL	167	175	175	140	152
STIP/NSM LAY WORKERS#					
Recommended	2	0	1	0	0
Not recommended	0	0	0	0	0
TOTAL	2	0	1	0	0
PERM. NSM LAY WORKERS#					
Recommended	0	3	0	0	0
Not recommended	0	2	0	0	0
TOTAL	0	5	0	0	0
TOTAL RECOMMENDED	453	505	582	548	537
TOTAL NOT RECOMMENDED	251	238	240	223	202
TOTAL ATTENDANCE	704	743	822	771	739

#From 1997 categories changed to Ordained Ministry (Stipendiary and Non-Stipendiary) and Ordained Ministry (Permanent Non-Stipendiary).

Diagram 8: Recommended candidates, 1984–2000

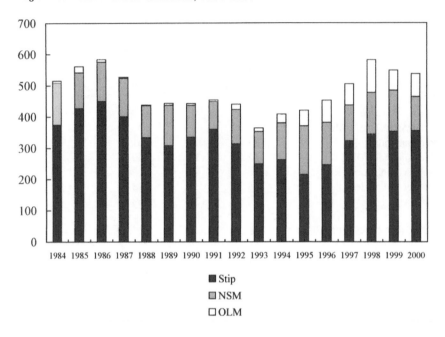

13

Care of non-recommended candidates: the 'but if not' question

Helen M. Thorp

How can candidates be supported by their dioceses when a bishops' selection conference does not recommend training for ordination? How can their experience be held, explored, given value and meaning? These are questions that continue to engage my thinking and challenge my practice as a vocations adviser working specifically with 'disappointed' candidates.

There are difficulties around the vocabulary of vocation. The process is one of discernment, but training is dependent upon a 'selection' conference – and if some are 'selected' what about those who are not? The language we use may compound the pain of rejection that candidates can feel deeply.

There are difficulties around disappointed expectations not just for the candidate but also for others caught up in the vocational journey. How can these be managed so as to negotiate the changes in perception, maintain supportive relationships, and lessen the feeling of stigmatization? Displaced anger, repressed emotion, withdrawing behaviour and other consequences of battered self-esteem can impact on and disturb relationships at home, work and church.

There may be difficulties around the spiritual life. A non-recommendation outcome can challenge previously held assumptions and theological convictions. Can God be held accountable for the actions of his Church? What kind of God allows this outcome? Prayer life may be thrown into confusion. Church services can be painful or meaningless.

The often heard cry: 'No-one ever prepared me for this' provokes reflection on how to familiarize candidates with the landscape of non-recommendation so that they can make some sort of personal map with which to negotiate its rough terrain. This is work to be done before a bishops' conference and may provide a searching contribution to the process of vocational exploration.

In the Durham Diocese we are developing different approaches to map-making, introducing candidates to the task through their vocational support groups and then at a later stage looking with the individual at the challenging scenario a non-recommendation outcome may present. These meetings with the Vocations Adviser who has specific responsibility for care of non-recommended candidates give opportunity to establish an open and safe relationship, which is the foundation of after-care should the candidate not be recommended.

Preparing a group of candidates

How can candidates be encouraged to engage with their own attitudes and possible reactions to non-recommendation? Group exercises can open up illuminating discussions and provoke challenging reflections. The following may be helpful:

In pairs, with Person A as the candidate, Person B as a close Christian friend: A tells B in their own words the news of their non-recommendation outcome. B responds, again in their own words.

In plenary explore together:

- What kind of language did A use? Where did it come from? What does it say about our attitude to the discernment process?
- How easy was it for B to respond? What was B feeling? What was B trying to express?
- How did we find this exercise? What learning might we take from it?

Invite the group to identify a particular loss and then to get in touch with how they felt at the time, and how they reacted. Write up responses and afterwards reflect together how the major loss of a vocation to ordained ministry might relate to the list.

Preparing the individual

A meeting is set up about a month before the bishops' conference – near enough to concentrate the mind, while leaving sufficient time both to engage with the implications of non-recommendation and then set to those reflections to one side before the immediate run up to selection.

The encounter is confidential to the Vocations Adviser and the candidate, and none of the content is fed back into 'the system'. We meet on an equal footing: I have no access to sponsoring papers or references.

I invite the candidate to think around some of the following questions:

What are you called to?
What are the distinctive details of your vocational canvas that will be there whether the frame of ministry is of an ordained or lay shape?
(This can provide useful material for future work following a non-recommendation.)
How do you understand the discernment process?
What is a bishops' conference about?
How would you explain it to someone outside the church?
(I am alert to language of pass/fail, success/rejection.)
Is there an image that describes your vocational journey this far?
Are you expecting to be recommended?
(I press the candidate to unpack their response.)
What are your previous experiences of loss (in its broadest sense)?
(We may then look at how the tentacles of a lost vocation might hook into and compound previous pain.)
How will you receive a non-recommendation outcome?
What is your usual response to difficult news?
How would you expect to feel? To behave? To think?
What might you want to say to God? What might God want to say to you?
How will you communicate a non-recommendation outcome?
Who are the significant people you will want to tell personally?
How will you do it and what language will you use?
How will you explain the outcome to those who have difficulty understanding discernment – children, the elderly, family and friends outside the Christian faith?
How will you manage the expectations of others?
Can you have a conversation with the key people (partner, children, parents, priest, spiritual director, close friends?) about how it will be for both of you if the outcome is non-recommendation?
What will you say to each other? How might others support you?
How can you best prepare for the conference and its outcome?
What can you plan into your diary that will resource you physically, emotionally, spiritually?
Who are the people to spend time with? – debrief the conference with?
Which situations, tasks and people drain energy and confidence or distract you from your vocational focus? How might you manage them around the time of the conference?

If you are recommended:
What have you to gain?
What have you to lose?

(I then turn the answers round, and reflect back what they would in turn lose and gain if not recommended.)

Brief notes of the meeting are kept, and a copy sent to the candidate, so that further reflection is encouraged and any inaccurate perceptions can be challenged.

Care following non-recommendation

Non-recommended candidates in the Durham Diocese have direct access to the Vocations Adviser, if and when they choose to make contact. To move on and out of the pain of non-recommendation demands a letting go, a search for meaning, and an integration of new and perhaps unwelcome discoveries of self and of God. The challenge to work through a bishops' selectors' report, courageously explore its critical elements, and move towards greater spiritual and personal integration is costly and demanding. Research suggests that most candidates understandably avoid such rigorous work, and that those with pastoral care tend to collude with them in this.

Journeying with candidates into the landscape of non-recommendation is demanding work. To put the full weight of pastoral care on the diocesan director of ordinands or parish priest is unrealistic. Those whose self-esteem has been battered by the selection process may need the support of skilled counselling even to begin engaging with the issues.

The challenge to the dioceses is to put in place structures that will prepare candidates for *both* conference outcomes, and offer confidential, professional and informed support after a non-recommendation. All candidates then have the opportunity to move into freedom and hope, growth and gain, and to fulfil their calling, whether the given shape of their vocation be ordained or lay.

Further reading

The Care of Candidates before and after Selection Conferences (ABM Ministry Paper No. 16)

On Being Not Recommended for Training and *Church of England: Obstacle or Opportunity?* (Church Pastoral Aid Society resource sheets)

Here I Am. Send Me! – a human inquiry group into the experience of non-recommendation following the testing of a vocation to the ordained Anglican ministry will shortly be available on the EIG web site (MA research by the author).

14

Pre-theological education

Marilyn Parry

Following a selection conference, bishops' selectors may recommend a candidate for training, subject to conditions. These conditions include those that relate to issues that must be addressed if a student is to make good use of the training that will be offered in preparation for ordination. A Pre-Theological Education condition relates quite directly to the current selection criteria and highlights particular areas that need attention from the candidate so that theological education can be useful and exciting rather than something to be survived. The Pre-Theological Education condition sets goals that must be achieved before a candidate enters training: it is a prerequisite for theological education.

The implementation of the devolved mode of pre-theological education (PTE) in January 1997, alongside the closure of the Aston Training Scheme in the summer of that year, signalled a radical shift in the thinking of the Church of England about the best way of preparing people for entry into theological education. Four main principles have been strongly influential in the developments over recent years:

1. Programmes should be tailored to the needs of the individual.

2. Any of the criteria for selection may usefully be the subject of a PTE condition.

3. The resources best used for PTE are regional and local.

4. The proper peer group(s) for those undertaking PTE are other adult learners and, possibly, other Christians.

A National Adviser was appointed to provide oversight, offer encouragement towards good practice and administer the scheme. An additional hope for the programme was that it might be more cost-effective than what had gone before.

Much of the early period of PTE was necessarily given to the development of the programme. Major attention focused on the criteria for selection and how they could be used in writing a condition paragraph which properly reflected candidates' needs. It was essential to develop guidelines which could be of use in articulating a condition that was clear, appropriate, attainable and assessable. Similarly, guidance needed to be offered which made it possible to distinguish between when a candidate should be placed on PTE and when a condition would be inappropriate. The Pre-Theological Education Panel (Pre-TEP) looked at the way in which a candidate's programme is developed and agreed in response to the condition paragraph. An important piece of work centred on the use of a portfolio both as an educational tool to accompany the work of a person undertaking PTE and as evidence to support the moderation interview at the end of the programme. The appropriate method for moderation and the method of reporting have also received considerable attention. Similarly, the fostering of open communication between all of the people involved in PTE has been regarded as crucial.

It needs to be noted that candidates undertaking PTE are *recommended* candidates who have prerequisites attached to their recommendation. If the sponsoring bishop chooses to endorse the recommendation, these conditions must be fulfilled if the candidate is to enter training. The pattern that has been developed moves from writing the condition paragraph, to the agreement of the programme between the diocese and the National Adviser, who then releases funds for the work. The candidate works through the agreed programme, using local and regional resources, and develops a portfolio which is presented at moderation. After the moderation interview, a report goes to the sponsoring bishop which offers advice as to whether the candidate has fulfilled the condition. This report informs the bishop's decision about the candidate's entry into training.

The programme and policy developed in all these areas have proved coherent and creative. The evidence of moderation suggests that candidates undertaking PTE have made considerable growth as a result. The review of the devolved mode of PTE, which took place during 2000, showed that the programme was essentially sound. The main change in the programme, now implemented, was a move to moderation rather than assessment. This reflects the adult education context in which PTE takes place.

The new form of PTE has enabled a group of candidates to enter training who would have been unable to do so in the past. Fewer than half of the PTE candidates would have qualified for the Aston Training Scheme because they are significantly older and/or are planning to train on courses and/or are sponsored for permanent non-stipendiary ministry. The effect of the availability of the devolved mode of PTE has been to increase the diversity of those training for ordination. Further, an examination of the candidate numbers shows that PTE has significantly advantaged women. The numbers of candidates undertaking PTE are relatively small: in the first four years of the programme, 105 candidates were recommended with a PTE condition. Of these, 59 have completed the programme, 24 are still on it, 21 conditions have been set aside (though the proportion of these is decreasing) and one candidate withdrew from PTE. Most candidates will spend slightly over nine months on the work. To date, all candidates who have been assessed have been deemed to have fulfilled their conditions.

It was envisaged at the outset of the new mode of PTE that the education programme and materials of the Aston Training Scheme would remain in use, perhaps with some revision. The programme itself has been re-validated in a new form as two Church colleges' certificates which can be undertaken by any adult learner in either a distance learning mode or in a taught mode. Undertaking these modules successfully allows an individual to demonstrate the ability to study at higher education level. The teaching materials are being entirely rewritten and published as a series of books, *Exploring Faith: Theology for Life*. Ten books are already in print and further volumes are being considered. This project is being undertaken in partnership between the Ministry Division, the Board of Education, the National Society, the Church colleges of higher education and the publishers Darton, Longman and Todd. The result has been the provision of an effective resource both for PTE and for the further education of adult Christians.

Issues which may warrant further consideration include:

1. ecumenical working at this level;
2. validation of the portfolio under the Church Colleges Certificate.

Further reading

Welcome to Pre-Theological Education, revised edition, January 2001
Pre-Theological Education and the Criteria for Selection, 2001

15

Adult education and formal lay ministries

Hilary Ineson and Ian Stubbs

Should the Church of England's provision focus on adult education in its broadest sense or on more specific lay training?

Christian Education and Training for the Twenty-first Century

- relates to the formation of all adults – focuses on those who understand themselves to be Christian and whose discipleship does not take the form of the ordained ministry;

- believes that nothing in our lives 'is exempt from the claims of the Gospel or the intelligent, sensitive application of Christian thinking and learning to it' (from *All Are Called*, 1985);

- asks questions to help dioceses 'choose between the good and the good' – recognizing that we cannot do everything.

Dioceses chose for the most part to move away from offering broad adult education for all lay people into lay training or lay ministry, training some lay people for specific roles in the local church

The document *Formal Lay Ministry Report* (1999) was offered as a resource for dioceses thinking about how to develop what was called 'formal' lay ministry, meaning ministry which was exercised at parish level and accredited or recognized by the diocese.

It has a clear link with collaborative or shared ministry and the document aimed to:

- produce guidelines on the selection, training, accreditation and use of lay people who undertake formal lay ministries in and through the local church;
- encourage the production of a directory of training schemes, produce models of good practice and foster the sharing of resources;
- share information with others working in this area, including ecumenical partners;
- examine the possibility of producing some form of validation/accreditation/recognition of schemes in order to facilitate Credit Accumulation and Transfer (CATS) across the C of E and to make recommendations for the future.

Using the term 'learning' has now blurred the difference between adult education and training which was clear in the early 1990s.

Questions about accreditation

Taking the Credit: National Vocational Qualifications (NVQs) and the Churches (1996): this document looked at the questions being asked about the national recognition of work experience and training undertaken in the Church. Since then the grassroots rise in the use of portfolio- and competence-based training in several dioceses (e.g. Oxford, Lichfield, Newcastle) needs to be noted. Here the move is away from putting training ministers through courses to helping people to acquire and demonstrate evidence of sufficient levels of knowledge, skills and personal qualities to undertake particular public roles. In principle, teaching may be from a number of different providers.

With respect to the accreditation and training of those involved professionally in adult education and training in the Church, the following were developed or recommended in co-operation with other agencies and other departments in Church House:

1. National Vocational Qualifications in Training and Development – offered through other religious and secular agencies.
2. The development of a scheme for professional development – now combined into a joint system for those working in adult, children and youth work in dioceses. The scheme includes recommended competencies for diocesan officers working with adults.
3. The development in co-operation with Chester College of a distance learning course offering awards at certificate, diploma and Masters levels in Adult Education with Theological Reflection. This course included the transformation into distance learning material of much of the board's work in designing educational events, understanding and working with process

and understanding how adults learn, which had been developed and used in training offered by the board since the 1950s. The material is also available as individual modules and will soon be available on the Internet.

Questions about the world and church contexts in which adult education and training is happening

Tomorrow is Another Country: Education in a Post-Modern World (1996): this document was the work of a Board of Education working party set up in 1993 to 'reflect theologically on the profound changes taking place in our post-modern world, in so far as they affect training and education, with a view to publishing practical help for decision makers in education at all levels'. It offers ways of understanding our postmodern culture and tools to help people reflect on the implications for education and training.

Questions about lay discipleship which is lived out in daily life and work

All Are Called: Towards a Theology of the Laity (1985). This was produced by a working group set up by the Board of Education. It is a series of essays giving individual perspectives on the importance of the baptismal call of all Christians and in particular those not called to ordination or specific ministry. This is the core document for much of the work that followed.

Called to be Adult Disciples (1989) was produced by a second Board of Education working party following on the thinking of *All Are Called*. General Synod debated this paper in 1989 and accepted its recommendations:

- that each parish finds ways of affirming lay vocation in its liturgy;

- that the Liturgical Commission produces material that values and celebrates the daily lives and experience of lay people;

- that parishes use the questions in Appendix 3 to ensure that there are opportunities for lay people to develop their discipleship in the 'dispersed' Church;

- that the Board of Education supports and encourages the further development and publication of work being done in the area of adult Christian learning;

- that the Board of Mission and Unity undertakes research into patterns of spirituality appropriate to lay vocation and looks at ways in which such patterns can be developed and disseminated;

- that ACCM co-operates further with the Board of Education in the areas of educational principles and practice with reference to theological education;
- that each bishop appoints a senior member of staff to share with him the responsibility to focus and develop the role of the laity in the dispersed church;
- that this person's terms of reference should be clearly indicated;
- that each diocese review its funding for ministerial and lay training so as to ensure that this specialized responsibility, in addition to staff salary and expenses, has adequate funding. This funding should be in the range of £2,000–£6,000 for each diocese;
- that the Faith and Order Advisory Group be encouraged to work further on the theology of the Church and the relationship between ordained and lay;
- that all boards and councils of the General Synod (and their working parties) should work towards having a significant proportion of lay people serving on them.

Called to New Life: The World of Lay Discipleship (1999) was produced by a working party of the board to see what had happened to this work in the ten years since *Called to be Adult Disciples.* It includes an overview of diocesan provision, resources offered by other agencies and the stories of six lay people from Peterborough Diocese, and it ends with a covenant between lay people and the Church.

The development of the Church of England as a learning church

A Learning Church for a Learning Age (1999): debated in Synod in July 1999, this document looked at the development of a learning culture in the Church in the context of the Government's stress on lifelong learning. It used GS Miscs 545 and 546 as background. Its recommendations were accepted by Synod.

The purpose of the report was to set out an agenda for a learning church in the context of a learning society. It addresses the Church's own learning needs as well as ways in which it both receives from and contributes to national provisions for lifelong learning. Key recommendations regarding a learning Church were contained in the *Called to New Life* and *Investors in People in the Church* reports.

Investors in People in the Church: The Introduction of the Investors standard in Dioceses, Parishes and Cathedrals (1999). The task group on Investors in the Church was set up by the Board of Education in order to assess the experience of churches using this national quality standard. The report recommended use of Investors as a theologically appropriate means of linking mission and training and of helping to develop a learning culture in the Church. As at February 2001 three diocesan offices are now recognized Investors in People (IIP) and about ten others are working towards the standard in some way. Use by parishes has been very slow.

Investors in People in the Church: Progress Report and Information on the New Standard (2000): an update on the progress of IIP in the Church and to update the General Synod on a major revision to the Investors' standard which was published in April 2000 and the work of the Investors in People in the Church Task Group to date.

Current issues and questions

Christian lifelong learning has its roots in our understanding of Christian baptism, vocation and discipleship. All Christians are called in the Gospels to learn and to teach. The term 'lifelong learning' embraces the notion that in the Christian community each is, at different times, both a learner and a teacher. Good teaching and good learning are both required if people are to fulfil their gifts and potential.

Adult Christian learning refers to the specific support and resourcing required by all people to fulfil their lifelong baptismal calling to serve God in Christ through the Church in the world. It involves several kinds of provision:

1. the provision of learning resources for all who are interested in the Christian faith and its application in the contemporary world. This can be understood in terms of a service and outreach of a national Church as well as that of evangelism – with a focus in our time on the needs of those who believe but do not now belong;

2. lifelong adult Christian education – with a focus on formation in the Christian faith and its application in different contexts and life stages;

3. lay discipleship training – with focus on ministry of daily life and occupation beyond the gathered church. This should not exclude the discipleship of clergy but is intended to focus on the particular character of the lay state to live and serve in the world;

4. formal ministry training – with focus on shared public leadership in the local church. This is increasingly seen in the context of shared ministry and therefore of the integration of lay and clergy training.

Where does this happen?

• informally in homes, families, communities, workplaces and among friends

– where the hidden role of committed lay disciples reaches those parts of contemporary life that the institutions cannot reach;

• in congregations and parishes as part of the corporate life and worship of the local church;

• on foundation and bishops' courses, diocesan courses, courses and programmes by other providers, theological colleges and distance learning programmes;

• in house groups, house churches, religious communities, cathedrals, chaplaincies;

• in schools, FE colleges, HE institutions, adult and continuing courses and workplace learning;

• via the Internet through web-assisted learning.

Further issues/questions

• Question of adult education in its broadest sense or more focused training.

• How to develop a culture of learning in church at all levels where people's contribution is recognized and they are helped to see and play their part in the mission of the whole.

• How to make the best and most recent understandings/interpretations of the Christian tradition accessible to church members – especially the contribution of biblical scholarship.

• Can learning resources be shared more effectively – e.g. Reader courses available to other lay people, bishop's certificate courses developed on a regional basis, etc?

• How can local churches be helped to support the ministry of the laity more effectively?

• How to ensure quality in Church adult learning provision – national guidelines.

• How to develop use of new learning methodologies and technologies, e.g. Web-based learning.

• How to balance sensible national co-ordination/networking/provision with local difference.

• Do we need some national systems of credit accumulation and transfer? How to help people move more easily between different systems of accreditation.

• How to support more research/evaluation/learning on what actually happens.

Further reading

Christian Education and Training for the 21st Century (GS Misc 389)

Formal Lay Ministry Report (staff level working paper), 1999

Taking the Credit: National Vocational Qualifications and the Churches (GS Misc 478), 1996

Tomorrow is Another Country (GS Misc 467), 1996

All Are Called, CIO Publishing, 1985

Called to be Adult Disciples (GS 794), Board of Education, 1987

Called to New Life, (GS Misc 546), The National Society and Church House Publishing, 1999

A Learning Church for a Learning Age (GS 1339), Board of Education, 1999

Investors in People in the Church: The Introduction of the Investors Standard in Dioceses, Parishes and Cathedrals (GS Misc 545), Church House Publishing, 1999

Investors in People in the Church: Progress Report and Information on the New Standard (GS Misc 604), 2000

16

Reader ministry

Pat Nappin

Current situation

One of the most encouraging developments in the Church of England in the last few years has been the growth of lay ministries and particularly of Readers. There are now over 10,000 active Readers who are not only engaged in a preaching and teaching ministry but increasingly in pastoral work. In parishes where collaborative ministry is the norm, Readers are involved in baptism and marriage preparation, pastoral visiting, bereavement visiting, in the taking of funerals as well as sharing in baptism and wedding services. They run parent and toddler groups, confirmation groups, Bible study and house groups as well as sharing in many other outreach projects and many other aspects of church life.

The main thrust of their work continues to be in the leading of services and in the preaching of the word. Many are involved week by week in a team situation and (hopefully) most are no longer used as a 'stop gap' but in a weekly sharing together by ordained and lay in a joint ministry to the people of God. But Readers who feel themselves to be a 'bridge' between Church and world value the opportunities that are a part of Monday to Friday lives. These vary from Reader to Reader and are as many and various as are the types of work both paid and unpaid. Many work quietly in their work situations while others serve as chaplains in hospitals and prisons, etc.

Over the years and particularly since the 125th anniversary of the 'modern' Reader 'movement' in 1992, Reader ministry has been recognized and affirmed by the Church. It is almost entirely a voluntary ministry.

Selection and training

Readers go through a selection process in each diocese and, if selected, are then trained by a diocesan scheme which is moderated regionally and nationally. The training is part-time over three or four years and when success-fully completed the Church of England Readers' Certificate is awarded. The revised regulations state clearly that Readers should not be admitted to office until this certificate has been awarded (Section 3.3). See further on training in Chapter 20.

However, training is not completed on admission but continues throughout the ministry. A number of dioceses offer 'CME' to clergy and Readers jointly and a number offer similar grants for both. The growth in recent years of courses leading to advanced awards by universities and colleges of higher education makes advanced study available to those Readers who wish to pursue it.The Archbishops' Diploma for Reader Ministry, which was the only further award available for many years, has now been discontinued in the light of the number of courses available.

The Central Readers' Council has for many years offered annually a week-long course at Selwyn College, Cambridge. Distinguished lecturers have given their services and enriched the ministry of those attending. In recent years the council has organized a number of national weekend conferences on a variety of topics. *The Reader* magazine, which was given a completely new look in 2000, provides useful resource material as well as interesting articles and book reviews and has a circulation of nearly 10,000.

Deployment

A number of dioceses include secondment to other parishes as a part of the training of Readers. Others make it clear that Readers may be deployed to another parish on the completion of their training in order to provide for the ministry of a deanery or area. The issue, which is discussed in the *Deployment of Readers* (published in 1999), highlights both the problems and the strengths of such a move. Readers who live and work and worship in one locality may find deployment a difficulty for themselves and their families since the family can then find themselves divided in their church attendance. For those who live in rural areas or areas where transport is poor the need to travel not only on Sundays but also for midweek events can present real problems especially at the end of a day's work.

However, it is possible to seek to be deployed when moving into a new area and before other social links have been built up. Some may be deployed for a short or longer period of time when a particular need arises in a parish or if they or the incumbent feels that their ministry has become stale or jaded. Whatever the situation it is important that the Reader's own spiritual development is provided for and the Reader is supported by the church family.

The future

The growth in Reader ministry is echoed in the growth of a number of other lay ministries, i.e. pastoral assistants, administrators of communion, evangelists, etc.

Interest in the whole area of Reader ministry has led to the planning of a 24-hour consultation on the theology and practice of Reader ministry. This consultation is planned for 2002 and will be built around a number of prepared papers written by well-known lay theologians.

The Central Readers' Council is also engaged in the planning of a book as an introduction to Reader ministry, with chapters on preaching, selection and training, collaborative ministry and parish and work life as well as a theological chapter.

Further reading

Bishops' Regulations for Reader Ministry, 2000
Reader Ministry leaflet, 2000 (text reproduced on pp. 134–5)
Selection for Reader Ministry, 1998
The Deployment of Readers, 1998
The Reader magazine, published quarterly

See also *Readers and Worship in the Church of England*, Grove Worship Series 115, 2000, book list at Chapter 20 (pp. 158–9), and Appendices 1 and 2.

Reader ministry

A challenging lay ministry for men and women in the Church of England

'Readers can be builders of bridges between the believing Church and the unbelieving world.'

Bishop Christopher Mayfield, Chair of the Central Readers' Council

'Never before has there been such a need for an alert, godly, effective Reader ministry in the Church.'

Archbishop George Carey

Who they are

The office of Reader has existed in its present form in the Church of England since 1866 and there are now 10,000 Readers, some in every diocese. Theirs is the only nationally accredited voluntary lay ministry which is governed by Canon and episcopally licensed.

Readers are lay women and men from a wide diversity of occupations and backgrounds – teachers, shop or office workers, accountants, machine operators, nurses, etc. They may be found in agriculture, government, industry, or at home. From such contexts Readers bring a rich experience of the community to the work of preaching and teaching which is at the heart of their pastoral ministry.

Their close contact with everyday situations helps them to interpret the gospel and to proclaim Christ's teaching in the Church and in the world. Readers work as members of teams with clergy and other laity, mainly in parishes, but also in prisons, hospitals and in the Armed Forces.

What they do

Readers' main duties include:

- preaching
- teaching
- leading worship
- assisting at Holy Communion
- pastoral work.

In many dioceses they may conduct funerals.

Readers are often active in teaching young people and leading discussion groups. They may also be involved in confirmation classes, youth work and marriage preparation. Their work includes outreach, helping people to grow in their faith and enabling others to explore a call to Christian witness. Readers' pastoral activity can involve visiting, counselling, comforting and generally showing the love and care of the Church for all, whatever their need. They may also be engaged in ecumenical work. Readers find many informal ways of ministering by their presence, witness and listening at their places of work, at home, and in their local communities.

Reader training

Each diocese has its own programme of training which is moderated by the Ministry Division of the Archbishops' Council. Those who successfully complete the training programme are awarded the Church of England Readers' Certificate.

Training usually lasts about three years and is designed to offer study and experience in important areas such as biblical study, Christian belief, pastoral studies, prayer and worship. The course is intended to develop both theological understanding and practical ministerial skills. After admission and licensing Readers are expected to continue their ministerial education through diocesan and other programmes.

What should you do if you are interested?

Pray
Pray that God will help you to know whether you are called to this ministry.

Consider
Consider the demands and the training involved.

Talk
Talk with your vicar, rector or chaplain to explore your calling.

Discuss
Discuss your ideas and feelings with your family, friends and other members of your church fellowship, and if possible with a Reader.

For more information

Contact the warden or secretary in your diocese; your vicar, rector or chaplain will know who they are.

The support of the parochial church council is needed before you can go forward for possible selection for Reader training.

The Central Readers' Council publishes a quarterly magazine, *The Reader*, to inform and resource Readers. It can be obtained via dioceses or direct from the Central Readers' Council.

Are you

- a confirmed and regular communicant member of the Church of England?
- keen to communicate your Christian faith?
- willing to train as a lay minister?

If the answer to these questions is 'yes' then Reader ministry may be for you.

Central Readers' Council and Ministry Division of the Archbishops' Council,
Church House, Great Smith Street, Westminster, London SW1P 3NZ
Telephone 020 7898 1415/1416   Fax: 020 7898 1421
http://www.readers@cofe.anglican.org
Email: sandra.fleming@mindiv.c-of-e.org.uk

17

Initial ministerial education

David Way

The then ABM provided an overview of initial ministerial education in its publication of October 1997 (with corrections 1998): *Issues in Theological Education and Training* (by Gordon Kuhrt). This chapter repeats some basic points and provides an update on that report.

The Church of England's provision for the education and formation of its clergy is made up of initial ministerial education to the point of ordination (the subject of this section) and the combination of apprenticeship with a training incumbent in the title parish and the first three to four years of CME. At this point stipendiary clergy are usually deemed ready to take up a post of incumbent level responsibility.

This chapter deals only with the initial ministerial education of those sponsored for ordained ministry and accredited lay workers in the technical sense (i.e. those sponsored to attend a national selection conference and selected against the national criteria). However, as there are at the current time only a handful of accredited lay workers, the focus will be on the initial training of ordinands. Within the synodical system, the House of Bishops has final responsibility for ministry issues. The role of the Ministry Division within the area of theological education and training is:

1. to advise the House of Bishops on issues in initial ministerial education as the need arises, and

2. to carry out key functions on its behalf, for example the setting of fees and approving of budgets, and approval of the curricula offered by the colleges, courses and OLM schemes. Through the Inspection Working Party the House of Bishops carries out inspections of training institutions every five years.

Initial theological education is provided by partnership between the House of Bishops, the Ministry Division and the individual colleges, courses and diocesan OLM schemes. Individual training institutions require the recognition of the House of Bishops in order to train ordinands for the ordained ministry of the Church of England. This in turn requires approval of the financial and educational proposals by the Ministry Division. Through this work it seeks to ensure that the money allocated by the Church to the training of ordinands is effectively spent and that a good and appropriate standard of education, formation and training is offered by all colleges, courses and schemes.

Bishops' Regulations for Training (available, among other places, in the *Church of England Year Book*) set out the basic regulations regarding the length of training in years and the mode of training (college, course, OLM scheme) according to categories of sponsorship of candidates. (For details on the category of sponsorship, see Chapter 12.)

Theological colleges offer two to three years of full-time training for those candidates who are sponsored to ordained ministry, which includes stipendiary ministry (i.e. sponsorship for the category stipendiary ministry/non-stipendiary ministry). In conjunction with their bishop or DDO, these candidates choose the college where they will be trained. Candidates over 30 and those who are theology graduates are required and enabled to do two years' training, while candidates who are under 30 and are not theology graduates will undertake three years of training. The purpose of these regulations is to ensure that all candidates who are presented for ordination are equipped, theologically, spiritually and personally, to begin public ordained ministry. As noted above, the whole training package includes the training offered by the first parish with a training incumbent and the provision of CME in these years. (This in turn is followed up by, hopefully, lifelong CME – see Chapter 26.)

Following the closure of the theological colleges at Chichester, Lincoln and Salisbury in the 1990s, candidates who qualify for full-time training have a choice of twelve theological colleges, including one in Wales. The colleges typically offer educational programmes at diploma, first degree and Masters level and can also offer higher degrees where this is appropriate, while at the same time being places of prayer and the fostering of community. Colleges seek to offer formation (personal development for the public ministry of the ordained), theological education and a basic level of appropriate skills to equip people for the first years of ministry and beyond.

The twelve *theological courses* are organized on a regional basis and offer a three-year initial training programme in a part-time mode for candidates over 30. They train candidates sponsored for permanent non-stipendiary ministry and candidates sponsored for stipendiary ministry/non-stipendiary ministry who opt to train in this way. As with college training, the purpose is to equip candidates to begin public ministry, with the title parish and the first three to four years of CME completing the initial training.

The twelve regional courses are each sponsored by a group of dioceses. Candidates from these dioceses will normally be expected to train on their regional course. All the courses now have university validation for their basic programmes, typically at diploma level. With the growth of the accreditation of prior learning, some candidates may achieve degrees or Masters level studies in theology for ministry in their initial training. Other candidates may be able to top up their pre-ordination studies to degree or Masters level after ordination. In terms of formation or development for ministry, courses make use of the community of prayer and learning on the course, especially the residential elements (weekends and summer or Easter schools), in conjunction with the candidate's continuing experience of work or home and his or her own parish.

As outlined in the report *Stranger in the Wings* (1998), dioceses of the Church of England may develop *ordained local ministry* schemes including the provision for the initial training of future OLMs. The diocesan OLM scheme may only train ordinands who are sponsored under the category of OLM. The training is often shared with Readers and/or members of local ministry or training teams. Some dioceses train their OLMs wholly or partly through regional theological courses (see above). As with the stipendiary and non-stipendiary categories, the purpose of the initial training is to prepare candidates to begin to exercise public ministry, but for these candidates in a specific local context.

At the time of writing 19 dioceses have OLM schemes approved by the House of Bishops. In general in the past OLM schemes have not sought or have been hostile to university validation. However, there is now a noticeable move to university validation at either certificate or diploma level. All OLM schemes emphasise two primary locations for the formation or development of candidates: the local ministry team or equivalent in the parish and, secondly, the educational programme in its setting in the life of the scheme.

Patterns of recruitment to the training institutions reflect a number of factors. These include the overall number of candidates, the rise in the number of older, often married candidates and the growth of OLM. This has resulted in a current pattern where there are roughly equal numbers in colleges and courses, with OLM candidates forming a smaller but growing group. The current figures for ordinands are (2000–01):

Colleges	622
Courses	578
OLM schemes	204
Total	1,404

However, it should be noted that a significant number of candidates whose sponsorship includes stipendiary ministry now train on the courses. Of the 578 candidates training on courses in the current academic year 2000/01, 257 are sponsored in the flexible category stipendiary/non-stipendiary. As a result the breakdown by category of sponsorship is as follows (2000–01):

Stipendiary/non-stipendiary	874
Permanent non-stipendiary	325
Ordained local ministry	204
Accredited lay worker	1

Following the closure of three colleges in the early to mid-1990s the twelve remaining colleges benefited from a modest upturn in candidates in the second half of that decade. This in turn led to a greater confidence within the colleges and gave a platform for some controlled diversification. Several colleges with evangelical foundations have always recruited additional, independent students who will offer themselves for Christian service in a variety of fields. Some of these colleges have now moved into the field of the training of Christian youth workers. Other colleges have developed Masters programmes suitable for clergy in service and other interested students. Where these programmes are successful they can help maintain or strengthen staffing levels. At the same time the colleges have to be careful not to be distracted from their main task of training ordinands and the demands on staff have to be carefully controlled. Where the proportion of ordinands and resident clergy in full-time training drops below 66 per cent of the student body, bishops' inspectors and the Church's validation service are asked to pay particular attention to this issue.

With regard to courses, the Church's commitment is to a nationwide provision of regional courses enabling all candidates wherever they live to train for ordained ministry while in their current employment or occupation. While the largest courses have grown to have around 100 students and up to five staff, inevitably some courses have remained small because of geographical and population factors. The Church has responded to this situation by encouraging co-operation with diocesan OLM schemes and Reader training schemes. In addition, all courses are either ecumenical in foundation or train ministers from other churches, particularly the Methodist Church and the United Reformed Church. This has financial, ecumenical and educational benefits. In addition the Church of England has developed a policy whereby courses should normally have at least three full-time members of staff who are primarily at the disposal of the course. This is to ensure a good quality of preparation for ministry for all candidates wherever they live.

As a relatively new movement OLM schemes are in a stage of growth, initial review and consolidation. As they are intrinsically a diocesan initiative the numbers of staff and students in each scheme are very small. Nearly all the schemes that have been inspected have been given recommendations to increase their staffing levels, and it may well be that this issue should be systematically reviewed. As with colleges and courses, OLM schemes are strongly encouraged to work in close partnership with other institutions providing theological education and ministerial training, at the diocesan level and at regional level. This strand of policy has to be attended to, however, with an equal care to ensure the coherence and appropriateness of OLM training.

In 1995 the House of Bishops approved a report on so-called *mixed mode training.* Permission was given in outline for five schemes which combined long-term parochial experience including lay ministry with appropriate theological training and formation for ordained ministry. While the overall take-up by candidates has not been great, two schemes have become established and have received positive comment from candidates and in official reports (for example, by Ministry Division moderators, see below). The St John's, Nottingham, scheme combines paid lay ministry with blocks of study at college, before and after ordination. The Peterborough Project, mounted by the East Anglian Ministerial Training Course, is a specialist scheme for theology graduates in which long-term placements are the basis for training which includes an MA in Contextual Theology. The East Midlands Ministry Training Course has also set up a scheme in association with a parish in Leicester. These mixed mode schemes will be reviewed by the Ministry Division in the coming two years.

All training institutions, especially colleges and courses, are faced with the considerable challenge of providing an appropriate *range of training options* to meet the needs of an increasingly diverse student body. Many candidates now come to their formal period of training and preparation with previous study in theology whether as Readers or through other vocational or academic routes, and nearly all candidates came with experience of lay ministry. The Ministry Division is currently carrying out a review of the issue of the accreditation of prior learning (APL). However, it is noticeable that small college and course staffs are being asked to provide an ever wider range of educational programmes from diploma to Masters level, and beyond, on similar staffing levels. This issue will continue to have implications for staffing levels but should lead in time to a better-trained clergy because training is being tailored to the needs of individual candidates.

Ecumenical partnership has become an increasingly important theme for initial ministerial education. As with many issues in theological education this means different things in different places. Colleges may be working closely with institutions sponsored by other Churches or may choose to appoint staff from different Churches. Courses are often ecumenical in terms of students or even in terms of their constitutions. The Ministry Division's educational validation service now works regularly with the Methodist Church and the United Reformed Church where we share educational programmes, and there have been some moves to work together in a more structured way in the financial area. At a denominational level, the Ecumenical Strategy Group for Ministerial Training, a group which usually meets at staff level, has been a useful forum for liaison and for promoting ecumenical partnership nationally and regionally. However, while much good work has been done in this area there remains much to do. Existing ecumenical relations need to be fostered and the range of churches working together needs to be widened.

Partnership with other educational institutions has also been a major theme of the past decade and continues to be so. Successive reviews of theological education have set in place a strategy of regional and national partnership between the providers of initial ministerial education, universities and colleges of higher education (see *Issues in Theological Education and Training*, pp. 7–8). These partnerships have grown in a variety of ways, ranging from university validation arrangements to full-blown schemes of federation. As with ecumenical partnership mentioned in the preceding paragraph, much has been gained from these partnerships but, in many cases, much remains to be done to get the full value out of often complex and time-consuming arrangements.

As noted above, the Ministry Division, through its Educational Validation Panel, scrutinizes and approves the curricula of theological colleges, courses and OLM schemes. Validation by the Church of England and, where appropriate, our ecumenical partners, takes place about every five years. Once the educational programmes of a training institution have received validation, the Ministry Division continues to receive annual reports on them from Ministry Division moderators who operate in a way somewhat analogous to university external examiners. In addition, every five years each institution has a full inspection, carried out by bishops' inspectors. These processes are designed to assure the Church that initial ministerial education is appropriate to its task of preparing candidates for ordained ministry and is of a good standard.

In turn, these processes have been reviewed and revised in two important ways recently. Firstly, the validation process has been co-ordinated with the quin-quennial inspections process in order to improve the quality of both, and to take some duplication out of the system. Thus, while they remain two separate processes because they have different lines of accountability (to the House of Bishops and the Ministry Division), inspection reports now inform the work of validation and moderation and, secondly, the same basic documentation underlies both inspection and validation.

Furthermore, the framework for validation, which used to be known as

ACCM 22, has itself been reviewed and revised. The three main changes brought in by *Mission and Ministry: The Churches' Validation Framework for Theological Education* (Archbishops' Council, 1999) are:

1. The former three basic validation questions which training institutions have to answer have been revised, partly for the sake of clarity and partly so that they reflect the ecumenical nature of much initial ministerial education.

2. While training institutions continue to be given the initiative in thinking about what type of training should be offered in each institution, a statement of agreed expectations for ordinands has been approved indicating what the Church expects of ordinands as they complete the pre-ordination phase of their preparation.

3. In order to give more guidance to training institutions in drawing up their validation documentation and to help the work of understanding and assessing them, much clearer guidance has been given in a set of 'Requirements for Validation'.

Both these sets of changes are being implemented as training institutions come to the five-yearly inspections and validation cycles. This has required a degree of flexibility on the parts of the inspectorate, the Ministry Division and the training institutions. Finally, it should be noted that all colleges and courses, and some OLM schemes, are subject to the various quality control procedures of the universities with which they work in addition to the Church processes described here.

Since 1990 the Church of England has had a policy of actively seeking to encourage the identification and training of potential theological educators, i.e. those who might, as part of their ordained ministry, teach in theological education or in comparable positions in the Church. This work continues to be focused in two main areas:

1. a provision for additional funding for well-qualified candidates who are over 30 (for example, those with good first degrees in subjects other than theology) to train at a college for three years, rather than two, so that they can complete a degree in theology as part of their training;

2. a provision for additional funding for suitably qualified candidates (for example, those with good degrees in theology) to take research degrees at Masters or doctoral level while training for ordination.

This work has continued and is beginning to attract additional and complementary funding from sources outside of central Church funds.

Following the Archbishops' Council's approval of the report *Managing Planned Growth* (see Chapter 18), the council set up a major working party to be chaired by Bishop John Hind. The remit of this working party, provisionally called the Structure and Funding of Ordination Training, was to look again at the fundamental theological, educational, organizational and financial issues of the Church's provision of ordination training. The group has started work, is in the process of consulting interested parties and plans to report to the Archbishops' Council and General Synod in 2003. The terms of reference and membership are reproduced as Appendix 3.

Diagram 9: Initial theological education in the Church of England

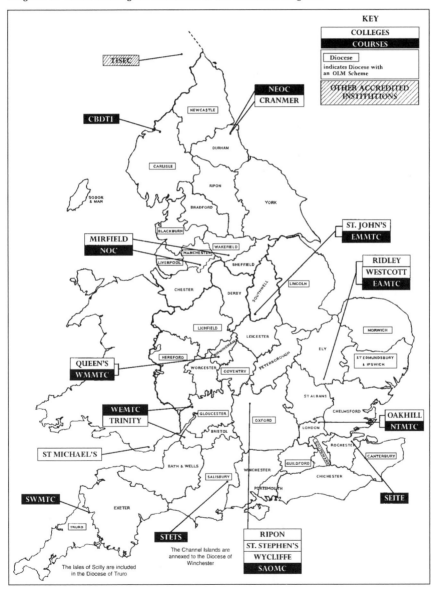

Theological colleges

Cranmer Hall, Durham	St John's College, Nottingham
College of the Resurrection, Mirfield	St Stephen's House, Oxford
Oak Hill Theological College, London	Trinity College, Bristol
The Queen's College, Birmingham	Westcott House, Cambridge
Ridley Hall, Cambridge	Wycliffe Hall, Oxford
Ripon College, Cuddesdon, Oxford	St Michael's College, Llandaff, Cardiff

---

Regional courses

Carlisle and Blackburn Diocesan Training Institute
East Anglian Ministerial Training Course
East Midlands Ministry Training Course
North East Oecumenical Course
Northern Ordination Course
North Thames Ministerial Training Course
St Albans and Oxford Ministry Course
South East Institute for Theological Education
Southern Theological Education and Training Scheme
South West Ministry Training Course
West Midlands Ministerial Training Course
West of England Ministerial Training Course

Dioceses with ordained local ministry schemes

Blackburn	Lichfield	Oxford
Canterbury	Lincoln	St Edmundsbury and
Carlisle	Liverpool	Ipswich
Coventry	London	Salisbury
Gloucester	Manchester	Truro (suspended)
Guildford	Newcastle	Wakefield
Hereford	Norwich	

Further reading

Education for the Church's Ministry: The Report of the Working Party on Assessment (ACCM Occasional Paper, Second Series, No. 22), 1987

Ordination Training on Courses: The Report of the Working Party on the Structure and Finance of Theological Courses (ACCM Occasional Paper, Second Series, No. 30), 1989

Theological Training, A Way Ahead: A Report to the House of Bishops of the General Synod of the Church of England, Church House Publishing, 1992

Theological Colleges, The Next Steps: Report of the Assessment Group on Theological Colleges, Church House Publishing, 1993

Steering Group for Theological Colleges and Courses: Final Report to ABM and the House of Bishops (ABM Ministry Paper No. 12), 1996

G.W. Kuhrt, *Issues in Theological Education and Training* (ABM Ministry Paper No. 15, GS Misc 507), 1997, revised 1998

Eucharistic Presidency: A Theological Statement by the House of Bishops of the General Synod (GS 1248), 1997

Beginning Public Ministry: Guidelines for Ministerial Formation and Personal Development for the First Four Years after Ordination (ABM Ministry Paper No. 17), January 1998

Stranger in the Wings: A Report on Local Non-Stipendiary Ministry, Church House Publishing, 1998

Mission and Ministry: The Churches' Validation Framework for Theological Education, Archbishops' Council, 1999

Theological Training in the Church of England, Archbishops' Council, 2000

Statistics of training

The training of ordination candidates has also diversified over the last 30 years. The graph below shows that in 1970 the vast majority of ordinands were training residentially (847 out of 899). By the academic year 2000/01 there were 622 ordinands at college, 578 on regional courses and 204 in diocesan OLM schemes.

Diagram 10: Numbers of sponsored candidates in training, 1970–2000

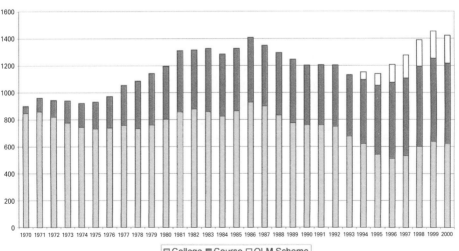

The detailed figures for ordinands in training for 2000–01 are given below:

Table 5: Total number of ordinands in training, 2000–01

	1	2	3	4	5	6	7	Other full-time students 2000/01
	Sponsored Students: 2000/01						1999/00 *TOTAL*	
	Men		Women		Lay			
Theological colleges	*Stip/ NSM*	*Perm NSM*	*Stip/ NSM*	*Perm NSM*	*Stip/ NSM*	**TOTAL**		
Cranmer Hall	33	0	21	1	0	55	*58*	31
Mirfield	31	0	0	0	0	31	*31*	7
Oak Hill	54	0	2	0	0	56	*57*	46
Queen's Birmingham	9	0	7	0	0	16	*25*	26
Ridley Hall	40	0	23	0	0	63	*62*	2
Ripon College	36	0	27	1	0	64	*67*	9
St John's Nottingham	62	0	30	0	0	92	*82*	14
St Stephen's Oxford	36	1	6	0	0	43	*47*	10
Trinity College	49	0	23	0	0	72	*80*	34
Westcott House	38	0	24	0	0	62	*58*	3
Wycliffe Hall	50	0	13	1	0	64	*68*	5
TISEC	0	0	0	0	0	0	*1*	
Llandaff	2	0	1	1	0	4	*2*	
TOTAL COLLEGES	**440**	**1**	**177**	**4**	**0**	**622**	*638*	**187**
Regional courses								
Carlisle & Blackburn	1	1	4	4	0	10	*17*	2
East Anglian	16	12	26	11	0	65	*72*	8
East Midlands	2	7	13	10	0	32	*34*	43
North East	4	10	15	3	0	32	*35*	8
Northern	15	11	20	23	0	69	*65*	20
North Thames	13	9	7	6	0	35	*34*	10
St Albans/Oxford	6	13	23	24	0	66	*70*	4
STETS	10	24	17	43	1	95	*91*	21
SEITE	11	28	15	27	0	81	*86*	7
South West	3	7	8	7	0	25	*23*	7
West Midlands	1	5	10	15	0	31	*26*	5
West of England	7	6	10	12	0	35	*36*	6
Other training establishments	0	1	0	1	0	2	*2*	0
TOTAL COURSES	**89**	**134**	**168**	**186**	**1**	**578**	*591*	**141**
TOTAL COLLEGES & COURSES	**529**	**135**	**345**	**190**	**1**	**1200**	*1229*	**328**
OLM Schemes (see below)	0	104	0	105	0	209	*200*	0
TOTAL in training	**529**	**239**	**345**	**295**	**1**	**1409**	*1429*	**328**

Table 6: OLM candidate numbers, 2000–01

Diocese	Men	Women	Total	*1999/00*
Blackburn	1	2	3	*3*
Canterbury	11	7	18	*13*
Carlisle	2	1	3	*5*
Gloucester	5	1	6	*5*
Guildford	4	3	7	*13*
Hereford	2	0	2	*5*
Lichfield	4	2	6	*15*
Lincoln	1	0	1	*1*
Liverpool	6	4	10	*15*
Manchester	9	12	21	*17*
Newcastle	3	1	4	*8*
Norwich	9	14	23	*16*
Oxford	10	18	28	*26*
St Eds and Ips	6	7	13	*30*
Salisbury	7	16	23	*0*
Southwark	16	13	29	*22*
Truro	4	1	5	*6*
Wakefield	4	3	7	*0*
TOTAL	104	105	209	*200*

18

The financing of training

David Morris and Mark Hodges

Introduction

The bulk of the costs of training candidates for the ordained ministry are met by the Central Fund for Ministerial Training (CFMT), which constitutes Vote 1 of the General Synod's annual budget (£8.9m in 2001 out of a total budget of £17.4m). The money is raised each year through the apportionment process, whereby each diocese pays its assessed contribution to the General Synod budget.

Vote 1 provides for the fees and personal grants of candidates undertaking college and regional course training and contributes to the cost of OLM training. (Ministry Division staff costs fall within Vote 2 of the General Synod budget.) The cost of the support of the dependants of married candidates in training is met primarily from diocesan budgets.

Fees system

Responsibility for the control of the training budget lies with the Ministry Division's Finance Panel in consultation with the Finance Committee of the Archbishops' Council's Finance Division.

Each year the Finance Panel invites each college and course to submit a detailed budget for the following academic year together with copies of accounts and other relevant information. The fee application format requires the costs to be broken down into specific categories of expenditure in order to facilitate the comparison of costs between institutions. The Finance Panel considers the overall position and scrutinizes each fee application individually within the overall confines of the Vote. The fee is then approved after taking into account any cost savings suggested by the panel. The approved fee applies to all sponsored ordinands and to other non-sponsored students attending the institutions.

Managing planned growth

Previous reports[1] on the structure and funding of ordination training have highlighted the budgetary problems – at parochial, diocesan and national level – resulting from fluctuations in the number of ordinands. Following the significant increases in the number of ordinands in 1997–9, the Archbishops' Council requested that a working party be formed with the following terms of reference:

with regard to the funding of ordination training within colleges/ courses and OLM schemes to make recommendations:

a) with regard to the specific handling of Vote 1 for year 2001;

b) to outline specifically any changes which may be required to the fee-setting mechanism/funding for the academic year 2000/01;

c) to highlight areas for further consideration and to report to the Archbishops' Council through the appropriate committees by the end of December 1999.

The working party's recommendations were accepted by the Archbishops' Council and implemented in time for the 2000/01 academic year. Among the report's significant recommendations were the following:

- that the 2001 Vote 1 budget should be drawn up on a realistic basis allowing for modest planned growth and that the budgets for 2002 and 2003 should be planned on a similar basis.

- a fee-setting procedure based on core funding principles be implemented for 2000/01 using the agreed budget for 1999/2000 as its starting point.

- a three-year rolling reserve to be created within Vote 1.

- colleges should not receive any fees for sponsored students in excess of their bishops' agreed maximum.

The result of the adoption of these recommendations has been that the Vote 1 budget and the budgets of colleges and courses are now very closely linked – the Finance Panel manages the allocation of fees by reference to the inflation and student number assumptions in the Vote 1 budget and by making discretionary allowances to take into account changes in institutions' individual circumstances. Any potential overspend on the training budget resulting from unbudgeted increases in student numbers is now minimized by limiting the cost to the training budget to the variable cost instead of the full fee cost. (This is 20 per cent of college student fees plus allowances and 35 per cent of course student fees plus allowances.) The creation of a three-year rolling reserve within Vote 1 has meant that such limited over-expenditure will be met from this reserve in this eventuality, thus avoiding the requirement for a Supplementary Vote and protecting the General Synod budget from unplanned fluctuations in costs.

Managing Planned Growth identified several issues requiring further exploration, some of which have been tackled in the working party's *Supplementary Report* published earlier this year. Others concerning wider training questions are included in the terms of reference of the Structure and Funding of Ordination Training Working Party set up by the council in the summer of 2000 (see Chapter 17).

Grants system

Grants from CFMT for college and regional course training make up 96 per cent of the annual training budget. All recommended candidates undertaking training within the Bishops' Regulations are eligible for funding. Training falling outside of the Bishops' Regulations may receive funding following approval by the Research Degrees Panel or the Candidates' Panel of the Vocation, Recruitment and Selection Committee. It is no longer generally possible for the local education authorities (LEAs) to make discretionary awards for ordination training. Candidates are only expected to apply to their LEA if undertaking a first degree course during training and they are thus eligible to receive a mandatory award towards college tuition fees. The level of the contribution made by LEA awards for the cost of ordination training has decreased very significantly in the last two decades. The graph on page 152 shows the steep decline in awards made since 1988 (Diagram 13).

A grant from CFMT for college training in the current academic year will normally consist of:

College tuition fees	approx £4,762 in 2000/01
College maintenance fees	£2,564
Personal allowance	£1,074
Short vacation allowance	£298
Long vacation allowance	£337
Travel allowance	varies

Grants from CFMT for regional course training normally consist of:

Course fees	approx £3,531 in 2000/01
Book allowance	£192
Travel costs	varies

Ordinands' grants from CFMT are paid through the colleges and courses on a termly basis; fees are paid to the colleges and courses in nine monthly instalments during the academic year.

Diocesan grants are made for the financial support of the dependants of married candidates entering college training and, where necessary, to single students requiring support beyond the level of the grants they receive from CFMT. In 1988 the *Report of the Working Group on the Support of Married Candidates* set out the guidelines to be followed in the allocation of diocesan family maintenance grants. These guidelines are now followed by all dioceses and updated annually.

A pooling arrangement exists so that diocesan costs in connection with both married and unmarried candidates are fairly distributed among dioceses. At the beginning of each year dioceses submit details of their expenditure in the previous year on the support of ordinands, based on the national guidelines. The total cost (£3.05m in 1999) is then apportioned between the dioceses in accordance with the approved system of apportionment for the General Synod budget and is taken into account in assessing each diocese's contribution to the General Synod budget in the following year. For example, diocesan expenditure in 2000 is reflected in the calculation of dioceses' contributions to the General Synod budget in 2002.

Ordained local ministry schemes are financed by a combination of local diocesan and CFMT funding. The contribution made by CFMT to each scheme approved by the House of Bishops, following the recommendations of the report *Strangers in the Wings*, consists of a basic grant (of £6,395 in 2001) together with the payment of a per capita sum (of £630 in 2001) for each selected ordinand. The balance of schemes' costs are met by the local dioceses concerned, which also in this case hold responsibility for the allocation of book and travel grants to OLM candidates in training.

Charities and trusts provide additional grant support for ordination training. Most notably, the *Church Times* sponsors the annual Lent Appeal for the Train-a-Priest Fund (which raised £133,236 in 2000 and has raised the equivalent of more than £8m since its inception in 1952). The TAP Fund, which is administered by the Ministry Division, is now open to both single and married ordinands in theological college training. The TAP Special Hardship Fund is open to all ordinands in special financial need, whether married or single and training at a college or on a course or OLM scheme.

Diagram 11: Contribution of LEA awards to college training, 1988–2000

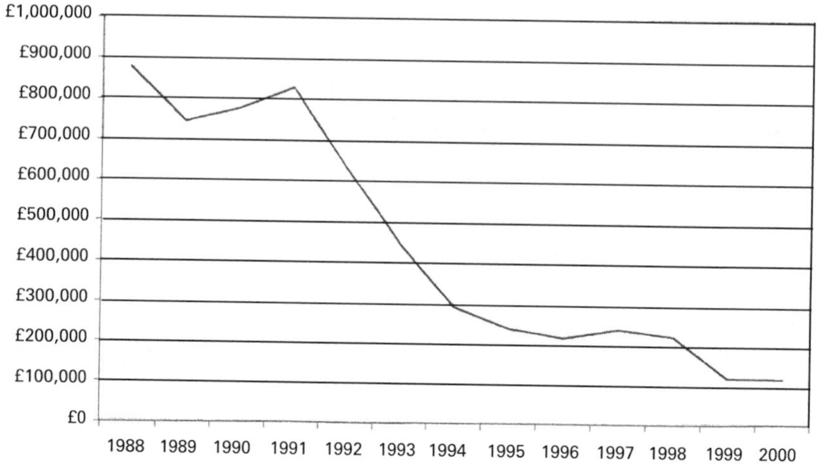

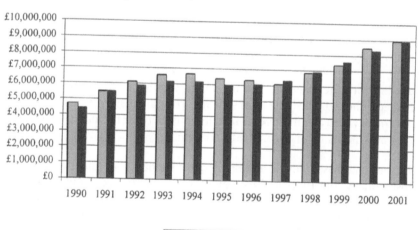

Further reading

Managing Planned Growth: A Report by the Vote 1 Working Party Review Group (GS Misc 597), January 2000

See also Appendix 4.

Diagram 12: Vote 1: budget and actual, 1990–2001

19

The Church of England colleges of higher education

John Hall

Eleven colleges in England are independently funded by one of the higher education funding councils and were founded by the Church of England for the purpose of training teachers. They train a quarter of all teachers but ceased to be known as teacher training colleges in 1963.

Table 7: Church of England colleges of higher education

College	Location	Foundation and date		Validating body
Bishop Grosseteste	Lincoln	Bishop Grosseteste, 1862		University of Hull
Canterbury Christ Church University College	Canterbury Tonbridge Thanet	Canterbury Christ Church, 1962	CBF	Degree awarding
Cheltenham and Gloucester College	Cheltenham	St Paul's 1847 St Mary's 1850		Degree awarding
Chester College	Chester	Chester College, 1839		University of Liverpool
University College Chichester	Chichester	Bishop Otter College, 1840		Degree awarding
King Alfred's College	Winchester	King Alfred's College, 1840		University of Southampton
Liverpool Hope	Liverpool	St Katherine's, 1844		University of Liverpool
College of Ripon and York St John	York	St John's, York, 1841 Ripon, 1861		University of Leeds
University of Surrey Roehampton	Wandsworth, SW London	Whitelands College 1842	Nat Soc	Degree awarding
College of St Mark and St John	Plymouth	St John's, 1840 St Mark's, 1841	Nat Soc	University of Exeter
St Martin's College	Lancaster, Ambleside, Carlisle	St Martin's College, 1963	CBF	University of Lancaster

The Anglican colleges reflect the diversity that is characteristic of British higher education. Teacher training currently represents, on average, only a third of their academic portfolio. The largest college, Canterbury Christ Church, has over 10,000 full- and part-time students registered in 14 of 19 recognized subject areas. The smallest, Bishop Grosseteste, has students in 4 of the 19. As well as teacher education, some of the colleges are major providers of health care and nursing; others are major providers of opportunities in business and administration, yet others in art and design.

There are flourishing religious studies and Christian theology departments. Through development in recent years, most of the colleges have professors within various Christian theology disciplines. There are strong links with ordination courses and schemes, often through academic validation, and with continuing ministerial education. For example, Cheltenham and Gloucester College provides the base for the distance learning Open Theological College, in partnership with, among others, three Anglican theological colleges. St Martin's College runs an undergraduate degree in Christian Ministry. As a group, the colleges are seeking opportunities to work more closely with the Church in ministry development. They are particularly well placed to make connections with education and youth ministry and with the ministry of health and healing but can offer a wide range of academic opportunities for lay and ordained people within open and well-founded Church institutions.

Further reading

An Excellent Enterprise: The Church of England and its Colleges of Higher Education (GS 1134), 1994

The Way Ahead: Church of England Schools in the New Millennium (report of the Church Schools Review published on behalf of the Archbishops' Council), Church House Publishing, 2001

20

Reader training

Wendy Thorpe

Introduction

Reader training today consists of a variety of training schemes devised by individual dioceses, the Armed Forces and the Diocese of Europe. The advantages of such a varied system outweigh those of having a neat, centralized, nationally approved course of training. Those who devise the schemes are enthusiastic about them and are highly motivated to make them work. Training can be made responsive to local needs and situations. It can be changed relatively quickly and easily to meet new diocesan needs and structures or to cater for the ongoing changes in Reader ministry. Good practice from other dioceses can be borrowed and tried out, new ideas piloted and then shared.

A centrally organized system of moderation ensures that, in spite of the variety, each training scheme meets national criteria and that good practice is widely shared and encouraged. National criteria are set out in Chapter 5 of *Reader Ministry and Training 2000 and Beyond*.

The present system has come a long way. When Reader ministry was revived in 1866, Readers had little, if any, training. The vicar would choose an upright, respected and well-educated man (*sic*) from the congregation to assist in leading services and preaching. Preaching in the early days often meant simply reading other people's sermons. Any training that was thought necessary was given by the incumbent.

As Reader ministry developed and women too were included (1969), an academic central training scheme was introduced based on a wide reading list and the writing of innumerable essays. The shortcomings of this scheme were soon obvious. It gave trainees a good academic grounding in theology, but it excluded those unable to cope with the high academic standards demanded and did nothing to train people to teach and preach well. Dioceses began to opt out and devise their own training schemes.

In 1989, after widespread consultation, centralized training was abandoned and the system we have today was set up, giving each diocese responsibility for devising and delivering its own training course subject to national moderation. This was set out in ACCM Occasional Paper No. 32, *The Training of Readers* (1989). There are currently about 1,300 men and women in training.

The organization of training

The most common arrangement is a diocesan curriculum provided for Readers only. This is delivered through lecture and seminar sometimes in a large group, sometimes individually, using a variety of tutors and lecturers, some clerical, some lay, some from academic institutions. But variations on this pattern are legion.

Several dioceses run a common course for all lay people which also forms the first, or first and second, year of a Reader's training. Some dioceses train Readers alongside trainees for ordained local ministry with some specialized modules for each group. A few train Readers alongside trainees for all forms of ordained ministry with appropriate variations for Readers. Other dioceses have chosen to buy in the whole or part of their training from higher education colleges. The Armed Forces and the Diocese of Europe also do this. Still others have developed, for trainees in remote areas, distance learning material which is studied with a local tutor.

Most courses are three years in length and require between four and eight hours per week of study.

Content of training

Courses include the Old and New Testaments, doctrine, worship, ethics and Church history. Attention is also given to sermon construction and delivery, the conducting of worship and pastoral and teaching skills. Many courses include working collaboratively and an understanding of group dynamics. Increasingly Reader trainees are given a parish placement in a church different from their own. Theological reflection is an important part of the formation of a Reader in preparation for Reader ministry in the world as well as for being part of a leadership team in the parish.

There is great variety in training for conducting funerals. Some dioceses provide it in initial training, others make it part of post-admission training.

Costs

Trainees are no longer expected to pay for their own training. Funding comes from the parishes of trainees or centrally from the diocese. Many Reader trainees, however, still pay for their robes, books and the cost of travel to initial and continuing training.

Tutors are usually licensed Readers or clergy with the appropriate skills and knowledge. Payment for their services is rare, although most dioceses give termly book tokens or a gift of money in appreciation. Incumbents of trainees are usually expected to share in the training of their Readers especially training them for preaching and leading services, but this is not to the same extent as in the past. It has been recognized that many incumbents do not have training skills, nor do they make available the required time to be good trainers.

Because of these factors, the cost of Reader training is very reasonable. In 1998 it was estimated that the average cost of three years of training was about £500 per trainee. The true cost, if premises had to be paid for and tutors rewarded at professional rates, was reckoned to be between £2,000 and £6,000 per trainee. Some would say Reader training is training on the cheap. Others would reckon it to be wise use of the Church's rich resources.

CME

Continuing ministerial training (CME) is considered essential for all Readers. Readers have such a varied ministry that it is not possible to provide all the skills, knowledge and formation they need in initial training. At licensing, Readers are not omni-competent. They have been given a good grounding in theology and have begun to practise their ministerial skills. But they need post-licensing support both from their parish and from the diocese. Their initial training should enthuse them for lifelong training and help them to take responsibility for obtaining it. Recent thinking on CME emphasizes that training needs to be linked to regular ministerial review (see Chapter 6 of *Reader Ministry and Training 2000 and Beyond*, and *Mind the Gap*, 2001). This is already happening in some dioceses.

Moderation of Reader training

The present system of moderation was set up in 1990 based on the guidelines set out in ACCM Occasional Paper No. 32. A few changes to develop good practice were introduced in 2000 in the report *Reader Ministry and Training 2000 and Beyond*. Moderation takes place every five years. The financing of it comes from a fee levied on each trainee at the beginning of training. At present this is £20. The fee is paid either by the trainee's parish or by the diocese. The moderation fund is administered centrally.

Each diocese appoints a moderator. The moderation exercise is carried out by at least two but preferably three moderators from adjoining dioceses in the region. Following moderation a report is presented to the bishop and those responsible for Reader training in the diocese. The report offers advice and recommendations to the diocese. Regional meetings of moderators are held at least twice a year. Reader training schemes in the army and air force will be subject to moderation from 2001. A slightly different way of working has been agreed to take into account the special circumstances of service life.

The honorary national moderator is appointed by the Ministry Division in consultation with the Central Readers' Council. The national moderator co-ordinates the scheme, attends regional meetings and contributes to the training and support of diocesan moderators. A report on Reader training, written by the national moderator, is published every five years. It comments on trends in training, shares good practice and makes recommendations for the future.

The national moderator issues the Church of England certificate for Readers to all those recommended by their dioceses as having completed their initial training satisfactorily in a training scheme which has been moderated and meets the national criteria. A Reader training panel, made up of representatives of those responsible for Reader training in the dioceses, oversees the work of moderation. This panel reports to the Theological Education and Training Committee of the Ministry Division.

Further reading (see also Chapter 16)

Ministry Division papers

The Training of Readers (ACCM Occasional Paper 32), 1989[1]
The Training of Readers (ABM Ministry Paper 9), 1994
The Moderation of Reader Training 1994–1999, 1999
Reader Ministry and Training 2000 and Beyond, Ministry Division, 2000

Central Readers' Council

Reader Ministry – slides on Reader ministry and accompanying script, 1998
Profiles: A Scheme for the Review of Readers, 1998
The Ministry of Readers: Holy Baptism and Extended Communion, 1998
The Central Readers' Council web page can be reached at: http://readers.cofe. anglican.org

Books

T.G. King, *Readers: A Pioneer Ministry*, Central Readers' Board, 1973[2]

R. Martineau, *The Office and Work of a Reader*, Mowbray, 1980[3]

Caroline Headley, *Readers and Worship in the Church of England*, Grove, 1991

Rhoda Hiscox. *Celebrating Reader Ministry: 125 Years of Ministry in the Church of England*, 1991[4]

H. Spence, *Decently and In Order: Practical Hints for Readers*, RSCM, 1995

21

Deployment of clergy

Margaret Jeffery

In 1972, the General Synod requested the House of Bishops to set up a working party to assist in 'the formulation of a scheme for the fairer distribution of clergy manpower'. The request grew out of concern about maintaining ministry to the whole nation, given projections of decreasing numbers of stipendiary clergy for some years ahead. In some dioceses the ratio of clergy to the population was four to five times greater than in others. The Synod's request was aimed at redressing the balance.

A working party was set up under the chairmanship of the then Bishop of Sheffield and its report, *Deployment of the Clergy*, was published in 1974. This recommended a formula which could be used to apportion the total number of stipendiary clergy between dioceses. For each diocese the formula would take into account four factors, namely, the population, area, the number of regular places of worship and the number on the electoral roll. Weightings were assigned to each factor as follows: 8 to population, 1 to area, 3 to the number of places of worship, 3 to electoral roll membership. (The 'membership' category was altered in 1988. It is now measured by one-third electoral roll members plus two-thirds usual Sunday attendance of people of all ages.) The greatest emphasis was given to population and reflected the priority given to the idea of the Church ministering to the whole nation, not just to its members. It would have been possible to have a different set of weightings but 8, 1, 3 and 3 gave results which meant that no diocese would be expected to relinquish or gain over 100 clergy. It was hoped that dioceses would achieve their targets by 1980.

The distribution of women deacons was governed by the Lambeth formula which was introduced in 1988. In order to take account of the fact that some dioceses had a stronger tradition of women's ministry than others, this formula

160

took 'historic' factors into account as well as those included in the Sheffield formula.

After the ordination of women priests in 1994, the Sheffield and Lambeth formulae were merged to become the Clergy Share Formula. Each year, the Ministry Division, with the help of the Church Commissioners and the Statistics Unit, advises dioceses of their current and predicted stipendiary clergy numbers. The formula is also used to apportion stipendiary candidates between dioceses.

There has been remarkable discipline in most dioceses in seeking to hold to their allocations. Most excesses are within 5 per cent of the diocesan allocation. Some dioceses do not take their full entitlement for a variety of reasons, which may be because the diocese cannot afford to pay or that people do not wish to live in particular parts of the country that they may perceive as being relatively inaccessible.

The formula does not apply to all clergy but only to those who are readily deployable by dioceses. Thus people in full-time chaplaincies in hospitals or prisons, for example, who are paid by agencies external to the Church, do not count. The total number of stipendiary clergy available for deployment is based on numbers on the central payroll.

The Diocese of London is allocated 15 clergy in excess of its notional total as a recognition of its role in the capital city.

Questions raised about the formula

The issue of who counts towards the formula is questioned frequently. In 1998, the House of Bishops decided that only people who had national, provincial or regional responsibilities, or responsibilities in more than one province or diocese, should be excluded. They also decided that part-time appointments should be amalgamated into full-time equivalents and thus count towards the formula.

There have been questions about whether university chaplains might be excluded from the formula on the grounds that universities are not evenly distributed between dioceses. Dioceses with several universities argue that chaplains should not form part of their total allocation. Many chaplains in Oxford, Cambridge and Durham are paid for by colleges. Similar questions might be asked about the exclusion of other unevenly spread ministries such as industrial missioners or agricultural chaplains.

There has been some pressure also to increase the number of factors included in the formula. Urban deprivation is one factor which might be taken into account on the grounds that the clergy–population ratio in UPAs needs to be higher in order to build confidence and leadership skills among local congregations.

Questions have been raised about whether the formula should take into account the distribution of ecumenical partners, ministers and priests. Another issue is whether people in first appointments might be excluded.

Projected stipendiary clergy totals against projected diocesan shares

Table 7 shows projected clergy totals against projected diocesan shares. In 1999 eight dioceses exceeded their clergy share by more than 5 per cent and nine dioceses were more than 5 per cent below their share.

In 2004, the number of dioceses expecting to be more than 5 per cent above their share is five and the number of dioceses expecting to be more than 5 per cent below their share is one.

In order to compile these figures dioceses were asked to indicate how many clergy they were planning to have in post in each of the years 2000–2005. In previous years dioceses have been asked to state how many clergy they needed and could afford.

See also the discussion in Chapter 6 on numbers of clergy (pp. 65–7).

Table 8: Stipendiary clergy: projected diocesan totals against diocesan shares, 2000–2005

	A	B	C	D	E	F	G	H	I	J	K	L	M	N	O	P	Q	R
		2000	Actual above share		**2001**		**2002**		**2003**		**2004**		PDT above share		**2005**		PDT above share	
DIOCESE	Share	Actual	B–A	C/A%	Share	PDT	Share	PDT	Share	PDT	Share	PDT	L–K	M/K%	Share	PDT	P–O	Q/O%
1 Bath and Wells	227	242	15	6.6%	227	240	225	238	223	236	222	234	12	5.4%	221	232	11	5.0%
2 Birmingham	203	207	4	2.0%	198	198	196	196	194	194	192	192	0	0.0%	191	191	0	0.0%
3 Blackburn	229	239	10	4.4%	228	236	226	233	224	230	222	227	5	2.3%	221	224	3	1.4%
4 Bradford	118	120	2	1.7%	117	121	116	120	115	120	114	120	6	5.3%	114	120	6	5.3%
5 Bristol	149	144	(5)	(3.4%)	148	150	147	150	146	148	145	148	3	2.1%	144	148	4	2.8%
6 Canterbury	172	179	7	4.1%	166	174	165	173	164	172	162	170	8	4.9%	161	169	8	5.0%
7 Carlisle	152	154	2	1.3%	151	152	149	152	148	152	147	152	5	3.4%	146	152	6	4.1%
8 Chelmsford	436	415	(21)	(4.8%)	432	411	429	411	426	411	423	411	(12)	(2.8%)	420	411	(9)	(2.1%)
9 Chester	285	276	(9)	(3.2%)	285	284	282	282	280	280	277	278	1	0.4%	276	276	0	0.0%
10 Chichester	313	338	25	8.0%	307	337	304	335	302	333	300	331	31	10.3%	298	329	31	10.4%
11 Coventry	144	151	7	4.9%	141	148	139	147	138	146	137	145	8	5.9%	136	144	8	5.9%
12 Derby	186	185	(1)	(0.5%)	184	185	182	182	181	181	180	180	0	0.0%	179	179	0	0.0%
13 Durham	236	240	4	1.7%	235	235	233	229	230	224	228	219	(9)	(3.9%)	227	214	(13)	(5.7%)
14 Ely	154	156	2	1.3%	154	154	153	153	152	153	152	153	1	0.7%	151	152	1	0.7%
15 Exeter	265	253	(12)	(4.5%)	264	267	262	263	260	259	259	258	(1)	(0.4%)	257	257	0	0.0%
16 Gloucester	158	160	2	1.3%	157	162.01	156	161.01	155	159.85	154	158.85	5	3.1%	153	157.85	5	3.2%
17 Guildford	175	203	28	15.0%	172	199	170	196	169	194	167	193	26	15.0%	166	192	26	15.7%
18 Hereford	124	117	(7)	(5.8%)	122	118	121	117	120	116	119	116	(3)	(2.5%)	119	115	(4)	(3.4%)
19 Leicester	166	169	3	1.8%	166	166	165	165	164	164	163	163	0	0.0%	162	162	0	0.0%
20 Lichfield	363	355	(8)	(2.2%)	362	364	358	363	355	362	353	361	8	2.3%	350	360	10	2.9%
21 Lincoln	242	227	(15)	(6.2%)	243	227	241	220	239	216	238	212	(26)	(10.9%)	237	210	(27)	(11.4%)
22 Liverpool	245	253	8	3.3%	243	249	241	244	238	239	236	234	(2)	(0.9%)	234	232	(2)	(0.9%)
23 London	524	557	33	6.3%	503	523	499	523	496	523	493	523	30	6.1%	490	523	33	6.7%
24 Manchester	304	299	(5)	(1.6%)	302	302	299	299	296	296	294	294	0	0.0%	292	292	0	0.0%
25 Newcastle	160	147	(13)	(8.1%)	158	158	157	157	155	155	154	154	0	0.0%	153	153	0	0.0%
26 Norwich	218	205	(13)	(6.0%)	218	207	216	207	215	207	213	207	(6)	(2.8%)	212	207	(5)	(2.4%)
27 Oxford	431	442	11	2.6%	430	436	428	431	425	426	423	420	(3)	(0.7%)	422	420	(2)	(0.5%)
28 Peterborough	168	168	0	0.0%	169	162	168	162	167	162	166	162	(4)	(2.4%)	166	162	(4)	(2.4%)
29 Portsmouth	125	119	(6)	(4.8%)	123	124	122	124	121	124	120	124	4	3.2%	120	124	4	3.3%
30 Ripon & Leeds	156	146	(10)	(6.4%)	154	154.5	153	153	151	151	150	150	0	0.0%	149	149	0	0.0%
31 Rochester	207	225	18	8.7%	209	230	207	225	205	215	204	214	10	4.9%	203	213	10	4.9%
32 St Albans	294	280	(14)	(4.8%)	290	290	288	286	286	288	284	284	0	0.0%	282	282	0	0.0%
33 St Eds and Ipswich	171	157	(14)	(8.2%)	170	158	169	167	168	156	167	156	(11)	(6.6%)	166	156	(10)	(6.0%)
34 Salisbury	240	229	(11)	(4.6%)	239	229	237	233	236	234	234	234	0	0.0%	233	236	3	1.3%
35 Sheffield	187	187	0	0.0%	185	185	183	181	181	184	180	180	0	0.0%	178	178	0	0.0%
36 Sodor and Man	19	20	1	6.3%	19	20	19	20	18	20	18	20	2	11.1%	18	20	2	11.1%
37 Southwark	359	374	15	4.2%	354	370	351	360	349	353.5	347	349	2	0.6%	345	344.5	(1)	(0.1%)
38 Southwell	182	172	(10)	(5.5%)	182	182	180	180	179	179	178	178	0	0.0%	177	177	0	0.0%
39 Truro	129	131	2	1.6%	129	126	128	123	128	120	127	117	(10)	(7.9%)	126	114	(12)	(9.5%)
40 Wakefield	177	180	3	1.7%	177	177	176	176	174	174	173	173	0	0.0%	172	172	0	0.0%
41 Winchester	247	240	(7)	(2.8%)	244	240.5	242	239.5	240	237.5	238	237.5	(1)	(0.2%)	237	237	0	0.0%
42 Worcester	155	152	(3)	(1.9%)	156	157	155	157	154	156	153	155	2	1.3%	152	154	2	1.3%
43 York	295	277	(18)	(6.1%)	293	279	290	279	288	278	286	278	(8)	(2.8%)	284	277	(7)	(2.5%)
Province of Canterbury	6,745	6,780	35	0.5%	6,677	6,753	6,623	6,700	6,578	6,645	6,535	6,608	73	1.1%	6,499	6,581	82	1.3%
Province of York	2,745	2,710	(35)	(1.3%)	2,729	2,735	2,704	2,707	2,677	2,679	2,657	2,659	2	0.1%	2,641	2,636	(5)	(0.2%)
CHURCH OF ENGLAND	9,490	9,490	0	0.0%	9,406	9,487	9,327	9,407	9,255	9,324	9,192	9,267	75	0.8%	9,140	9,217	77	0.8%

'PDT' is the Projected Diocesan Total of stipendiary clergy.   'Share' is the projected supply of stipendiary clergy, distributed between dioceses according to the share system.

Note: Two dioceses (Birmingham and Newcastle) did not supply information as to the number of clergy that they expected to have in post in the years 2001–2005. Consequently, in order to ensure that the information was as accurate as we could get it, we took the assumption that they would be 'on share' for those years.

22

Remuneration of the clergy

Patrick Shorrock and Roger Radford

The work of the Central Stipends Authority (CSA)

The CSA was set up to ensure that the system of clergy remuneration is:

- flexible enough to ensure (a) that the Church can pay its clergy in the places and positions where they can best be deployed, and (b) that mobility of clergy is not impeded by financial uncertainty;

- nationally coherent, while allowing an element of diocesan flexibility;

- equitable, with a high degree of conformity between one diocese and another and one level of responsibility and another;

- adequate, so that clergy are relieved of undue financial anxiety.

Each year the CSA:

- consults dioceses about stipend recommendations by post (in February) and at the Inter-Diocesan Finance Forum (in April/May);

- issues stipend recommendations during the summer to take effect the following April;

- submits an annual report to the General Synod, and publishes statistics of diocesan stipend levels.

The CSA also issues general advice and publications on a variety of subjects, including: *The Parochial Expenses of the Clergy: A Guide to Their Reimbursement*; maternity and paternity provisions; Council Tax; and housing allowances. It also provides advice on request in specific cases, and collaborates closely with the staff of the central payroll on matters affecting clergy pay.

The legal position of the CSA

Under the CSA Regulation 1972, which was subsequently replaced by the CSA Regulation 1982, the Church Commissioners were appointed Central Stipends Authority by the General Synod. Under the CSA Regulation 1998, the functions of the CSA have been transferred to the Archbishops' Council.

Under this regulation, the CSA is required, among other things:

1. to establish and publish recommended forms and levels of the pay of clergy, deaconesses and licensed lay workers;

2. to consult diocesan authorities and the Church Commissioners at least once a year on stipends policy and arrangements;

3. to submit an annual report on its work to the General Synod;

4. to have due regard to any resolution of the General Synod in respect of matters of general stipends policy.

It should be noted that the CSA's powers cover parochial, diocesan and cathedral clergy, and deaconesses and licensed lay workers. They do not extend to stipendiary non-parochial clergy, such as prison, forces, hospital or educational chaplains. Furthermore, the CSA only has power to make recommendations. If a diocese chooses to disregard the CSA's recommendations, the CSA is only able to exert moral pressure, and has no legal sanction. The most effective remedy, if a diocese chooses to disregard recommendations agreed after consultation, is, therefore, likely to be peer pressure from other dioceses.

The question of adherence to the CSA's recommendations was considered in 1982 in GS 498 *The Central Stipends Authority: A Review*. The Church Commissioners had been making their allocations of new stipends money conditional upon adherence to CSA recommendations, and the General Synod concluded that this practice should cease, and that the Commissioners should not contemplate withdrawal of allocations as a sanction for disobedience. However, GS 498 also went on to say: 'Dioceses in a strong financial position should not exceed upper limits on stipends ... Such dioceses could well contemplate a transfer of surplus resources to poorer dioceses.'

Since 1982, the proportion of the diocesan stipends bill contributed by dioceses and parishes has risen from 42 per cent to 76 per cent. As a result, dioceses are, inevitably, assuming an increasingly active role in stipends policy. This is entirely within the spirit of the CSA Regulation, which requires the CSA not only to consult, but also 'to have due regard to the views of diocesan authorities'. Although it is a matter for serious concern when dioceses choose to disregard the CSA's recommendations, which are adopted after consultation with all the dioceses, the CSA also has a duty to address concerns raised by such dioceses about stipend adequacy.

Although the CSA's recommendations have never been universally accepted by dioceses, in practice, the great majority of dioceses adhere to them, particularly where the national minimum stipend for incumbents is concerned.

Much work remains to be done in the area of clergy stipends, and there is clearly no room for complacency. There has, nevertheless, been some moderate progress since the CSA was set up in 1972:

- Disparities in stipend levels have been significantly reduced. The gap between the highest and lowest diocesan stipend (adjusted for inflation) fell by 54 per cent between 1972 and 1997.
- The level of parochial expenses unreimbursed has fallen from 55 per cent of declared expenses to 9.2 per cent.
- A new stipends system was introduced in April 1998 which takes account of regional variations in the cost of living.

The current stipends system

The current stipends system is based on proposals contained in the Leigh Report (CSA(96)7), which were discussed by dioceses at conferences in 1996, and which came into effect on 1 April 1998. Under this system, the CSA recommends each year a national stipend benchmark (NSB) for clergy of incumbent status. It is intended that it should be close to the national average stipend. The NSB is then adjusted for regional variations in the cost of living, and a regional stipend benchmark (RSB) is provided for each diocese, which indicates the level of stipend required for each diocesan stipend to have the same purchasing power as the NSB.

Dioceses are asked to use their RSB as a guide in reaching their own stipend decisions. After discussion at the Consultative Group of Diocesan Chairmen and Secretaries, dioceses expressed their support at the Inter-Diocesan Finance Forum on 4 May 1999 for the principle that they should set their stipends at a level not less than 1.5 per cent below, and not more than 2.5 per cent above, their RSB.

The figure used for the purposes of comparison with the RSB is the diocesan basic stipend, which is defined as the stipend paid to the greatest number of clergy of incumbent status in a diocese. In most dioceses, this will be the diocesan minimum stipend for incumbents.

RSBs are calculated by obtaining details each year of the cost of a package of goods and services in nine different economic regions of the country from the Reward Group (an organization specializing in remuneration data for personnel purposes). This is based on typical expenditure by a family of two adults and two children living in a three-bedroomed semi-detached house ('income standard B'). Housing and travel costs are excluded. From this data, an index of the relative cost of living in each diocese is compiled, which is then applied to the NSB to produce the RSB for each diocese.

In addition to the NSB, the CSA also recommends a scale for assistant staff of between 89 per cent and 96 per cent of the NSB. This scale is increased in line with the national average stipend, as agreed by the General Synod in 1989. The CSA also recommends that no full-time clergy of incumbent status should receive less than its national minimum stipend, unless there are special circumstances. The national minimum stipend is also used to calculate the value of the clergy pension, with a full service pension being set at two thirds of the previous year's national minimum stipend. The national minimum stipend is increased each year by the same percentage as the increase in the NSB and is 94.8 per cent of the NSB.

The CSA also recommends a stipend for dioceses to pay to archdeacons, and makes recommendations to the Church Commissioners about the level of stipend for residentiary canons, deans and provosts, bishops and archbishops.

Review of clergy stipends

This far-reaching review was established by the Archbishops' Council in 1999. See Appendices 5 and 6 for its terms of reference and the consultation document issued to interested parties. The group carried out a survey of all clergy and lay workers on the central payroll, and the results of this survey have already been published. The group's final report will appear in October, and will be debated at the November General Synod. The review group's recommendations include a new definition of the stipend. It continues to see a role for the CSA, although there is more emphasis on the need for diocesan flexibility.

Parochial fees

Parochial fees are set each year by issuing a parochial fees order. Additional information is provided in *A Guide to Church of England Parochial Fees.* Issues which have recently arisen in connection with parochial fees include: the destination of parochial fees; the conduct of services at crematoria; fee guidelines for retired clergy, NSMs and Readers; a survey of burial space undertaken by the Churches' Group on Funeral Services at Cemeteries and Crematoria; and the recent General Synod debate on funerals. Some of these are considered in more detail below.

The destination of parochial fees

Fees are legally payable to the incumbent of the benefice whether s/he takes the service or not. However, the amount of fees received should not make any difference to the overall level of remuneration. Either the incumbent signs a deed, assigning his/her fees to the diocesan board of finance, and passes all fees received to the diocese; or s/he retains the fee, and reports the fees received to the diocese, which takes them into account in calculating the level of stipend. Thus all incumbents in the same diocese should receive broadly the same stipend, regardless of the fees they receive, whether or not they assign their fees to the diocese.

At the request of the General Synod Clergy Conditions of Service Steering Group and dioceses, consultations have recently been held with dioceses and other bodies on various matters connected with parochial fees including whether the current structure of fees should be retained (with fees being payable to the incumbent), or changed so that fees are payable to the diocesan board of finance or parochial church council. The results of those consultations indicate that there is a broad spread of views on this question. The steering group, therefore, concluded that there is currently insufficient consensus within the Church to propose changes to the Ecclesiastical Fees Measure 1986 (which stipulates that fees are payable to 'a PCC, a clerk in Holy Orders, or to any other person performing duties in connection with a parish ... as may by law or custom be included in a Parochial Fees Order').

Conduct of services at crematoria

Concern has been expressed about the handling of funeral services at crematoria and especially about the pastoral considerations surrounding the issue of crematoria 'chaplains' (mainly retired ministers who take large numbers of crematorium services without providing adequate pastoral care) and the associated diversion of fee income away from the support of the stipendiary ministry. We hope that the recently issued Guidelines on Parochial Fees will go some way to dealing with these issues.

Fees guidelines for retired clergy, NSMs and Readers

These guidelines were produced in response to a request from dioceses and the General Synod Clergy Conditions of Service Steering Group, and have been the subject of extensive consultations with, among others, dioceses, the Central Readers Council and the Retired Clergy Association. Note the following points:

• all expenses are to be reimbursed fully;

- retired stipendiary clergy are to receive two thirds of the usual fee for incumbents;

- NSMs and Readers are not to receive fees, as their ministry is essentially voluntary.

See Table of Parochial Fees (Ministry Division of the Archbishops' Council, 2001).

Pensions for clergy and others in the stipendiary ministry

A brief history

Up to 1954, there was a separate pension fund, to which contributions were paid by clergy, dioceses and the Church Commissioners. The 1954 Pensions Measure made the Commissioners responsible for meeting the cost of clergy pensions, on a 'pay as you go' basis. The existing fund, amounting to £8.5m, was added to the Commissioners' assets. Contributions ceased.

There was no provision for widows' pensions, so a separate fund (to which clergy contributed) continued for this purpose. Widows' pensions were included in the main arrangements in 1961. The separate fund for widows was closed to new entrants in 1967. (Contributions were ended for all remaining contributors in 1988, but benefits, which are additional to the main scheme widow's pension, are still payable in respect of all those who contributed.)

A retirement lump sum, in addition to the pension, was introduced in 1967.

The 1980 'aspirations'

A detailed paper on clergy pensions, produced jointly by the Pensions Board and the Church Commissioners, was considered, and accepted, by the General Synod in 1980. It set out an underlying philosophy:

- pensions are part of remuneration in the form of 'deferred pay' and there should be a defined relationship to national stipend levels and to years of service;

- allowance needs to be included in recognition of housing needs in retirement;

- pensions should increase in payment by the same percentage as stipends;

- there should be the same arrangements for all in stipendiary ministry – clergy, deaconesses, licensed lay workers;

- a widow's pension of one half of the member's is not enough;
- the retirement lump sum should be improved;

and established 'aspirations' for the three main benefits:

- member's pension for full service – two thirds of the national minimum stipend in the previous year;
- widow's pension – two thirds of the member's pension (or of prospective pension for those who die in office);
- retirement lump sum – three times pension, calculated for all at the basic rate (i.e. ignoring higher pension rates for certain dignitaries).

The reason for 'aspirations' was that the Commissioners did not feel able to make a specific commitment to the timing of being in a position to meet the full projected costs.

The Regulations – the formal documentation of the scheme – did not contain the formulae for calculating benefits, but continued to leave a substantial discretion with the Commissioners. In the event, the targets were achieved in stages over the following ten years and since then have been maintained.

Recent developments

The effect on the Commissioners' income of the investment difficulties encountered in the early 1990s meant that pension costs took up a higher proportion than expected – and projections indicated that the proportion would continue to rise – whereas previous projections had suggested greater stability.

In July 1995, the General Synod accepted the proposal that a separate pension fund should be established, to receive contributions to provide for benefits arising from future pensionable service. The Commissioners would retain responsibility for the cost of all benefits arising from service prior to the date of commencement of that fund.

In July 1996, the Synod received a report from the Pensions Board regarding the calculation of benefits for future service and the contributions to be payable. It was agreed that:

- the existing benefit basis would continue to apply;
- the scheme documentation would state:
    1. the formulae relating benefits to national minimum stipend at the point of retirement;
    2. that post-retirement increases would reflect limited price indexation ('LPI' – i.e. price inflation but a maximum of 5 per cent in any one year);

- the balance of post-retirement increases, up to the objective of matching rises in stipends, would remain discretionary (but the rate of contributions payable would reflect that objective).

The Commissioners agreed to the proposal that the Regulations governing the 'past service' part of the scheme should be amended to mirror the Funded Scheme Rules. The Funded Scheme came into operation on 1 January 1998.

Derivation of the formula for calculating the pension and retirement lump sum

The starting point was the national minimum stipend – defined as an adequate living allowance so long as housing is provided and expenses of office are reimbursed. Basic expenditure in retirement should not be significantly different except that National Insurance contributions are no longer payable but, on the other hand, housing costs must be met. Part of retirement income will come from the State pension.

The result of mathematically following through the philosophy was then applied to the benchmark – the national minimum stipend – to produce an ongoing formula. The formula has been retested at subsequent reviews. The arithmetic has continued to support it.

Key features

The pension formula was tailor-made to reflect the particular situation of those retiring from the ministry, who must meet the costs of housing in retirement, whereas accommodation is provided while in office.

The scheme is uniform for all service covered, no account being taken of variations in stipends between dioceses. There are limited differential pension rates, agreed by the General Synod, to reflect the holding of certain offices within the provinces of Canterbury and York. (Individuals can increase their prospective benefits, within statutory limits, by paying voluntary contributions.)

The same basic pension is in payment, at any given point in time, to all those in retirement with the same length of service, whatever their year of retirement. This 'generation uniformity' is a long-standing request of the House of Clergy. Details of the benefits are set out in an explanatory booklet for scheme members.

See also the annual reports of the Pensions Board.

23

Clergy conditions of service

Margaret Jeffery, Gordon W. Kuhrt and Bryan Pettifer[1]

Deployment, remuneration and conditions of service

The Deployment, Remuneration and Conditions of Service Committee inherited in 1999 the work of the General Synod's Clergy Conditions of Service Steering Group. The group was set up in 1992 to 'co-ordinate the consideration of issues relating to clergy conditions of service, including a review of the ecclesiastical freehold'.

The setting up of this group was prompted in two ways. A joint meeting in February 1990 of the convocations of York and Canterbury discussed the legal and financial arrangements associated with clergy 'conditions of service' and asked for consideration to be given to the issue of the ecclesiastical freehold. Subsequently representatives of the convocations identified a wide range of issues requiring further consideration. These included matters to do with leasehold appointments, appraisal, voluntary severance, an investment fund for clergy to contribute to in preparation for retirement, stipends differentials at regular intervals, and a clergy dependants' allowance.

The second stimulus came from the Diocese of Southwark, which sent a motion for debate by the General Synod in 1991 asking for a review of all freehold tenure of office. Following this debate, the Synod's Standing Committee set up the steering group.

The steering group produced a consultation document in 1994 (GS 1126). This set out some general principles for determining the conditions of service which might be appropriate for clergy. They are as follows:

1. they should be such as to free the clergy to undertake what is required of them without, for example, fear of want or arbitrary action;

2. they should recognize the dignity of individual clergy and embody Christian standards of equity;

3. they should reflect the Church's duty of pastoral care for those who have devoted their lives in its service;

4. they should be proportionate, not only to individual needs, but to what the Church will afford;

5. they should help ensure that individual clergy can discharge their vocation in a way which uses their talents as fully as possible;

6. they should enable the bishop in council to deploy the human and other resources of the Church in a way that ensures that the need of the Church for a strategy of mission and pastoral care can be met for the benefit of the whole community;

7. they should be capable of flexible adaptation to suit individual circumstances; and

8. they should embody the best of secular practice where this is possible and appropriate.

The consultative document discussed stipends, differentials, working expenses, ministerial review, clergy discipline and the issues raised by the convocations.

Some 130 responses were received to the document, mainly composite replies (e.g. from 43 dioceses). *Improving Clergy Conditions of Service* (GS 1173, 1995) contains a summary of the responses. It was concluded that there was insufficient consensus in favour of abolition or reform of the freehold of office to warrant pursuing this in the near future. Areas were identified where there was significant room for improvement and these should be addressed first before coming back to the issue of the freehold of office. These are listed below:

- improving clergy discipline (and possibly grievance) arrangements (voluntary severance arrangements might also be further investigated);

- reviewing some or all stipends and pensions differentials for 'senior clergy';

- continued attention, within the bounds of affordability, to the adequacy of current stipend levels;

- dioceses putting in place adequate systems of ministerial review, support structures for the clergy and their families and, together with the national Church, effective 'personnel management' arrangements (where these do not exist already);

- the House of Bishops setting up a procedure for monitoring the development of ministerial review arrangements;

- looking at ways of reforming the incumbent's freehold of property, while safeguarding the clergy's security of housing;

- looking at ways of improving the security of tenure for those without the freehold;

- considering ways of improving appointments procedures;

- improving the care for clergy between posts at a national and diocesan level;

- clarifying the mutual expectations of clergy and diocese in such matters as working hours, etc., e.g. through the introduction of diocesan 'staff hand-books', and disseminating examples of good practice;

- in due course, reviewing the conditions of service of NSMs;

- reviewing the conditions of service of specialist ministry and chaplaincy posts;

- considering ways of abolishing 'Guaranteed Annuities', etc. and allocating the funds released on a basis of need;

- (as a medium-term objective) a separate review of the need for insurance for clergy against legal action;

- a review of the implications of joint ministry.

The General Synod debated the report in November 1995 and endorsed the conclusions.

Following the publication of the survey results and recommendations, the Clergy Conditions of Service Steering Group commissioned work in the following areas.

Improving conditions of service for those without the freehold

Considerable preliminary work had been done in this area by the Ministry Development and Deployment Committee. The group recommended that the Ministry Division set in train a major piece of work to look at what level of security unbeneficed clergy should have, how that security should manifest itself, how other developments such as the reform of clergy discipline legislation affects clergy security, what the expectations of the clergy should be, and so on. One of the major considerations in this area was how to ensure an appropriate degree of security of tenure without inadvertently entering into a contract with the clergy person. In this context the group carefully studied the implications of the Coker case (see pp. 177–8).

The group hoped that in the long run revised conditions of service for unbeneficed clergy might be a model which, suitably adapted, might be an alternative to the freehold for beneficed clergy.

Stipends adequacy and differentials and the philosophy of the stipend

The group strongly supported the philosophy of the stipend as the foundation for clergy remuneration. The group was concerned about adequacy particularly for clergy with dependants and no other source of income. It had mixed views on differentials. One area which received particular attention was the stipend differentials for residentiary canons. Stipend differentials were debated by Synod in February 1996 (see Chapter 22).

Review of freehold ownership of benefice property

A working party was set up in 1996 to review this issue. The steering group endorsed the conclusions of the working party that the freehold of benefice property should be retained. However, other action was recommended to tackle problems with unsuitable housing. One possibility which emerged was to review the Repair of Benefice Buildings Measure 1972, which the Church Commissioners are undertaking in 2001 (see Chapter 25).

Ministerial review

The group welcomed ABM's and the dioceses' initiatives over this and recognizes them as a key development (see Chapter 26).

Support structures for the clergy and their families

The group produced a draft summary of the various support structures for the clergy, for use possibly as a checklist for dioceses and possibly as the basis for a review. This work was passed to the Ministry Division to take forward.

Voluntary severance arrangements

The group produced a draft summary of the various voluntary severance arrangements for the clergy, for use possibly as a checklist for dioceses and possibly as the basis for a discussion as to whether these measures are adequate. This is work in progress which was passed to the Ministry Division to take forward (see Chapter 31).

Parochial appointment practices

The group recognized the importance of effective and fair selection procedures for clergy and therefore the need for good practice at parish level. The work of the Clergy Appointments Adviser in encouraging good practice is crucial, especially his notes of guidance in this area and his efforts to publicize the various diocesan initiatives. The work of the Archbishops' Adviser on Bishops' Ministry is also relevant. The group looked at whether there was more that could be done to encourage good practice at the local level. This is ongoing work for the Ministry Division to consider taking further (see Chapter 24).

Clergy handbook

The group looked at a number of diocesan handbooks for the clergy. There may be scope for suggestions about sharing examples of good practice in the dioceses and guidance (e.g. ensuring that the document does not equate to a contract). If these matters were to be developed, it would be necessary to do so in conjunction with diocesan secretaries and others in the diocesan structures. Two dioceses have recently requested advice on this matter. This is ongoing work for the Ministry Division to consider taking further.

Clergy discipline, grievance and minor complaints procedures

The group welcomed the work of the *Under Authority* implementation group that resulted in the preparation of the Clergy Discipline Measure. The outcome of this work will be highly relevant to the work on establishing appropriate levels of security for those clergy without the freehold (see Chapter 28).

Other matters

Insurance: the group encouraged the Central Board of Finance to work with the Ecclesiastical Insurance Group over the provision of a Clergy Legal Expenses scheme. This scheme was launched in 1998.

Abolition of guaranteed annuities: it has been agreed with the Diocesan Chairman and Secretaries that a review of the existing arrangements for distribution of guaranteed annuities should be conducted towards the end of the transitional period for the introduction of pension contributions.

Review of conditions of service of NSMs, those in multi-role ministry, married couples working together as ministers and those in specialist ministries and chaplaincy posts.

Creating a personnel/human resources framework for the clergy: a working party did some preliminary work on drawing up a matrix of clergy conditions of service – looking at what the elements were of the clergy conditions of service package, who was responsible for them and what work was underway to improve those conditions.

Relations with the MSF Union's clergy and churchworkers sector: the group kept a watching brief over relations between Church House and the MSF and considered reports on meetings that had taken place. The group considered that the office-holder status of clergy, as confirmed by the Coker case, was worth retaining. The group did not accept the MSF's contention that employee status was an essential element of improving clergy conditions of service.

During the course of its work, the group reached a number of conclusions regarding clergy conditions of service. These included:

- that conditions of service should strike an appropriate balance between the needs of the Church and those of the clergy and their families. In some areas the balance was tipped too far in the direction of the Church – e.g. lack of security for assistant clergy, in others too far in the direction of the individual – e.g. the protection that the freehold offered to beneficed clergy who were significantly underperforming;
- that the work on clergy conditions of service needs to be viewed in strategic context rather than simply dealing with each item piecemeal;
- that providing appropriate conditions of service for the clergy, particularly appropriate levels of security of tenure and housing, is crucial for their morale;
- that development of the Church's personnel or human resource practice should be a high priority at national and diocesan level.

The Employment Relations Act and its implications for the Church

The Government intends through its Employment Relations Act to extend employment rights to people who are not technically employees. The purpose of this is to give protection to anyone who works for another person, not just those employed under a contract of employment. Clergy are held in law not to be employees because they are not regarded as having contracts of employment. Neither are there 'legal persons' with whom contracts can be concluded. This was made clear in the judgements emanating from the proceedings brought by the Revd Dr Coker in 1997 against the Diocese of Southwark, the bishop and the Diocesan Board of Finance.

The main points of the judgement are:

1. the relationship between the Church and a minister of religion is not regulated by a contract of service;

2. the duties owed by the Church to a pastor are not contractual;

3. there is a lack of intention to create a contractual relationship;

4. the law requires clear evidence of an intention to create a contractual relationship in addition to the pre-existing legal framework. That intention is not present on the appointment of an assistant curate;

5. the relationship between bishop and priest, cemented by the oath of canonical obedience, is governed by the law of the established Church which is part of the public law of England, not by a negotiated contractual arrangement.

The Government has made it clear that clergy will fall within the scope of the legislation. In a reply to a question in the House of Commons on 16 December 1998 as to whether the Government had plans for legislation which would affect the employment rights of clergy, the Minister of State for Trade and Industry replied as follows:

> The *Fairness at Work* White Paper contained a proposal for an order-making power enabling the Government to extend the coverage of employment legislation to categories of workers not currently covered. It also indicated that the Government would consult fully on specific changes before exercising this power. The position of the clergy is one of the matters to which consideration will be given during the course of the consultative process.

See Appendix 7 for an extract from the Explanatory Note prepared for the House of Commons about the Employment Relations Bill which sets out the intentions of the legislation.

The Secretary-General wrote to the Minister for Trade and Industry to register the Church of England's interest and willingness to be consulted. This issue affects all denominations (and other faith communities). The Churches' Main Committee therefore will play an important part in any discussions with the Government.

A group including members of the Archbishops' Council and senior staff has considered how to respond.

There are complex arguments (theological, ecclesiological, pastoral and legal) for and against changing the employment status of clergy. A radical change of employment status would raise questions about the current arrangements over patronage, parochial appointments practices, senior clergy appointments practices, selection for ordination training, clergy discipline, and so on. It is also recognized that clergy who have the freehold might be unlikely to welcome becoming employees since this would lessen their security of tenure. There would be problems in defining the employer.

The view from the group mentioned above is that there is much that can and ought to be done to give clergy the rights they could expect if they were employees without effecting a radical change in their status. This would point to the adoption of a code of practice. Unless the Church is able to demonstrate that there is good practice in its 'employment' relations, the Government could, if it chose, radically change the legal position of clergy and much of the Church's 'employment' practice.

The Clergy Conditions of Service Steering Group spent much time considering good practice, but compliance to its recommendations has remained voluntary. It identified a number of areas where work is needed, including:

Appointment practices

The group considered issues such as: Should all posts be advertised? How can equal opportunities principles be incorporated? What should be done about interviewing procedures particularly in parishes? Should there be written job descriptions? (The Ministry Division will now consider working on a code of practice for the House of Bishops.)

Conditions of service issues

The steering group hoped that a way could be found to ensure that all clergy were clear about matters such as:

- the tenure of their office;
- the basis on which housing or housing allowances are provided;
- the payment of stipend, pension and retirement provisions, expenses and insurance provision;
- availability of pastoral and other support;
- ministerial review arrangements and expectations;
- a statement of the benefits available for clergy from the diocese and elsewhere;
- guidance about holidays and practice over days off;
- training provision and guidance on sabbaticals;
- disciplinary and disputes procedures;
- grievance procedures;
- procedures to be observed towards the end of any time-limited term of office;

- arrangements for maternity and paternity leave and pay;
- arrangements for voluntary severance;
- expectations of compliance with policies of child protection, harassment and bullying.

Some of these matters would be covered in the diocesan handbook. Questions about the legal status of written material, namely whether it constituted a contract, would need to be carefully addressed.

The issue of security for clergy without freehold

The report *Improving Clergy Conditions of Service* (GS 1173) concluded that 'the security of clergy without the freehold has been revealed by the review as one of the priority areas for attention ...'.

There are three main categories of full-time stipendiary clergy who do not have the freehold: (a) those employed by non-Church bodies, e.g. armed services, prisons, hospitals and some educational institutions; (b) those employed by dioceses through diocesan boards of finance or education or employed by ecumenical bodies, e.g. industrial chaplains employed by a county ecumenical council; (c) those paid through the Church Commissioners' payroll with a licence and who neither hold a contract nor have the freehold of office. These will include assistant curates, cathedral canons, priests-in-charge, team vicars and team rectors (with the exception of some team rectors appointed before the passing of the Team and Group Ministries Measure 1995) and some sector ministers. The issue is also relevant to some in dual or multiple ministries involving a combination of the three categories.

Table 9 shows cathedral, diocesan and parochial clergy, paid through the Church Commissioners' payroll, with and without the freehold, at July 2000.

Table 9: Categories of clergy with and without 'freehold'

	With freehold	Without freehold
Assistant staff		1,672
Incumbents	5,256*	100*
Team vicars and team ministers		676
Priests-in-charge		1,205
Curates in charge		30
Cathedral clergy	121	39*
Assistant bishops		1
Other bishops/archbishops	106	
Archdeacons	107	
Non-parochial clergy		369
Part-time clergy		206
TOTAL	5,590	4,298

*Estimate. The Commissioners do not record this information.

Also, there are:

- 128 full-time parochial licensed lay workers
- 68 non-parochial full-time lay workers
- 14 parochial part-time lay workers
- 17 non-parochial part-time lay workers

making a total of 227 licensed lay workers. The grand total of staff is 10,115. It has been assumed that all bishops (except one assistant bishop), archdeacons, deans, provosts and commissioners' residentiary canons are freehold posts.

'Non-parochial clergy' covers those clergy paid through the Church Commissioners' payroll, that is, university and industrial chaplains, other chaplains, and other diocesan appointments. Those clergy paid through external agencies, such as hospital, prison, school or forces' chaplains, are not included here.

This means that about 57 per cent of clergy have the freehold and 43 per cent are without it. By contrast, in 1959, in the equivalent categories, only 25 per cent were without the freehold. There are a number of contributing factors to this increase, notably: (a) the need for pastoral reorganization has meant that some livings have been suspended; (b) since the Pastoral Measure 1968 introduced team ministries there has been a steady growth in their number (and hence the number of team rectors and vicars without the freehold); and (c) since the Team and Groups Ministries Measure 1995, appointment of team rectors on a freehold basis can no longer be made in team ministries. (Team vicars have always been appointed for a term of years.)

Of the three categories listed above, conditions of service for (a) and (b) are agreed with their employing bodies. They have the security of tenure provided by employment law and we see no case for saying they should have something more, though our comments below about housing may be relevant in some cases. In category (c) some team rectors and some cathedral canons have the freehold. The remaining team rectors and cathedral canons together with all team vicars have a leasehold of office for a term of years. Standards for the Church of England for clergy in teams and groups have been set by the Teams and Group Ministries Code of Practice. *Priests-in-charge remain the group where the least work has been done on their conditions of service and who usually have the least security.*

Any system has to meet the needs and expectations of the clergy and the needs and expectations of the wider Church. The lists which follow are in fact relevant to all clergy. There are differences between these needs and expectations but they are not necessarily in conflict.

The main clergy needs and expectations include the following:

- regular feedback on how their performance is perceived;
- early warnings of any problems that are seen, indication of where any improvements are expected, a timetable for any action, and a clear indication of the basis on which any assessment may be made;
- a grievance procedure to operate where they believe judgements being made about them are unfair;
- a degree of security which reflects the dependence on tied housing, and in particular a sense that no change will be made to their appointment without respecting a minimum period of notice;
- an assurance that they will not face unreasonable pressures to move themselves and their families to situations they consider unsuitable;
- a written statement of the reason for discontinuing a licence;
- a sense of belonging to a body that takes them, their situation and their needs and expectations seriously, and which demonstrates this in the way it treats them.

The main needs and expectations of the wider Church include the following:

- well-motivated clergy with reasonable security who do not regard their relationship with those in authority as being 'us and them';
- the knowledge that the Church is following recognized good practice in the way it treats its clergy;
- some basis on which the small number of personnel problems which are impairing the mission of the Church can be resolved without unreasonable time and cost;
- some basis on which movement between posts can be achieved for the good of the posts and the post-holders;
- a major say for lay people sharing in and associated with the life of the Church;
- a system where movement and change cannot be vetoed by the clergy making unreasonable demands or holding unrealistic expectations.

24

Patronage and appointments

David Parrott and John Lee[1]

Appointments to benefices

The appointment of clergy to benefices in the Church of England is still made under the system known as patronage. An article by Peter Smith on the history of this system is in the *Ecclesiastical Law Journal*. However, during the 1970s and 1980s, it became clear that the system needed a good overhaul. There had been some changes made earlier in the century[2] and in 1972[3] but there was still a perceived need for a more comprehensive change. Some argued that the system should be abandoned entirely while others argued that there was still good merit in having a three-party process involving the patron, the bishop and the parish. Most felt it would be good to involve parishes to a greater extent than had been the case under the older system.[4] As a result of this revision process, the law governing the process now is the Patronage (Benefices) Measure 1986. Each parish still has a patron or patrons, whose rights are now registered with the diocesan registry. The registered patron has the right to present to the bishop candidates for the incumbency. The patron is not, however, responsible for stipend or housing once the appointment has been made.

The provisions of the Patronage (Benefices) Measure 1986 set out the procedures for filling benefices that become vacant in the Church of England. This is affirmed by Canon C 9 (1), which says:

> A vacancy or impending vacancy in any benefice shall be notified by the bishop of the diocese to the patron and to the parochial church council, and the provisions of the law from time to time in force relating to the filling of such vacancy shall be complied with.

The Measure applies in most but not all circumstances: for example, it does not apply where the patron is the Crown, the Lord Chancellor or the Duchy of Lancaster or when the bishop has suspended the right of presentation under s.67 of the Pastoral Measure 1983. The full details are set out in detail in the Measure and in the Patronage (Benefice) Rules 1987. Further guidance is described in the Patronage (Benefices) Measure 1986 Code of Practice issued in 1988.

Each diocese has an appointed 'Designated Officer' and the first step in the process is for the bishop to notify the Designated Officer that a vacancy has occurred. The Designated Officer then has to notify all registered patrons of the benefice and the PCC secretary. The registered patron, if an individual and not a clerk in Holy Orders, must either make a declaration of being an actual communicant member of the Church of England or of a Church in communion with the Church of England, or must appoint another, who can make such a declaration, to act in place of the patron. If the patron is a body of persons corporate or unincorporate, they must appoint an individual who is able to make such a declaration to act in connection with the vacancy. The Designated Officer must then pass the name of the person dealing with the vacancy on behalf of the patron to the PCC secretary. As in the law before the Patronage (Benefices) Measure, if the patron is a clerk in Holy Orders or is married to such a clerk, that clerk is disqualified from presentation to that benefice.

The PCC secretary must then call a meeting of the PCC within four weeks. The purpose of this meeting is, according to s.11(1)(a) of the Patronage (Benefices) Measure 1986, to prepare a statement of the conditions, needs and traditions of the parish, to appoint two lay members of the PCC to act in connection with the appointment of a new incumbent, to decide whether to request the patron to consider advertising the vacancy, to decide whether to request a joint meeting of the PCC with the bishop and the patron, and to decide whether to request a statement in writing from the bishop describing, in relation to the benefice, the needs of the diocese. There are provisions as to the number of representatives to be appointed from multi-parish benefices. There are also guidelines as to how the parishes may be helped to prepare a s.11 statement. These will be referred to at a later stage.

The PCC may make the request mentioned above that there be a joint meeting of the patron, the bishop and the PCC. The patron or the bishop may also make such a request and, when anyone does so, this meeting must happen. The patron or the bishop may send a representative to the meeting and need not attend in person. The rural dean and lay chairman of the deanery synod must also be invited to attend this meeting. Its purpose is to discuss the PCC's statement of needs and any such statement prepared by the bishop at the PCC's request.

One further formal requirement has been added to the process since the passing of legislation for the ordination of women as priests. PCCs are required at the s.11 meeting to consider whether to vote on two formal resolutions designed to describe their attitude to women's ministry (see further Chapter 37).

From that point onwards the selection of an incumbent is, in general terms, in the hands of the patron. When the patron has chosen the priest to be offered the benefice, he must notify the PCC representatives and the bishop. They have a discretion to approve the offer before it is made. They may refuse such approval in which case the patron may refer the matter to the archbishop or select another candidate. There are no grounds set out in the Measure as to why the bishop or a PCC representative may refuse to approve.

Under Canon C 10(3)(a), however, grounds are set out. This Canon states:

A bishop may refuse to admit or institute any priest to a benefice (a) on the grounds that at the date of presentation not more than three years have elapsed since the priest who has been presented to him was ordained deacon, or that the said priest is unfit for the discharge of the duties of the benefice by reason of physical or mental infirmity or incapacity, pecuniary embarrassment of a serious character, grave misconduct or neglect of duty in an ecclesiastical office, evil life, having by his conduct caused grave scandal concerning his moral character since his ordination or (b) in the case of a presentee who has not previously held a benefice or the office of team vicar in a team ministry on the ground that he has had no experience or less than three years' experience as a full time curate or curate in charge licensed to a parish.

After the formal presentation has been made by the patron to the bishop procedures are begun for the institution or collation of the priest to a new ministry. The mode of institution is covered by Canon C 10(6) which states:

The bishop, when he gives institution, shall read the words of the institution from the written instrument having the Episcopal seal appended thereto; and during the reading thereof the priest who is to be instituted shall kneel before the bishop and hold the seal in his hand.

The current form of the oath of allegiance, oath of obedience and declaration of assent are all set out in the Canons.[5]

As in the law prior to 1986, after institution or collation has taken place the bishop instructs the archdeacon to induct. This is covered in Canon Law[6] and the archdeacon is obliged thereupon to induct. The archdeacon may authorize the rural dean or other member of the clergy beneficed or licensed in the archdeaconry to induct. The mode of induction is that the archdeacon shall take the priest to be inducted by the hand and lay upon it the key to the church or place a hand on the church door. At the same time the words of induction are read. The priest shall then toll the church bell to make the induction known and public to the people.

There is also provision in the Measure regarding lapse. The complex rules of lapse valid before the introduction of the Measure have been simplified. There is now one simple lapse procedure. After the period of nine months from the notification of the vacancy, the right of presentation lapses to the archbishop, who shall act in the place of the patron.

One other area that needs to be noted in order to understand the whole process is the use of s.67 of the Pastoral Measure 1983. Under this Measure the bishop, after consultation, may suspend the right of presentation of the patron so as to enable other matters to be taken into consideration. The three usual reasons are:

1. that pastoral reorganization is in process;

2. that the parsonage house needs major attention or replacement; and

3. that the post is proposed to be held jointly with a diocesan post.

In each case it is assumed that there is justifiable need to remove the right of presentation from the lawfully registered patron into the hands of the bishop. When this happens the bishop may appoint a priest-in-charge to the post, so it need not suspend the ministry itself.

The current state in the Church of England is not 'usual'. There is a tendency, identified by patrons, and on the whole denied by bishops, that s.67 is being used too freely, sometimes as a means of financial management. This is not entirely fair to the bishops, but is clearly a worry to patrons. It is clear that the tendency has been noted by all and has been to some extent curbed. Where there are financial considerations these normally result in pastoral reorganization. Good practice demands that when s.67 suspension is in place the principles of the Patronage (Benefices) Measure should be followed, even though the strict letter of the law has been avoided.

In an unpublished work on the Patronage (Benefices) Measure by this author, I argue that some areas of the current law and practice need review. The time limits within the Measure are very tight, especially when appointing to multi-parish benefices. There is not always sufficient time for the reflective process required if parishes are to be ready to move on to the next phase of their life, and if good appointments are to be made. Further, most dioceses, and indeed the guidelines in the Patronage (Benefices) Measure Code of Practice, seem to guide parishes towards preparing their s.11 statement as a factual document, but do not encourage people to consider deeply the nature of the church and the nature of the ministry. Most problems which arise after appointment are not to do with the facts of the parish (it had three schools not two!) but are more deeply rooted in people's models of ministry and models of the Church. Clearly the Measure pre-dates many of the current developments in the nature of ministry explored elsewhere in this book, and patronage legislation and practice must be kept under review if the Church of England is to avoid finding the 1986 Measure falls into the same disrepute that patronage had fallen into prior to that Measure's introduction.

The Clergy Appointments Adviser's office

Background

The office was originally set up by Peter Bostock (a former CMS missionary), who felt that clergy should have some sort of clearing house for opportunities in parochial ministry outside their diocese. This was particularly important for those ordained here but serving abroad, who did not have access to the usual routes of appointments back in this country.

Development

Through the stewardship of Prebendary Royall and Canon Hardaker the office has developed into an information centre for vacancies and clergy that most major patrons use today. There is much more mobility and sense of choice (rather than a bishop's direction) in the minds of clergy. Some people see this as a forward step and others still look for a sense of discernment in those who are set above them. There is a certain clash of expectations at the time of an appointment and this will continue for the foreseeable future. The CAA office tries to steer a kindly path between these different approaches to appointments, and there is the hope that God's guidance is always close at hand.

Key features

The vacancy list
A list of all those parishes which are vacant and have been brought to the attention of the office by a patron, a bishop or a team leader. These will not necessarily be the same posts that are advertised in the Church press. The list usually contains considerable detail about the post and is available electronically and in hard copy. We estimate it is looked at by at least 800 people every month.

The General Circulation

A compilation of brief CVs of all stipendiary clergy who are looking for a move within, or into, the Church of England. Clergy are included in this list for a year and then they are withdrawn. It is hoped that many other avenues (such as the society patronages or the Lord Chancellor's Ecclesiastical Secretary) will also be explored at the same time. We 'process' about 300 clergy a year.

Training days

The Adviser is available to give clergy advice on appointments systems, writing CVs, interviewing skills, etc., and he travels around the country providing one-day seminars.

Bishops' staff meetings

These are important contact points for the diocese to make its feelings known, and for the Adviser to give guidance if it is requested. The world of clergy appointments is idiosyncratic and unpredictable. This is a chance for the senior staff to let the national officer know what their worries are and the centre to say what the national picture looks like.

Interviews

All candidates for the General Circulation are interviewed by the Adviser (allowances are always made for those coming in from abroad) because he needs to know something about them so that, on occasion, recommendations can be made. However, there are quite a number of other interviews that have no other purpose than to allow someone to take stock of their life and ministry. During last year the Adviser talked to nearly 400 clergy about their future (and several had more than one appointment).

The future

As the climate of openness develops in the secular world, so will the expectations of a greater number within the Church of England. The changes we see operating in society cannot help but be felt in ministry and how that ministry is deployed. The General Circulation is still seen by some as being the last resort of the hopeless and the 'difficult to place'. This is a diminishing point of view and representative of a time when clergy had little or no say in where they were directed. Whether by divine guidance or some very astute thinking on the part of our predecessors, this office can only be increasingly useful to those who are seeking new work. It remains to be seen whether the somewhat idiosyncratic system of appointments can make full use of the department's potential!

See Appendix 8 for a leaflet on curacy appointments prepared by Gordon Kuhrt, and approved by the Bishops' Committee for Ministry in March 1999.

Further reading

Canons of the Church of England, 6th edition, Church House Publishing, 2000 (esp. Canons C 9, 10, 11, 13, 14 & 15)

Mark Hill, *Ecclesiastical Law*, Butterworths, 1995, Chapter VI

Lynn Leeder, *Ecclesiastical Law Handbook*, Sweet & Maxwell, 1997

David Parrott and David Field, *Situations Vacant: A Guide to the Appointment Process in the Church of England*, Grove Books Pastoral 65, Cambridge, 2nd impression, 1999

David Parrott, *Patronage (Benefices) Measure 1986: An Analysis of its Working in Practice, Ecclesiastical Law Journal*, vol. 6, 2001–, p. 12

David Parrott, *Situations Vacant: A Guide to the Appointment Process in the Church of England*, unpublished dissertation for the LLM in Canon Law of the University of Wales, 2001, available in Cardiff Law School Library.

P. M. Smith, *The Advowson: A Most Peculiar Property, Ecclesiastical Law Journal*, vol. 5, 1998–2000, p. 320

Relevant legislation

Benefices Act 1898 (Amendment) Measure 1923

Pastoral Measure 1983

Patronage (Benefices) Measure 1986

Priests (Ordination of Women) Measure 1993

Team and Group Ministries Measure 1995

Patronage (Benefice) Rules 1987, Statutory Instrument 1987

Patronage (Benefices) Measure 1986, Code of Practice 1988

25

Clergy housing

Martin Elengorn

Clergy housing: the Parsonages Design Guide

The current *Parsonages Design Guide* is the sixth in the series and dates from 1998. It was prepared after consultation with, among others, dioceses, clergy, clergy spouses, architects and the Fire Brigade and Police. The guide recommends a slightly larger property (1,950–2,050 sq. ft) than that advocated before, mainly as a result of a larger study to accommodate small meetings (*not* as a substitute for a proper parish meeting place elsewhere). The guide also includes recommendations on security, sustainability, disabled access and the need for flexibility in design. It also underlines the view that the Church should design, build and manage its new buildings responsibly, economically and efficiently, minimizing their environmental impact.

More recently further advice has been offered to dioceses on the implications for parsonages of the Disability Discrimination Act.

Clergy housing: the freehold ownership of benefice property

In January 1996 the Clergy Conditions of Service Steering Group invited the Commissioners to set up a Staff Working Party to examine further, in consultation with dioceses, the basis on which benefice property was held, bearing in mind the need to provide secure housing. The working party included a Ministry Division representative and a diocesan assessor. In May 1998 it reported that problems arising from the need to obtain the incumbent's express consent to sales of unsuitable parsonages were not sufficient to justify the comprehensive reform or removal of the incumbent's freehold of benefice property. Evidence suggested that only 2 per cent of parsonages in the country could not be replaced due to an unwilling incumbent. Planning restrictions caused greater problems in this respect. The administrative and flexibility arguments advanced by the proponents of change could to a certain extent be met by alternative means/initiatives. It was also clear that there would be formidable opposition to change. The working party's conclusions were broadly accepted and a review of the Repair of Benefice Buildings Measure is currently in hand with a view to streamlining parsonage management.

The suggestion that all parsonages should be sold and that the clergy should provide their own housing out of a larger stipend is raised from time to time. Regular reviews have continued to show that this is financially unattractive quite apart from the serious deployment problems that would arise.

Housing for curates

The Commissioners offer dioceses 'value-linked' loans for the long-term provision of housing for curates. The loans are made under the Commissioners' general investment powers and some £32m net has been invested since 1986. The Commissioners take a share in the equity of the property purchased. The current initial interest rate is 5 per cent. This is set at a level which is intended to match the expected returns on the remainder of the Commissioners' investment portfolio. The normal maximum loan is £50,000.

Housing for deserted clergy spouses

This scheme was also introduced in 1986 with the backing of the House of Bishops to assist with the housing of clergy spouses whose marriages had broken down. The scheme was set up as a 'safety net' to be used where all other avenues, including renting, had been exhausted. The initial rate of interest is one of 4 per cent, with a normal maximum loan of £75,000. Around £7m net has been advanced. Again, the Commissioners take a share in the equity of properties purchased.

Further reading

Parsonages: A Design Guide, 6th edition, Church Commmissioners, 1998
Report of the Working Party on the Freehold Ownership of Benefice Property,
    1998

26

Continuing ministerial education

Tony Chesterman, Gordon W. Kuhrt and Neil R. Evans[1]

Continuing ministerial education

When we were working on *Mind the Gap* (see 'Further reading' below) we drew heavily upon a questionnaire sent to CME advisers at the end of 1998 which asked a series of questions related to the current condition of CME in their corner of the vineyard. We also discussed the matter at regional meetings during 2000 and with officers for Readers and local ministry.

It became clear that in most dioceses CME had become further established over the past five years by:

- an almost universal acceptance of the nominal 1 per cent of stipend for individual grants;

- increased demand for learning opportunities (82 per cent of CME officers reported such an increase);

- most CME officers being seen as senior diocesan staff working closely with the bishop.

It is also the case that over a third of dioceses now have a director of training, a number of whom came out of the CME 'stable' but who now have a wider brief that encompasses the education and training of both clergy, accredited lay ministers and lay people. Such posts are reflective of two relatively recent developments:

1. the Church moving into home mission mode in what is now a post-Christian society, and

2. the dawning realization that it is the committed lay disciples who are the missionaries, not just the clergy or other accredited ministers.

The knock-on effect for CME is profound. For such a mission endeavour to succeed there needs to be a confident, well-trained and articulate laity who are being educated, trained, supported and encouraged by competent and confident clergy/ministers. So, whereas in times past it was assumed that the clergy offered the ministry to the world on behalf of the Church, with lay people 'helping', it is now being acknowledged that it is the committed disciples who are called to offer that ministry, with the clergy 'helping'. That effectively means turning the Church upside down. Obviously this is a very difficult process which frustrates and confuses conventional expectations of both clergy and lay people, from both within and outside the Church. Nevertheless there has been a significant rise in 'every member', 'collaborative' or 'shared' ministry in most, if not all, dioceses over recent years.

This ministry has clergy and lay people sharing the ministerial functions of the 'royal priesthood' which, some of us think, calls for an 'episcopal' understanding of ordained ministry. For the specific role of the clergy in shared ministry is to do at a local level what the bishop does at a diocesan level, i.e. 'Take this cure which is both mine and yours'. That is, to exercise a servant leadership of caring oversight that will enable the 'priesthood' of the committed baptized. For instance in this diocese the bishop and I conducted two clergy CME training days on *How to be a Bishop*!

Other changing patterns of CME drawn from the answers to the questionnaire are:

- an increasing link between ministerial reviews/appraisals and individually designed CME programmes;
- increase in requests for sabbaticals;
- increase in requests to engage in courses offering further qualifications;
- growth of interest in courses on spirituality, worship, biblical studies, preaching, counselling, theology (contextual), management skills (time, administration, dealing with volunteers, etc.), gender issues, divorce/marriage, information technology;
- help and resourcing in handling the increasing number of multi-parish benefices;
- coping with ongoing financial stringencies.

To which I would add in conclusion the following future trends:

- the impact of the concept of lifelong learning, now embraced by the present Government, which has always been at the heart of adult education and CME within the Church;
- the development of ecumenical regional consortia offering ministry training;
- CME linked to the implementation of diocesan policy;

- the rise, in some dioceses, of ongoing training in competencies/portfolio learning/individual development plans;
- CME for all accredited ministers being jointly planned and resourced.

Ministry review

The term 'ministry review' is widely preferred to the word 'appraisal' and is strongly recommended in the key report listed below. That 1994 report both reflected considerable development across the Church of England, and was a catalyst for further reconsideration. It argued for review schemes on the grounds of both pastoral care and accountability, although it recognized significant differences between the 'work' of most parochial clergy and that of people in other walks of life. It discussed the pros and cons of both peer and hierarchical systems and proposed guidelines for good practice. Review schemes are in operation across almost every diocese now and many have been carefully evaluated and revised.

The 1994 recommendations are worth quoting in full:

1. All dioceses establish schemes for 'ministerial review' (para. 12) and that the term 'Ministerial Review' be used as the standard name for the practice (para. 14).

2. For trust to be maintained in a scheme it should be owned by the bishop, his staff and the diocesan clergy (paras. 39–42).

3. All reviewers should receive initial and ongoing training and the CMESC should advise on suitable training for reviewers and on the training of trainers (paras. 43–48).

4. The objectives of a scheme should be concerned with the welfare of the ministry of individuals and of the diocese, be carefully determined, achievable, positively framed and listed clearly at the beginning of literature describing the scheme; the choice and design of a scheme should reflect those objectives (paras. 49–59).

5. A scheme should only be introduced in a diocese after careful planning and thorough consultation (paras. 82–83).

6. In a diocese operating parallel schemes, where the hierarchical scheme is mandatory the peer scheme should also be mandatory (para. 62).

7. The choice of reviewers should meet the objectives of the scheme and there should be a strong element of continuity in who conducts a minister's review (paras. 65–77).

8. In a hierarchical scheme no reviewer should conduct more than 50 reviews a year and the use of consultants acting on behalf of the bishop should

be seen as preferable to overloading members of the bishop's staff; the use of area or rural deans as reviewers should be considered with caution (paras. 67–70).

9. Ministerial review should be applicable to all the ordained including bishops, and to appropriate diocesan lay staff; spouses should not be invited to the ministerial review discussion (paras. 72–78).

10. All ministers should participate in some form of ministerial review at least every two years (paras. 79–81).

11. Preparatory questionnaires should encourage reflection on ministry; means for using the perspectives of others who know the person's ministry should be adopted (paras. 85–89).

12. Attention should be given to the practical arrangements of the ministerial review discussion (para. 90).

13. Written reports should be required in all schemes, and the report should always be seen by the person reviewed; when a minister moves diocese agreed reports should be passed on to the new diocese only with the minister's permission (paras. 91–93); there should be a mechanism by which training needs identified in the review are, with the minister's agreement, communicated to the diocesan CME officer (para. 54).

14. All ministerial review schemes should be regularly evaluated (para. 94).

15. The Ministry Development and Deployment Committee of the Advisory Board of Ministry should be asked to review the situation in five years' time and report further to the House of Bishops (para. 95).

The 1998 report does *not* replace its predecessor. It is a supplement which clarifies and reinforces in certain areas. The recommendations were:

1. That dioceses consider moving towards a common terminology for the type of ministerial review being undertaken:

   Consultant's Review when the review is carried out by a lay or ordained person who has been specifically commissioned by the bishop. This person is not usually a member of the bishop's senior staff. A report to the bishop, agreed by both consultant and reviewee, ensures that the process is recorded, although the depth of detail may vary.

   Episcopal Review when the review is carried out by the bishop or a member of his senior staff.

2. That the context of ministerial review must be part of a holistic process of professional support for the clergy alongside other opportunities for pastoral care and spiritual direction.

3. That the purpose of the ministerial review is clearly explored and stated in any paperwork that is sent to clergy prior to the event.

4. That those completing post-ordination training are fully integrated into the ministerial review scheme of the diocese.

5. That the principle of mutual accountability be explained in the statement of the purposes of the review scheme.

6. That dioceses which are in the process of introducing a scheme or reviewing their present scheme are advised to use an external consultant to bring wider perspectives into the discussion.

7. That all reviewers (lay and ordained) are required to undertake training in listening skills and in the particular features of the review scheme.

8. That dioceses appoint a co-ordinator to monitor the operation of the scheme, to arrange the training of reviewers and to ensure that regular dialogue occurs with reviewers and clergy to ensure that schemes are modified to take account of new developments.

9. That a record be placed on the person's file noting the date and type of review undertaken, along with any salient points agreed between the reviewer and reviewee.

10. That training needs are identified at the time of the review and a separate form sent to the Continuing Ministerial Education Officer.

11. That attention be given to consideration of how non-stipendiary ministers, sector clergy and accredited lay workers and Readers can be integrated into a diocesan scheme.

Ministerial Development Programme

Introduction

The Ministerial Development Programme (MDP) is aimed at encouraging Church of England clergy to think and act constructively for a lifelong ministry. Although based upon the concept of career and personal development, the MDP recognizes, and builds on the fact, that the C of E has no career structure. It also takes into account the extent to which personal and ministerial life will often be integrated.

One of the principal aims of the MDP, then, is to help clergy plan intelligently for, say, 30 years as a parish priest, and to see this as offering a wide variety of opportunities. It is intended that the programme be a major contribution in preventing 'burn-out' or 'rust-out' in mid- to later ministry.

Lifelong learning and development are major themes of the MDP. Currently the programme is best aimed at those in mid-ministry, although the principles encompass all clergy, and future developments will take this into account.

The MDP is a joint venture between Careers and Training International (CTI) and Kensington Episcopal Area of the Diocese of London. The Revd Margaret Jackson of the Ministry Division of the Archbishops' Council gave helpful support and encouragement throughout the process. The programme was piloted with a generous grant from the Jerusalem Trust.

Background

The MDP has been in the process of development since 1998. An initial needs survey was undertaken, and as a result of this a pilot programme took place in February–March 2000. The pilot was run over a two-day residential, with a one-day follow-up. There were eleven participants, with two trainers from CTI and two enablers from Kensington Episcopal Area. The course combined teaching input with group work, drawing on individuals' own experience. It was based on a well-presented workbook, provided for each participant.

A number of areas for improvement were noted following this pilot. Principally it was agreed that theological reflection should take a prominent role; that individuals' own experience should be a key feature; and that the programme would best be extended to the inside of a week, with a follow-up day.

The pilot proved to be a great success, with all participants showing a high degree of positivity towards both the course content and the process. The Bishop of Kensington fully supported the principle that the programme be run on an annual basis for clergy of the Kensington Episcopal Area.

Content

The MDP offers a selection of models and tools for participants to explore and apply to their lives and ministries. It uses many well-tried and tested management and personal development techniques, but allows participants to take and use those which are most applicable to their own situation and personality.

Theological reflection is an integral element of the programme, encouraging participants to explore their ministerial and personal situations in the context of theological imperatives and models.

Additionally, participants bring with them a description of something of their current situation to work with, alongside theoretical input. Working together as a group, and in small groups, ensures that participants are both supported and challenged through the process.

Process

All of the recommendations following the pilot were integrated into the first full run of the programme in February 2001. The programme was led on this occasion by a trainer from CTI (Stuart Mitchell) with a theological consultant as co-trainer (Dr Nicola Slee). It ran from Monday lunchtime to Friday lunchtime, with a follow-up day in May 2001. Participants completed a package of pre-course material (either on disk or on paper). They also submitted a one-page summary of a current issue in their ministerial situation, which was explored with other participants in small groups.

It is intended that the small groups should continue to give mutual, ongoing support into the future, and they will be encouraged to meet perhaps once or twice a year to review.

The residential week proved a great success, with all participants indicating that they had received great benefit from the programme.

Future development

The Bishop of Kensington is committed to the programme being available annually for clergy in the area. The bishop and his staff will undertake the programme in 2002. Twelve people will be invited, by the bishop (in consultation with the CME Officer), to take part each year.

Gloucester Diocese ran a programme over three days, with a one-day follow-up, in May 2001.

A national consultation for CME Officers will take place on 1–2 October 2001, when Kensington Area, CTI and Gloucester Diocese will present the various models of the programme used to date. So far, twelve dioceses have indicated that they will be represented at the consultation (more than 20 participants).

As a part of the development of the package CTI and Kensington, with others, are working on a *Training the Trainers* package, so that dioceses can run the programme locally, without the ongoing use of professional trainers, but using local expertise.

Conclusion

It is clearly a considerable financial investment, with the programme running at around £800 per participant using professional trainers. These costs would be reduced considerably using in-house trainers, with an initial outlay being a significant factor to train the trainers.

However, the benefits of MDP are recognized as being manifold. Clergy feel newly motivated and equipped with a new range of skills and tools to assist them in personal and ministerial development over a lifelong ministry.

Further reading

The Continuing Education of the Church's Ministers (GS Misc 122), 1980
Beginning Public Ministry: Guidelines for Ministerial Formation and Personal Development for the First Four Years after Ordination (ABM Ministry Paper No. 17), 1998
Mind the Gap: Integrated Continuing Ministerial Education for the Church's Ministers, Church House Publishing, 2001
Ministerial Review: Its Purpose and Practice – The Report of a Working Party on Clergy Appraisal (ABM Ministry Paper No. 6), 1994
Servants and Shepherds: Developments in the Theology and Practice of Ministerial Review (ABM Ministry Paper No. 19), 1998

27

Code of professional conduct for the clergy

Michael Hodge and David Jenkins

On Thursday, 18 November 1999, at a meeting of the House of Clergy Standing Committee, the Ven. Gordon Kuhrt, Director of Ministry, spoke about issues arising from the Employment Relations Act, as a result of which it was decided to convene meetings of the convocations to consider the matter.

At meetings of the Lower House of the Convocation of Canterbury and of the Convocation of York, held on 28 February 2000, the following motion was carried:

> That this House approves the proposal of the Standing Committee of the House of Clergy that a joint Committee of the two Lower Houses be set up to prepare a Code of Professional Conduct.

A working group of six has been established, consisting of the two persons then serving as prolocutors and two other proctors from each of the convocations. The synodical and the synodal secretaries service the committee. One member is a woman priest, who is also an NSM.

Being anxious not to reinvent the wheel, the secretaries wrote to all diocesan secretaries asking for copies of any existing documents on the subject. Copies of six codes were received: from Gloucester, Norwich, Oxford, Rochester, Sheffield and Southwark. Articles in the Church press were noted and made available to the members of the working party.

The secretaries also wrote to the chairmen of diocesan houses of clergy and to the secretaries of various clerical organizations. Subsequently, letters were sent to the *Church Times* and the *Church of England Newspaper*. The purpose of this correspondence was not only to give opportunities for witnesses to be heard but to enable the members of the working group to ascertain what areas needed to be covered by the code. At the same time, the members of the group hoped that this would help avoid negative criticism at a later stage regarding what was or was not included in the code.

One of the members prepared a draft document, taking into consideration the documents supplied by the six dioceses and other material that had been received. The draft is based on the Ordinal from both the Book of Common Prayer and the *Alternative Service Book*. The group has been in touch with the Liturgical Commission regarding a new Ordinal to be prepared for use with *Common Worship*.

It is hoped that a 'green paper' type document will be produced towards the end of 2001 or early in 2002. This could then be the subject of discussion in the constituent Houses of the General Synod and elsewhere.

Given that the diocesan bishop will have a central role in the implementation of the new Clergy Discipline Measure and that the episcopate has the primary responsibility for the care of the clergy, the members of the group were agreed that the House of Bishops should be invited to consider what contribution it would wish to make at this stage of the process. The working group will give consideration to whether guidelines might be preferable to a code.

A final version of the code of professional conduct would be prepared in the light of all these discussions. This would be brought to the convocations, who set up the working group, and then to the General Synod. It might be appropriate to declare it an Act of Synod.

The code of practice

The code of practice might cover the following:

Introduction

1. Purpose and scope (all clergy) including an underlying theology.
2. Who is the code for?
3. What is the code for? – educational; regulatory/advisory; ministerial development; protection.
4. The need for ongoing training.
5. The need to know oneself – both strengths and weaknesses.
6. Honesty in assessing the gifts and skills of those we work with – clergy, laity and other professionals.
7. The need for a consultant and/or a confessor.

Good ministerial practice

1. Accountability – God, Church, self, family, law (ecclesiastical and civil).
2. An exemplary life (Ordinal).
3. Behave and act in a professional manner.
4. Relationships – parishioner or client; the wider community (including schools); the family (the working day/week; leisure; holidays; the use of the home and how much should one share with one's partner); bishop, colleagues, other professionals – how much should one share with them?; working collaboratively (including the laity); personal relationships (friendship, attraction and sexuality); gender issues; the single person in ministry.
5. Specific matters – confidentiality: is there an absolute bar to the sharing of a confidence even when someone's safety is threatened (child abuse)?; listening; touching and kissing; trust and reliability; where should people be seen, ever alone (given the fact that many spouses work; that the study is sometimes upstairs?; that the priest has to visit the sickbed; are things different for a woman priest?); the timing of visits, both the length and the time of day or night; punctuality; record keeping – written, computer and other methods; the management of parochial visiting – can there be/ should there be a strategy?; the apology, when one has forgotten or failed to do something or failed someone; inappropriate behaviour – oneself, a colleague, a parishioner or another professional; finance – personal, the family, the parish (degree of involement?).

Ministerial standards

1. Worship, preaching and the office.
2. Rhe occasional offices.
3. Prayer, Bible reading and study.
4. Absolution and the seal of the confessional.
5. Support for Church structures.
6. Working relationships with colleagues, including the courtesies to be observed.
7. Relationship to one's bishop and other senior staff.
8. Ecumenical relations.
9. Retreat and spiritual renewal.

28

The Clergy Discipline Measure

Alan F. Hawker

In November 2000 the General Synod gave final approval to the new Clergy Discipline Measure. It is inevitably a lengthy and major piece of ecclesiastical legislation. It relates to an area of concern that is always going to be sensitive and controversial. Yet it received a 91 per cent majority, and is clearly viewed as offering a new way forward.

Why a new disciplinary procedure?

The current procedures are laid down in the Ecclesiastical Jurisdiction Measure of 1963. But this has long since fallen into disrepute and disuse. The EJM 1963 is complex and confusing. It is inflexible, expensive and very slow moving. It is little understood and generally unsatisfactory. So it is very rarely used. As a consequence, a significant number of complaints have been left unresolved, which is highly unsatisfactory. Alternative approaches to discipline have been followed.

Bishops have been driven to handle discipline informally, outside of the procedures provided. This has resulted in variability of process and adjudication and also a confusion of the episcopal roles of pastoring and disciplining, and the 'cutting of corners' on occasions so far as the natural rights of the clergy are concerned. In short, for the last 38 years we have had a highly unsatisfactory situation.

The principles behind the new Measure

The new Measure has been carefully crafted over five years. There has been extensive consultation, examination of practice elsewhere in Christendom, and an analysis of best modern practice in the professions and employment legislation. The aim has been to provide a unitary procedure for all clergy, of whatever rank or experience: a procedure that is flexible, yet time-constrained, easy for all to understand in general overview, and which properly balances the competing interests of different constituencies. Above all, it is designed to be a procedure that allows appropriate responses to handling alleged misconduct by clergy, while protecting and supporting all the clergy who are exercising their vocation in appropriate and responsible ways.

Complainants will find the procedures for laying a complaint have been simplified. A complaint must be made in writing to the bishop (verbal complaints are unacceptable). Where complaints are adjudicated to be frivolous, malicious or vexatious, they will be set aside. Beyond this it will be the responsibility of the complainant to provide the evidence to support the complaint. There is provision for a complainant to appeal if a complaint is set aside and not proceeded with.

Clergy against whom complaint is lodged must be fully informed of what is being alleged. They must have time in which to make a considered response, and not be rushed or strong-armed into ill-considered responses. They are to be encouraged to take advice, and support systems for them and their families are envisaged.

Bishops have to be clear about their conflicting roles (pastoral and disciplinary) and take steps with their support staff to avoid confusion. A nationally provided commission will be in place to assist consistency across the two provinces. They will be obliged to use the new procedures, and no others, when handling discipline. And because any exercise of discipline must involve discretion, each discretionary power is identified, ring-fenced to clarify its extent, and provided with appeals where people feel it has been abused. In this way the bishops are to be provided with an important measure of support and security whilst carrying out disciplinary procedures.

What the new disciplinary Measure does not do

What is provided is a procedure for handling alleged misconduct in the areas of personal behaviour, performance of authorized duties, and response to the Canons and ecclesiastical laws and regulations. The areas of doctrine, ritual and ceremonial are temporarily excluded (continuing to follow the 1963 EJM provisions) while a further detailed examination of how best to handle this area of discipline is carried out.

It is a procedure to be used. It does not specify the standards expected of the clergy. A working party of the convocations is currently seeking to determine what advice and guidance can be offered in this area (see Chapter 27).

It is a methodology for handling complaints that should be able to respond to all cases, however small or serious. But it is, ultimately, only as good as the persons who operate the procedures, and their goodwill. However, the temptation to short-cut or ignore the procedures will, in and of itself, be a disciplinary offence.

It does not attempt to do the secular authority's job for them. Allegations of a civil or criminal nature that are within the jurisdiction of the secular courts will be determined in those courts, with the resulting adjudication being accepted by the Church authorities.

Further reading

Under Authority: Report on Clergy Discipline (GS 1217), Church House Publishing, 1996

29

Dual role ministry

Nigel Peyton

Dual role ministry (DRM) is a particular response by Anglicans and other churches to changed times. A working definition is: 'dual role ministry describes posts which formally combine two sorts of ministerial work, frequently with divergent foci of responsibility and accountability'. The bishop licenses the minister into dual roles, usually on an unbeneficed and time-limited basis, and resignation has to be from both posts, unlike, for example, from the office of area/rural dean. Unlike the many-role parochial clergy, dual role ministers (DRMs) cannot choose to neglect either part of their fundamental role division.

In essence it means deploying a stipendiary minister in two different areas of ministry, often with contrasting expectations. Typical examples might be: priest-in-charge in a rural multi-parish benefice and diocesan tourism officer, team vicar in a market town and half-time hospital chaplain. DRMs are frequently required to cross boundaries, juggle roles and employ a range of skills. In deploying clergy who 'do more than one job' the Church is implicitly expecting two ministries for the price of one. It is a model of pastoral organization, which until the 1990s was not always recognized as such.[1]

Research undertaken in 1995–7 suggested that 10 per cent of stipendiary Anglican clergy were in dual role. Three types of role combinations were identified: parish(es) plus chaplaincy posts – in education, health care, prisons, industry, the community, etc.; parish(es) plus diocesan advisory posts – in mission, training, ecumenism, social responsibility, etc.; and miscellaneous role partnerships – including cathedral and diocesan links. The combinations that dioceses conjured up were imaginative.[2]

The rationale for DRM is a mixture of expediency and choice: such appointments are a means of maintaining both parochial and sector ministry at a time of diminishing stipendiary clergy resources. In many ways DRMs are at the sharp end of the search for the right strategy for a Church serving the whole nation. The combination can be stimulating, joining up the intra-mural church with engagement with the world, spreading sector and advisory expertise around deaneries, linked to ministry in the local church. On the other hand, dual role appointments can be a mixed blessing. They clearly bring their own pressures, intensifying the normal trials that clergy endure.

Particular care therefore is needed in the making and sustaining of dual role ministries if they are to succeed. Experience shows that where DRM is not the first choice it is unlikely to be the best choice. DRM can expose weaknesses in pastoral reorganization and in individual clergy in a pretty ruthless way and senior diocesan staffs need to be aware of this. Careful supervision in the first year can make all the difference.

Most DRMs, however, enjoy their varied work and are appreciated for the added value they give to the Church. Parishes have responded increasingly creatively to the challenge of what it means to have a half-time vicar. DRMs themselves often express a refreshing excitement about their ministries and display the priestly qualities sought after by the Church's selection criteria. Effective DRMs are great improvisers amid the role complexities of ministry – imaginative yet realistic, flexible yet robust.

The growing number of DRMs in the 1990s gradually developed a professional self-consciousness, sharing common concerns and good practice through a national network and an annual residential consultation. Much of this activity is now devolved to dioceses and interest groups. The publication in 1998 of a Grove Booklet[3] about dual role ministry, placing the research, practical advice and theological reflection under one cover, remains the key reference for all those responsible for setting up or engaging in DRM.

See the author's *Dual Role Ministry: First Choice or Mixed Blessing?* (Grove Books, 1998)

30

Two-clergy couples

Lesley Bentley

Two-clergy couples make up a significant proportion of the clergy of the Church of England. A recent survey conducted by the Deployment, Remuneration and Conditions of Service Committee of deans/advisers in women's ministry and diocesan secretaries identified 333 couples where both members are ordained or accredited lay ministers. Some 364 full-time stipendiary clergy are part of such couples, perhaps 4 per cent of the stipendiary clergy.

Significant numbers of those in two-clergy couples have not obtained stipendiary posts but are available for this. Of 333 couples only 83 have both members paid full stipends. (There will be others excluded from that figure who are full-time in ministry but paid by others, e.g. chaplains.) Responses indicate that nearly two thirds of the 666 clergy/ALMs concerned participated in the recent survey conducted by the Clergy Stipends Review Group. (Stipendiary spouses of non-stipendiary clergy were invited to indicate to their partners that they could obtain a copy of the survey for their own response.) Some 42 clergy/ALM spouses were identified as NSM other than by choice (i.e. around 10 per cent of the clergy who replied).

Inability to secure a stipendiary post has further effects on the clergy couple. Pension contributions are not made. The diocese is unlikely to provide funding for CME.

There appears to be a gender bias in appointments. In the DRACSC survey, where one of a couple was NSM and the other stipendiary 87 of the NSMs were women and 16 were men. In a recent survey of deans/advisers in women's ministry through NADAWM (National Association of Diocesan Advisers in Women's Ministry) and the Ministry Division the deployment of couples was one of the most frequently expressed concerns. Anecdotal evidence suggests that dioceses are far more likely to 'find a suitable post' for a male priest moving with an ordained spouse who is changing post than vice versa.

In the recent past there have been accounts of dioceses refusing to pay more than one stipend or paying less than two stipends even when both partners in a two-clergy couple are in full-time posts. This was not stated in any current policy but may still be a hidden assumption. The current definition of stipend, now likely to be challenged by the Clergy Stipends Review Group, has been used to considerably disadvantage two-clergy couples where both are on diocesan stipends, when compared to couples with one partner employed by a secular body.

In the recent past there have also been stories of poor pension provision or people being paid a stipend but no pension. We found no sign of this. Legislation would now make it illegal.

Housing has sometimes been a matter of contention. In some dioceses bishop's dispensation of residence is given so that both partners may occupy an incumbency (or equivalent) post in different parishes. Calls have been made for imaginative use of the 'spare' vicarage to benefit the parish and the partner. Concern has been expressed about the 'loss' to the remuneration package of the partner not resident in their own vicarage. Expense of travel from the parish of residence to the parish of work can be an issue in some situations.

There are important issues for couples about days off and time off. It is clearly important that couples are able to organize their work in such a way that these coincide or dovetail (according to the couple's choice and family situation).

There are significant issues for two-clergy couples in the case of a divorce. If one partner is receiving a diocesan stipend but the other is remunerated from elsewhere, albeit by virtue of their licence from the bishop, there seems a strong argument that that partner should be given the same help as any other clergy spouse.

There is little evidence of dioceses being proactive in the encouragement of couples into suitable posts. The patronage system and lack of consistency in advertising posts mean that it can be difficult for couples to find an appropriate move for both partners. Few dioceses have policies for clergy couples. Some suggested in the DRACSC survey that there were informal policies, but it was not clear what status they had. Others said they dealt with each couple individually. (DRACSC is currently working on a document recommending a diocesan policy. The Carlisle policy has been given consideration as an example of good practice.)

Alternative patterns of working may now be considered a possibility but we found little evidence of 'job-sharing' in the DRACSC survey (six couples only were identified). (The Carlisle guidelines for the appointment of couples discourages the use of this secular terminology because clergy cannot reasonably be expected to 'cover' for the holidays and days off of their partners.) Other forms of flexibility may also be of particular value to the clergy couple – for example, the opening of part-time posts to individuals rather than combining posts so that a full post is always made.

Clergy couples would want to point to the benefits to the parish of a joint ministry. These include mutual support, reduced expenses, the challenge they offer to stereotyped images of marriage and ordained ministry.

Two-clergy couples have been the subject of two consultations at St George's House, Windsor. The report *Marital Bliss and Ministerial Enigma* (1998) resulted from one of these. A report was published of the 'Double Vision' conference in February 1992, but no formal network was established from this. The ABM Ministry Paper No. 11, *Partners in Marriage and Ministry* (December 1995), raised issues concerning the training and deployment of two-clergy couples. Sue Waldron-Skinner's book *Double Vision* (London, 1998) contained an academic analysis of the experience of two-clergy couples over the period of the ordination of women to the priesthood set against a control group of clergy couples.

The editor comments: 'In a considerable number of instances where one spouse has a stipendiary parochial or cathedral appointment (with parsonage or housing provided), the other spouse either has a chaplaincy or sector appointment or exercises NSM ministry of some kind.'

The two issues which inhibit both spouses being incumbents of parishes are:

1. Is there genuine deployability?
2. The requirement to live in the parsonage house.

The problems which inhibit both spouses being appointed to the same parish or team ministry are:

1. Are there genuinely two posts?
2. Has there been genuine openness about the appointments?
3. Issues about power and confidentiality.
4. Inevitably they will want to have the same day off and holidays.

31

Moving out of full-time ministry (voluntary severance)

Gordon W. Kuhrt

There are some clergy who will leave full-time ministry before the normal retirement age. This will happen for a variety of reasons. These include:

- those who are unable to find an appointment;
- those whom the bishop is unable to recommend for a further appointment;
- those who wish to move into another career.

Most clergy are not employees but rather 'self-employed office-holders'. Some have freehold security, others have term agreements and others have licences that can be terminated at fairly short notice. At the request of the House of Bishops' Standing Committee, the Advisory Board of Ministry re-convened the Voluntary Severance Working Party 'to advise on the nature of the relationship entered into with the Church by clergy at ordination and to advise on guide-lines for bishops in respect of a severance package for clergy who reach the end of an appointment'. The group produced the report entitled *Moving Out of Full-time Ministry*.

The House of Bishops endorsed the five recommendations:

1. That any severance payment (apart from any housing provision) should have regard to that which is statutorily required under legislation for redundancy.

2. That ABM ensures that a central list of professional career counsellors who are willing to be called on to assist dioceses is maintained.

3. That when Church funds are being allotted to retraining, or time allowed for a substantial course of training, formal agreement to vacate the post by a fixed date should be a condition before the training is funded or permitted.

4. That any costs involved in a severance package described in Chapter 4, other than those borne under the Pensions Measures, should be the responsibility of the diocese where the minister is licensed.

5. That a record of each arrangement, agreed by the minister, should be kept in the form suggested, a copy to be placed in the minister's file and a copy sent to the Advisory Board of Ministry. That the House of Bishops be invited to ask ABM to monitor progress.

As the Bishop of Hereford (then Chair of ABM) said in the Preface:

> For some the provisions will offer the opportunity to move into a part-time ministry. This could enable them to develop specialist skills that can be offered on a freelance basis. Others will see possibilities for a light-duty post towards the end of a life-time's ministry. In some cases these provisions suggest how a caring Church could help clergy to explore a vocation outside full-time ministry and to move into this with respect and encouragement, often continuing as non-stipendiary ministers.

Further reading

Moving Out of Full-time Ministry: Arrangements for Clergy who Move out of Full-time Stipendiary Ministry in the Church of England (ABM Policy Paper No. 4), 1994

32

The parish system

Michael Turnbull

I believe we need to think radically about the parish as we now have it. In many areas the parish hinders mission rather than enhancing it. This suggestion is not abandoning the geographical elements of the present system but changing present perceptions of what a parish is.

I believe that in some areas the parochial system is collapsing because:

- clergy have become isolated in a 'failure' situation;
- there is a low morale among clergy and laity;
- small, elderly, poor congregations make lay training and lively worship difficult or impossible and young people are alienated;
- pensioner/unemployed congregations are not viable even when there is sacrificial giving.

On the other hand parishes are strong when:

- teams of clergy are working collaboratively;
- there is strong, prayerful, visionary leadership – both clergy and lay;
- there is clear teaching and well-planned worship;
- giving is close to the tithing requirement;
- They recognize the essentially eclectic nature of most congregations because they take seriously how most people live – that is in a locality which is much wider than the present parish. They travel to amenities such as school, shops, adult learning, team sport activities, etc.

In the past we have, because of the shortage of clergy, used the Pastoral Measure to link several parishes under one incumbent. But bolting parishes together cannot go on without taking a look at the consequences. This policy has had a severe effect on the working patterns of clergy – probably to the detriment of pastoral care and evangelism – since clergy time is taken up with leading too many services, a huge burden of occasional offices without the time to use the teaching opportunities they offer, looking after several buildings and supervising duplicated electoral and administrative structures. Such arrangements have had consequences for the health and morale of clergy and active lay people, all of whom are ministering in an increasingly secular context, the consequent reduction of congregational numbers and an effect on active lay participation and financial support. We cannot continue on that road as ministry in an alien situation will overwork and oppress the clergy, especially when they are working in isolation and running hard, at best, to stand still.

But change should not be regarded as despairing response for we have the opportunity to follow where God is leading our missionary church. We are a people called to reflect God's nature to the world. And his nature is not hierarchical and distant but relational and inclusive. That becomes a model of being the Church.

The marks of such a people are precisely those that Gordon Kuhrt has described in Chapter 8 – collaborative, waiting on God's grace, and relating to the real social structures in which people operate.

So I suggest we:

1. emphasize the value of *locality* but recognize that for most people this is not the *parish* as we have known it;
2. look to establishing locality ministries rather than current parish ministry.

Locality ministries may include neighbourhood worship but wider learning activities and engagement with the community and church administration would be on the scale of locality.

To service this, a group of, say, three stipendiary clergy, Readers, lay minister, NSMs, OLMs and sector ministries would be established. Many dioceses already have underway a shared ministry programme which could be enhanced to reduce the number of present parishes – probably by as much as 60 per cent – and thus enable us to reduce the number of clergy without the consequent stress and also bring under control diocesan finances which are under enormous pressure.

I realize that this could not be done quickly but, fully explained to the Church in terms of the current shared ministry language and of the old Tiller language, I believe people would respond with a huge sigh of relief that at last someone was listening to what was actually happening in most of our parishes and not just talking up what is the experience of a few, largely suburban, middle-class parishes. I emphasize that this is not a north/south debate nor one of urban/rural. It is common across the country.

Unless we take bold measures now we shall go on seeing many of our churches empty and many of our clergy showing increasing signs of chronic stress.

It would, of course, have important consequences for clergy formation. Only by some bold leadership from the Archbishops' Council and House of Bishops will the Church become:

- collaborative rather than isolationist;
- a praying church rather than a hyperactive church;
- ready to use *all* people's gifts and enable them to take responsibility;
- sacrificial givers because people will be confident in what they are supporting;
- conscious of the missionary nature of the Church in an alien and secular society.

See Chapter 40 on the Pastoral Measure and also Appendix 9 for material from the Durham Diocese on *Redefining the Parish* and *Building Localities*.

33

Accredited lay workers

Hilary Unwin

History

In the late nineteenth century, most women wishing to work in the Church became part of a religious community, deaconesses, or Church Army Sisters. According to Sean Gill, in his book *Women and the Church of England* (SPCK, 1994), there were also Biblewomen and Parochial Mission Women who may well have worked full time. With the move towards professionalism in the early twentieth century, consideration was given to training. From 1919 certificates were issued to women who had undergone training in theology, teaching and social studies, but pay for the work was very low. In 1930, a three-year course was set up to obtain the Inter-Diocesan Certificate (IDC), which is the qualification held by most of the older workers today. In 1966 there were said to be 307 lay parish workers. By this time, licensed lay workers were allowed to take part in services other than Holy Communion, prepare people for baptism and confirmation, conduct courses and missions, and take funerals and baptisms. The Deaconesses and Lay Ministry Measure of 1972 threw open the office to men and women.

The present situation

With the ordination of women to the diaconate and later to the priesthood, the numbers of what were now called accredited lay workers (ALW) fell sharply and the number now licensed is probably below 30. There are also a number holding permission to officiate, perhaps in excess of ten. Some of these are elderly but very active!

Candidates come forward for selection conferences most years and about one per year is selected for training. While this used to be very much a parish-based ministry, the new ALWs often have a specialized ministry. One, a man, works with ethnic minorities in Slough, another is used by her diocese to counsel clergy and their families, a third works with a pastoral foundation and is a highly trained counsellor, and two are involved in vocational advice and selection. Sector ministries also benefit from a university pastoral worker at Exeter and an industrial chaplain in Liverpool. Only a few receive payment for their work.

Selection, training and afterwards

Candidates offering for this ministry are selected and trained in the same way as ordinands. The criteria for selection used are the same, but candidates need to be clear about their motives for looking at this ministry. They are entitled to the same training grants as ordinands.

When training is completed, the candidate is admitted and commissioned. In recent cases, this took place at the ordination service with fellow students.

The traditional dress for an ALW is a burgundy coloured robe or cassock and scarf with a medallion on a burgundy ribbon. There is a silver lapel badge as well.

It is appropriate that the new ALW should be licensed to a training parish even if the focus of his or her work is elsewhere. Care needs to be taken in planning the job description that a balance is kept between the different aspects of the work, but basic training in parish duties needs to be covered in the three years. CME needs to be tailored to the needs of the individual.

A contract must be drawn up for the protection of paid ALWs and the diocese or other body as employer. The licence, contract and job description must tally. The legalities are covered by Canons E 7 and 8 and are not listed here. More recent legislation places ALWs on their deanery synods.

Why lay and not ordained?

There are some lay ministries where the theological training and the authority given by the Church enable people to carry out their work more effectively and yet where ordination is not appropriate or necessary. In many cases there is a diaconal aspect to the work; ALWs may well work for the bishop directly. The ALW who is delegated by her bishop to counsel clergy in need of help says that it helps that she has been through the same training as her clients, yet is not 'one of them'.

Although ALWs can and do lead worship, for most of them this is not the focus of their work or their principal calling. When they preach they bring experience from the other part of their work.

Looking for a theological model for their work, a group of ALWs felt they wished to follow the example of Christ on the Emmaus road; to be able to walk alongside people in their time of need and to have the training to be able to reflect theologically on the situation.

It can be a very lonely ministry, a sort of hybrid between the clergy and the laity, misunderstood by both. The people who choose this path have to be very sure that it is for them.

Issues for the Church

If the Church considers that this is a ministry option it wishes to keep it might choose to do more to recognize those who have chosen this path. The majority of people in the Church have never heard of it. This includes DDOs. Most diocesan yearbooks do not distinguish between ALWs and other lay people who have been given a bishop's licence. It is relatively easy to find statistics of NSMs and Readers in the national Church. It proves very difficult to find numbers of ALWs. Even recently trained ones disappear from the figures. Yet the Church has selected these people and spent money on training them for ministry.

There is a need for the care of ALWs to be part of the Ministry Division's portfolio. Since the ordination of women it has been very difficult to find anyone at Church House, Westminster, who has oversight of ALWs. When I tried to get hold of a badge for an ALW a few years ago, I was told they were now in the archives.

There may be very few ALWs, but they are not merely part of the Church's history yet.

34

Non-stipendiary ministry

Mark Hodge and John Mantle [1]

Non-stipendiary ministry

The *Regulations for Non-Stipendiary Ministry* define two main categories of NSMs as follows:

1. Those in secular employment whose chief area of ministry is in the context of their employment, commonly called ministers in secular employment (see 'Ministry in secular employment', below).

2. Those in secular employment, and those retired from or not engaged in secular employment, whose chief area of ministry is in the context of a parish or chaplaincy.

Non-stipendiary ministry has played an increasingly important part in the life and ministry of the Church in recent decades. Since the establishment of the Southwark Ordination Course in the 1960s over 3,500 men and women candidates have been selected, trained and licensed to non-stipendiary ministry. Ordinations to non-stipendiary ministry in the last four years have numbered between 130 and 160 each year. Ordained local ministry (OLM) is a variant of non-stipendiary ministry (see Chapter 35).

Selection

Candidates for non-stipendiary ministry are selected according to the same basic procedures as stipendiary candidates – they are sponsored by a diocesan bishop for attendance at a bishops' selection conference. The selection criteria are the same, although some different emphases may be placed in the application of the criteria.

Candidates must normally be aged over 30. An upper age limit may apply in dioceses at the discretion of the diocesan bishop. Candidates are expected to be well established in their community, local church and occupation. For candidates who anticipate a parish-focused ministry, the sponsoring papers must always include an expression of opinion from the PCC of the candidate's parish of their willingness to accept and support the candidate's ministry, if recommended. For candidates who foresee a work-focused ministry, there needs to be an indication of the attitude of the employer and the likely reception of the candidate's ministry at the workplace.

An important change was made in January 1996 following the House of Bishops' acceptance of the recommendations of the working party report, *A Review of Selection Procedures in the Church of England.* Since then candidates for non-stipendiary ministry have been sponsored within one of two categories: ordained ministry (permanent NSM) or ordained ministry (SM and NSM). The first category is used for candidates where the perception (of the bishop and the candidate) of vocation relates to a ministry that will be permanently non-stipendiary. The second category is used where it is perceived that at a future date the candidate may transfer from non-stipendiary to stipendiary ministry, or vice versa. (This category therefore allows movement between non-stipendiary and stipendiary ministry without seeking the advice of the Candidates' Panel of the Ministry Division's Vocation, Recruitment and Selection Committee.)

Training

The vast majority of candidates who will be ordained to non-stipendiary ministry undertake a three-year course of ordination training with a regional course. The type of training undertaken by candidates aged 50 and over is a matter formally at the bishop's discretion, and in some cases special tailor-made courses have been designed for candidates in this age group. In some cases it has been possible for older candidates, retired from secular employment, to undertake a shortened period of training on a full-time basis at a theological college. (There are five such cases of NSM candidates undertaking college training in the 2000/01 academic year.)

All the regional courses train for both stipendiary and non-stipendiary ministry, to equal standard. There are currently 257 candidates in course training sponsored in the permanent NSM category and 320 on courses in the SM/NSM category.

Deployment

The majority of NSMs are licensed as assistant curates to parishes, most usually their home parishes. In some cases they have been given pastoral charge of a benefice. In these situations it may be possible for the NSM to move into the parish, sometimes residing in a parsonage house. In general, however, there are practical limits to the deployability of NSMs and it is this factor that has inhibited their inclusion in the formulae used for calculations in the Stipendiary Clergy Share System.

The distribution of the 1,796 NSMs in licensed ministry (as at December 1999) is shown in Table 10, page 222. In general the current distribution of NSMs is far more even between the dioceses than has hitherto been the case, particularly in the early years of the development of this ministry when there were marked differences in the policies and approaches taken by dioceses. The table also shows in a separate column the distribution between the dioceses of OLMs in licensed ministry. In some dioceses the presence of an OLM scheme will have had a bearing upon NSM numbers.

As noted above, a significant proportion of candidates ordained to non-stipendiary ministry do later transfer to stipendiary ministry.

Nomenclature

It should perhaps be noted here that there has been much expressed dissatisfaction with the terms 'non-stipendiary ministry' and 'non-stipendiary ministers'. There has, however, been no common agreement reached on any alternative term, for they have all been claimed to carry unsatisfactory con-notations. In November 2000 the General Synod was asked through a Southwell Diocesan Synod motion to consider the use of one such alternative term, 'self-supporting ministers'. At the end of the debate the following amended motion was carried:

> That this Synod request the Archbishops' Council, in consultation with the House of Bishops, to examine the designation 'non-stipendiary ministry and ministers' with a view to ending the usage of the designation altogether except for administrative purposes.

The possible consequences are now under consideration.

Ministry in secular employment

Ministry in secular employment (MSE) may be seen as a 'branch' of non-stipendiary ministry. The majority of NSMs who normally earn their own living and expect to live their faith at work, nevertheless see their ministry as focused *in the life and witness of their parish church*. To this end they assist an incumbent in the administration of word and sacrament, and participate in

Table 10: Distribution of NSMs and OLMs, 1999

Ref. no.	Diocese		Non-stipendiary clergy			Ordained local ministers		
			men	women	total	men	women	total
1	Bath & Wells	C	25	16	41			
2	Birmingham	C	17	7	24			
3	Blackburn	Y	18	8	26			
4	Bradford	Y	7	5	12			
5	Bristol	C	21	7	28			
6	Canterbury	C	32	15	47			
7	Carlisle	Y	17	9	26			
8	Chelmsford	C	39	44	83			
9	Chester	Y	20	12	32			
10	Chichester	C	45	18	63			
11	Coventry	C	10	11	21			
12	Derby	C	27	11	38			
13	Durham	Y	11	12	23			
14	Ely	C	20	10	30			
15	Exeter	C	34	16	50			
16	Gloucester	C	30	10	40	3	3	6
17	Guildford	C	29	13	42	10	4	14
18	Hereford	C	17	10	27	3	2	5
19	Leicester	C	27	10	37			
20	Lichfield	C	17	14	31	11	4	15
21	Lincoln	C	17	10	27	13	8	21
22	Liverpool	Y	21	2	23	2	6	8
23	London	C	90	29	119			
24	Manchester	Y	34	6	40	25	17	42
25	Newcastle	Y	14	13	27			
26	Norwich	C	15	14	29	17	13	30
27	Oxford	C	128	44	172	12	17	29
28	Peterborough	C	12	5	17			
29	Portsmouth	C	24	31	55			
30	Ripon & Leeds	Y	8	3	11			
31	Rochester	C	19	13	32			
32	St Albans	C	48	33	81			
33	St Edms & Ipswich	C	19	10	29	18	16	34
34	Salisbury	C	31	22	53	13	9	22
35	Sheffield	Y	14	3	17			
36	Sodor & Man	Y	9		9	3		3
37	Southwark	C	70	27	97	24	10	34
38	Southwell	Y	28	24	52			
39	Truro	C	21	8	29	7	3	10
40	Wakefield	Y	18	10	28		1	1
41	Winchester	C	31	24	55			
42	Worcester	C	14	11	25			
43	York	Y	16	7	23			
44	Europe	C	17	8	25			
Totals Province of Canterbury (C)			946	501	1447	131	89	220
Totals Province of York (Y)			235	114	349	30	24	54
Totals CHURCH OF ENGLAND			1181	615	1796	161	113	274

the teaching and pastoral care of the congregation. In contrast, MSEs, while maintaining a relationship with their parish church and its incumbent, see their ministry focused *in their place of work*, be it school, shop, lab or factory. They enter – in the face of the Church's public faith and public failings – with substantial theological comprehension, pastoral know-how and an authoritative sign and voice *because* they are ordained.

This ministry has a variety of origins including Roland Allen, missionary and visionary, who in the 1920s called for 'voluntary clergy' in places of work. More recently, and sometimes inappropriately, it is said to go back to the French (and a handful of British) worker-priests who from the 1940s through to the 1990s entered mines, factories, docks and other worksites, in order to share (simply by their presence) the gospel with the working class. This history was often cited as one of the models for introducing NSM across Britain and was one of the reasons for Mervyn Stockwood, Bishop of Southwark, starting the Southwark Ordination Course in the 1960s. He wanted worker-priests in his diocese too. Yet working-class candidates rarely came forward for ordination, and the newly ordained from Southwark and other courses simply returned to their middle-class occupations and professions. An increasing number, disenchanted with not having a 'real ministry', have joined the ranks of stipendiary parish clergy.

Nevertheless ministers in secular employment have some affinity with worker-priests. They often understand their role as rooted in incarnational theology. It is about the Church – in the person of its ordained clergy – supporting the laity at work, or remaining, perhaps permanently, in environments where there may be no Christians. The MSEs' daily environment is 'other people's territory', often alien and hostile. This is a unique ministry and deserves to be recognized and encouraged in a special way.

Further reading

Advisory Board of Ministry, *Regulations for Non-Stipendiary Ministry* (ABM Policy Paper No. 5), 1994

Advisory Board of Ministry, *A Review of Selection Procedures in the Church of England* (ABM Policy Paper No. 6), 1995

Mark Hodge, *Non-Stipendiary Ministry in the Church of England* (GS 538A), 1983

James M. M. Francis and Leslie J. Francis (eds), *Tentmaking: Perspectives on Self-Supporting Ministry*, Gracewing, 1998

John Mantle, *Britain's First Worker-Priests*, SCM, 2000

35

Local ministry and ordained local ministry

Ferial Etherington

Introduction

The comprehensive view of the Church's shared source of ministry in Christ expressed in the 1983 Tiller Report[1] required a collaborative style. That style was seen as not being limited to formal teams of ministers but acknowledging the gifts of the whole people of God in a shared partnership, where both lay and ordained exercise a corporate leadership of the Church in the local community.

Increasingly throughout the last two decades, development of this vision for 'every-member ministry' has found expression in the growth of collaborative ministry teams and in the concept of ordained local ministry. The term ordained local minister [OLM] refers to those local ministers who are priests or deacons called by, and from within, their local community, who hold the bishop's licence to serve specifically within and for that local community in the context of a local ministry team.

The current situation

At present[2] 19 dioceses within the Church of England have ordained local ministry schemes approved by the House of Bishops upon advice from the Ministry Division. These dioceses (in which nearly 300 OLM priests are serving) are: Blackburn, Canterbury, Carlisle, Coventry, Gloucester, Guildford, Hereford, Lichfield, Lincoln, Liverpool, Manchester, Newcastle, Norwich, Oxford, St Edmundsbury & Ipswich, Salisbury, Southwark, Truro and Wakefield. The guidelines, regulations and recommendations governing the content and construction of a scheme are set out in the key policy documents, ABM Policy Paper No. 1: *Local NSM,*[3] and the report on local non-stipendiary ministry, *Stranger in the Wings.*[4] Each diocesan submission will also be required to answer the questions set out in ACCM Occasional Paper No. 22[5] which deal with vision for ministry, evidence of catholic order and provisions for training.

Other dioceses, while committed to the concept of collaborative ministry, have decided to pursue the development of local ministry teams without addressing the additional aspect of *ordained* local ministry, other than that already encompassed within the existing category of non-stipendiary ministry.

Principles

Ordained local ministry carries three distinctive marks:[6]

- catholic order in the service of the local church and community;
- the collaborative ministry of the whole local church; and
- a commitment to working in teams.

Every Christian community needs someone to fulfil the dual task of the priest expressed in the Ordinal, representing Christ's presence in the world and among his people, seeking, feeding and serving his sheep; and representing the people before God, praying for them and with them. Against this background, parishes have in recent years found fresh value in accepting a greater measure of responsibility for the provision of ministry as part of their mission in and to the local community, and to call ministers from among themselves. Recognition of a particular ministry is by both bishop and the parish (or parishes) it will serve.

Ordained local ministry must be the fruit of a commitment by the local church to the ministry of the whole congregation. This means that congregation and church council share the work of the local church and responsibility for it with the incumbent, working in a collaborative way. Local ministry teams, containing both lay and ordained members, express a practical working out of the priesthood of all believers[7] for the building up of the body.[8] The concept of a partnership of ordained and lay is integral to the idea of local ministry.[9]

In increasingly complex societies, the isolated stipendiary minister cannot provide all the varieties of skills and needs called for. Ordained local ministry is exercised in close relationship with other ordained and lay leaders in the local church, and this organized collaboration offers a way to develop more effective ministry and mission. The local church, as the local expression of the Body of Christ, has a vast variety of work to do,[10] and gifts of leadership within the church and gifts for ministry in the community are there among both clergy and laity. Local ministry teams are an opportunity for ministry of the whole people of God."

Strategy

The model of ministry for local teams is that of collaboration, and an understanding of this is expressed elsewhere in the Anglican Communion in such titles as 'circular', 'total', 'mutual', 'every-member' ministry and so on. The progress towards development of ministry teams (and ordained local ministers if appropriate) is through a discernment process involving the expressed desire of the parish, the guidance and encouragement of a local ministry development officer, and the mandate from the bishop. The precise manner in which this progress will be made will vary according to the diocesan context and needs. Once mandated, teams train together for ministry, and any ordinand discerned from within the team would be included in that team training process.

Candidates for ordained local ministry, who must be at least 30 years old, should be well established in their community, local church and occupation. Their circumstances should, as far as possible, assure that they will remain in their present locality.

Sponsorship for training as an ordained local minister is always the responsibility of the diocesan bishop, and assessment of candidates takes place either at a local bishops' selection conference within the diocese, or at a central conference at which special provision for such candidates is made.

Training takes place over a period of at least three years and is specific to the candidate's category of sponsorship. This is by means of a diocesan course for ordained local ministry, or by an adaptation of or participation in a recognized part-time theological course or of a theological college, together with the ongoing training of the team of which the ordinand is a member. A variety of training models is used. Typically an integrated approach will be taken – training lay and ordained together for local ministry teams. Other ordinands will train within local groups that are *not* local ministry teams, or in diocesan groups with other local ordinands *only*.

After ordination, ordained local ministers hold the bishop's licence, which relates the holder specifically to ministry within a designated parish or group of parishes and is for a set period of years in the first instance, renewable thereafter as the bishop considers appropriate. Ordained local ministers are not deployed outside their own local community, however that may be defined.

Vision

> Ordained Local Ministry is part of the ministry of Christ which he shares with all baptised members of the Church. Those called to this ministry by the local church need to have made the calling their own. For its effective operation, Ordained Local Ministry requires the local church's commitment to shared ministry, including the collaboration of local Church leaders, ordained and lay. It is a development in ministry open to parishes and candidates of all social backgrounds.[12]

This 'basic statement' forms the underlying principle of all diocesan ordained local ministry schemes, and is set out in every submission for which approval is sought from the House of Bishops. The practical expression of this statement is borne out under the criteria required for mandate:[13]

- The local church, as represented by its parish or district council, needs to be clear about its priorities for mission and about the kind of ministry it needs to enable it to fulfil those priorities.

- It needs to be understood that the relationship between clergy and laity is based on partnership and mutual support, and expressed in collaborative ways, promoting and developing the shared ministry of all baptized people.

- The incumbent and church council need to be clear and agreed about the desirability of a local leadership team and, if applicable, *ordained* local ministry. This agreement will arise out of awareness about, and ownership of, the new development among church members.

At the heart of the vision of local ministry is the idea that each local community takes responsibility for its own faith journey, acknowledging that the call of God is *to* them, but is also *for* other people, and above all for other people in their community. Training for ministry needs to know the context and to take it seriously.

The key issues in implementing this vision are:

- to work hard at looking at the distinctive role of individuals and groups within the life of the Church. If this work is not done then collaboration slips into merely thinking everybody can do anything now.

- to take seriously the fact that the process is dynamic, and teams need to go on developing and growing ministers, lay or ordained. Ministry – collaborative, local, shared, circular, total, whatever its name – raises more questions, even as it provides some of the answers. But the strategy of local ministry, both ordained and lay, is to ensure that 'the ministry of the Church of England is responsive to the demands of mission to the nation and not merely limited to the necessary requirements of maintenance'.[14]

See also Chapter 5 and Appendix 10.

Further reading

ACCM Occasional Paper No. 22, *Education for the Church's Ministry*, Church House Publishing, 1987

Advisory Board of Ministry, Policy Paper No. 1, *Local NSM*, Church House Publishing, 1991

Advisory Board of Ministry, *Stranger in the Wings*, Church House Publishing, 1998

Archbishops' Council Ministry Division, *Statistics of Licensed Ministers*, 1999

Robin Greenwood, *Practising Community*, SPCK, 1996

John Nightingale, 'God So Loved the World', in Board of Mission, *A Time for Sharing*, Church House Publishing, 1995

John Tiller, *A Strategy for the Church's Ministry*, CIO Publishing, London, 1983, pp. 49–69

36

The diaconate

Gordon W. Kuhrt and Paul Avis

Some recent history on diaconate in the Church of England

For many centuries the Church of England has had a 'transitional' diaconate for men, i.e. a one-year term as deacon before ordination as priest.

The 1968 report *Women in Ministry* demonstrated the confusion over the status of deaconesses.

The 1974 report *Deacons in the Church* proposed abolition of the diaconate as unnecessary and inhibiting lay service.

The 1977 report *Ministry of Deacons and Deaconesses* debated with the previous report, and expounded three options – the status quo, abolition or extension. The General Synod voted against abolition, but was unclear about extension.

The 1985 report *The Distinctive Diaconate* sought to bring this (and especially the Portsmouth scheme) within Bishops' Regulations for NSM and/or LNSM.

In 1987 women were ordained deacon. The Liturgical Commission published *The Liturgical Ministry of Deacons*.

The 1988 report *Deacons in the Ministry of the Church* argued strongly for a distinctive ordained diaconate.

The 1990 report *Deacons Now* reviewed the three years' experience of women deacons. It encouraged good practice for the development of their ministry.

In 1992 General Synod approved legislation for the ordination of women to the priesthood. Until this point, the debate on diaconate had been distorted by the following:

- the confusion about the status (lay or ordained) of deaconesses;

- most women who were ordained deacon had a vocation to priesthood;

- deacons who were permanently so by choice have been few.

The House of Bishops has a working party on a renewed diaconate which is just completing its report. It is no secret that it will be recommending a renewal of the ministry of a distinctive diaconate. Arguments include the recent biblical scholarship on *diakonia*, the ecumenical opportunities, and the vocation and experience of some deacons in recent years.

Rediscovery of the biblical idea of diakonia

Recent biblical scholarship – especially the pioneering work of the Australian scholar John N. Collins – has shed new light on the original meaning of some key New Testament Greek words and of the ideas that lie behind them. The richness and subtlety of the Greek is often obscured in translation. These findings have major implications for our understanding of the 'diaconal' aspect of the Church's mission and for the office of deacon in particular.

The inherited understanding of *diakoneo* was 'to serve or wait at table' and the diaconate was identified with humble service. In *Diakonia: Reinterpreting the Ancient Sources* (OUP, 1990), John N. Collins explored the meaning of *diakonia* in secular Greek usage and then applied it to the New Testament references. He came to the conclusion that the primary meaning centred around message, agency and attendance. The crucial point is that, in classical Greek, the *diakonia/diakonos* group of words refer to responsible agency on behalf of a person in authority and involve the fulfilling of a vital task. These Greek terms certainly do not have connotations of inferiority or of menial service.

This fundamental meaning is carried through into New Testament usage. The central sense is to do with responsible agency and an authoritative commission. The apostles themselves are entrusted with a *diakonia* or ministry (Acts 1.17; 6.4; 20.24) which stems from the Lord's commission to carry the good news into the world. St Paul refers to himself as *diakonos* in the sense of an instrument of Christ to bring others to faith in him (1 Corinthians 3.5). In upholding his authority against his detractors, St Paul insists that he is truly a *diakonos* with the Lord's commission, a minister of the new covenant in the power of the Spirit (2 Corinthians 3.6; 6.4; 11.23). (The New Testament word for servant or slave is not *diakonos* but (usually) *doulos*.)

These new insights provide the Church with categories which can apply to the ordained ministry. *Diakonia* is a flexible concept that embodies being commissioned by God or the Church to carry out a task or to convey a message. All Christian ministry, ordained or lay, is grounded in *diakonia* because it is all dependent on the divine commission of the Church in the service of the kingdom. Therefore all ministry is commissioned to have that connecting, bridging role, reaching out in the name of Christ, whatever else it may be called to be and to do.

The transition in New Testament times from this general sense of authoritative commissioning for service to the distinctive ministry of those called deacons is not clear. However, deacons (*diakonoi*) are specifically mentioned as a separate 'order' of ministry, along with overseers (*episkopoi*), in Philippians 1.1 and 1 Timothy 3.1-13. Women deacons may well be mentioned in Romans 16.1 (Phoebe) and in 1 Timothy 3.11. Associated with overseers, deacons clearly have a respected and defined role in the Christian community. The historic connection between deacons and their bishop can be traced back to this New Testament link between *diakonoi* and *episkopoi*.

It was in keeping with this emphasis that, early in the second century, St Ignatius of Antioch, on his way to be martyred in Rome, instructed the Trallians: 'all should respect the deacons as they would respect Jesus Christ' (Trall., 3.1). The close association of the deacon with the bishop is first found explicitly in Ignatius, but builds on the New Testament's link between *diakonoi* and *episkopoi* (overseers) (Philippians 1.1; 1 Timothy 3.1-7).

A renewed diaconate

Recent insights of biblical interpretation enable us to see the office of deacon in a new light. The deacon is an instrument of God's purpose, of the kingdom of God. The deacon is invested with authority by Christ through the Church, in the person of the bishop. The deacon is not set apart for menial service, is not expected to exhibit humility more than others, and is not called to bear more than his or her fair share of suffering for Christ's sake. All Christians are called to present themselves as a living sacrifice in God's service for Christ's sake (Romans 12.1).

Of course, the self-emptying humility of the Son of God, evoked by St Paul in Philippians 2, is the benchmark for Christian attitudes and behaviour. The ideal of obedient and compassionate service remains fundamental. We should not react so far against the received interpretation that we lose sight of the servant character of all Christian ministry. That is still crucial to the understanding of *diakonia*.

Above all, however, the deacon is a person on a mission, a messenger or ambassador, making connections, building bridges, faithfully delivering his or her mandate. As such, the deacon says something about the nature of the Church as Christ's body, becoming indeed a sign of what the Church is called to be. The Church is at its most visible when it is exercising its *diakonia*, its commissioned service in the world. Deacons can be understood as the persons who represent to the Church, and therefore to the world, its authoritative calling as servant (a service that takes many forms, including liturgical and proclamatory ones). In the language of *Eucharistic Presidency*, their office, like that of all the ordained, is to promote, release and clarify the nature of the Church. Deacons do this in relation to the *diakonia* of the Church as they model, encourage and co-ordinate the diaconal ministry of the people of God.

A deacon may be regarded, therefore, as an ecclesial sign, embodying a truth about the whole Church and about all its ministries. The deacon receives a particular ecclesial identity before God through the Church. That identity relates to the kingdom of God that has dawned in Jesus Christ but remains to be fulfilled, and to the place and role of the Christian Church in God's coming kingly reign. Christ is himself the embodiment of the kingdom. But he is also the archetypal baptized one, as well as the archetypal deacon, priest and bishop. In himself he holds together kingdom, Church and ministry.

This particular ecclesial identity is, however, true of the Church as a whole and of all her ministries. It is true of presbyters and bishops as well as of deacons. All three orders are given to embody in a visible, public and representative way what is true of the Church as such. In ordaining men and women, the Church is witnessing in a concrete way to how it understands its God-given mission. Presbyters and bishops have ministries that, while they are distinctive, overlap in various ways, both with each other and with the ministry of the deacon. The three orders of ordained ministry overlap also with the ministry of lay people. This is inevitable because the work entrusted to the Church is an integrated whole, not a random assortment of discrete functions. All according to their vocation and ministry play their part. The orders of ministry are distinctive without being exclusive.

See also 'Further reading' in Chapter 3 and the report of the House of Bishops' working party, *For Such a Time as This* (Church House Publishing, 2001).

Further reading

Deacons in the Church, C10, 1974
Deacons in the Ministry of the Church, Church House Publishing, 1988
Deacons Now, ACCM, 1990

John N. Collins, *Diakonia: Reinterpreting the Ancient Sources*, OUP, 1990

Ministry of Deacons and Deaconesses (GS 344), 1977

The Distinctive Diaconate (report to the ACCM Council), 1985

The Liturgical Ministry of Deacons: A Discussion Document from the Liturgical Commission (GS Misc 281), 1987

Women in Ministry: A Study, C 10, 1968

37

Women and ordained ministry

Gordon W. Kuhrt and Lesley Bentley[1]

Women priests: the legislation

The legislation was given final approval by the General Synod in November 1992, and subsequently by both Houses of Parliament. On 12 March 1994 the first women were ordained priest in Bristol Cathedral followed by about 1,500 others in cathedrals throughout the country.

There were two measures in the primary legislation. The first, Priests (Ordination of Women) Measure, made provision for the ordination of women as priests. In addition, it provided Resolutions A and B for parishes who were opposed to the development. Resolution A is that the PCC 'would not accept a woman as the minister who presides at or celebrates the Holy Communion or pronounces the Absolution in the parish'. Resolution B is that the PCC would not accept a woman as the incumbent or priest-in-charge of the benefice or as a team vicar for the benefice.

The second was the Ordination of Women (Financial Provisions) Measure. This made financial provision for those who resigned from office or employment because they could not accept women priests in the Church of England.

I have written elsewhere (*An Introduction to Christian Ministry*, pp. 64ff):

> In addition, and quite separately, the House of Bishops proposed an Act of Synod which included the provision of 'extended episcopal care' and the appointment of Provincial Episcopal Visitors (PEVs, popularly known as 'flying bishops'). The work of the Forward in Faith movement has maintained the issue's high profile, and debate continues as to the propriety of the Act of Synod's provisions and/or how long they should continue.

Since women have been licensed as Readers, and ordained as deacons and priests, it is inevitable that attention is increasingly turning to the next issue of women in the episcopate. There are women bishops in other provinces of the Anglican Communion, and there are women in very senior positions in other churches.

Finally, there has been a very significant reaction among some conservative Evangelicals in recent years. Evangelicals in the Church of England (like Anglo-Catholics) were divided about the women priests' proposals. Many felt particularly marginalized because they thought the debate was largely conducted on catholic and/or liberal premises. Since 1992, conservative Evangelicals have increasingly distanced themselves from those sometimes called 'Open' Evangelicals who supported the ordination of women proposals. They have expressed their views through the organization Reform. These developments have been strongly influenced through conservative elements in the Diocese of Sydney in Australia. Far from being seen as a (secondary) matter of Church Order, the issue has been magnified into both an assault on the authority of Scripture and the nature of the Triune God. On Scripture's authority, because, it is argued, the Bible is clearly against women exercising leadership/headship over men. On the Trinity, because it is argued, the Persons of the Trinity are equal in dignity while Christ is subordinate to the Father, and this is the model for the male/female relationship. Some in these groups are also prohibiting women from preaching or teaching to congregations or audiences which include men. The issues of women in authority have, thus, become associated (even entangled) with suspicion about the Church's confidence in, and exposition of, Scripture, its commitment to credal orthodoxy, and, particularly, its alleged liberalizing views on homosexual practice.

The present position, in summary, is that:

- two positions on women's ministry may be held with integrity;
- women are ordained priest and able to fill any appointment other than those requiring episcopal orders;
- provisions are in place to protect the consciences of those opposed to the ordination of women (i.e. Resolutions A and B and the Financial Provisions mentioned above and the Act of Synod, see Chapter 38);
- there is to be no discrimination on the ground of views on this issue.

There has been considerable anxiety about the issue of discrimination both ways. With regard to the selection processes, the House of Bishops approved in June 1993 a Statement entitled 'A Fair, Open and Welcoming Selection Process: Arrangements for Selection after the Synod Decision on Women Priests'. The text is reproduced here as Appendix 10.

As mentioned above, the Church of England is now turning its mind to the issue of women in the episcopate. This development has already been received in some other Anglican provinces and in other Church denominations. The House of Bishops is, at the time of writing, setting up a working party to address the issues. This is in response to an overwhelming vote of the General Synod requesting this action.

Because of the controversy and sensitivities surrounding these issues, there now follow (on pp. 236–9 and in Chapter 38) two considerations from very different standpoints.

Women in ordained ministry

In 1992 the Church of England agreed that women should be ordained as priests. Already almost 12 per cent of the stipendiary clergy are female. Of those in training for stipendiary/non-stipendiary ministry nearly 40 per cent are female. Female priests report a widespread acceptance and welcome of their ministry in society at large. Opposition appears to come mainly from a relatively small number within the Church.

Six years after the first ordinations of women as priests within the Church of England there are now 1,796 female priests licensed within the Church of England: 1,068 are stipendiary, 569 are of incumbent or team vicar status.[2] The percentage of female clergy will continue to rise in the foreseeable future.

Deployment across the dioceses is, however, very uneven. The percentage of females of incumbent or team vicar status varies across the dioceses, from 0 per cent in the Isle of Man to 15.4 per cent in the Diocese of Southwell. While not all dioceses where the diocesan bishop is known to be opposed to the ordination of women as priests have a low percentage of incumbent status females, those which have the lowest percentage are known to have, or have had until recently, an unsympathetic bishop.

There are issues about how vocations of females are discerned and supported within parishes where the incumbent is opposed to the ordination of women. There is a gender bias among the training institutions:

• Courses have a disproportionately high number of female students.

- Mirfield does not train female ordinands. A few colleges have had very low numbers of female ordinands even in recent years.

There are two important issues here:

1. The type of training received probably has an effect on future ministry. Is the Church disadvantaged by gender bias in training?

2. Can a male ordinand be sufficiently prepared for ministry in the Church of England if he has not trained alongside female ordinands? While the conscience of those who cannot accept the ordination of women as priests is protected, no ordained male can avoid contact with female priests. If the preparation for living with this conflict is not made in training the ordinand will not be prepared for ministry in the C of E.

For the gifts of women to benefit the Church fully it is important that more women are theological educators. How is this to be encouraged particularly in the academic disciplines of theology?

There are few women at senior levels within the Church (currently three archdeacons, one dean, six residentiary canons). There are issues concerning preferment:

1. the valuing of ministry prior to ordination as priest;

2. the decision-making process concerning preferment is strongly male dominated.

Few women priests are involved in decision-making at diocesan level. Few bishops' staff meetings contain a female although there are some notable exceptions where the bishop has appointed the dean/adviser in women's ministry to his staff meeting. The balance and representation that was sought for in the ordination of women is not therefore gained. Curiously this also means that appointments of women to posts beyond first curacy are often made solely by men.

Many dioceses have a post of Dean of Women's Ministry or Adviser in Women's Ministry. While women continue to be disadvantaged in the existing systems such an appointment is the only effective way of enabling the voice of women as women to be heard both in 'women's issues' and more importantly in the broader scope of Church decision-making.

In the Measure that was put before Parliament and in the subsequent Act of Synod there were provisions to protect the consciences of those who could not accept the ordination of women to the priesthood. Respect for conscience is important in Anglicanism. This, however, created a tension. Respect for conscience was quickly turned into a right to a parallel belief that the Church had acted in error. The Church was at once seen to ordain women but also to accept that some people believed that this was wrong and give validity to this belief. The frequent use of the term 'two integrities', the practice of continuing to ordain those who cannot accept the decision of the Church and the acceptance of bishops who are not in communion with each other all foster a picture of two alternative belief systems.

In a Church that ordains women this is often felt to undermine women priests. While Canon A 4 is quite clear that women are ordained lawfully and fully within the Church, the Act of Synod makes it feel that the Church somehow denies this.

In the opinion of many, the Act of Synod has failed in its aim of promoting unity. There are fears that PEVs encourage parishes to opt for their pastoral oversight rather than that of the diocesan. PEVs have refused to receive Communion at celebrations by their brother bishops, giving rise to suspicions that they support a theology of 'taint'. (Although this is vigorously denied no other theological explanation has been offered.) Many would welcome the PEVs being more active in promoting unity.

Questions have been raised about the cost of PEVs in times of increased pressure on dicoesan budgets. It is to be noted that only 296 parishes[3] have opted for their oversight.

The experience of women in ministry has by definition been different from that of men. The life experience of women within our culture is also by nature very different from that of men. It is important that this experience and its associated development of gifts are used for the furtherance of the kingdom of God. As a Church we face an issue about how this experience, ability and gifting are best harnessed and how they can be used to bring changes to established structures and traditions.

As a society we traditionally expect women to take responsibility for child-care, if not for delivery of this. Issues arise for women about the appropriate-ness of established work patterns of clergy. These often seem to presuppose a wife at home to look after the children, e.g. breakfast chapters, clergy meetings, and the Office being said directly before the appropriate time for an evening meal. There are issues about the willingness of bishops to offer incumbencies to women with young children.

Issues of personal safety are relevant for all clergy but perhaps heightened for women who are more likely to suffer attack or harassment. An equal problem is the presuppositions about this made by others. Supposition is best replaced with a proper risk assessment involving the persons considered at risk them-selves. Two publications have looked at the risks and possible safeguards.[4]

There are a host of issues around deployment of two-clergy couples which are dealt with elsewhere (see Chapter 30). Suffice it to note at this point that it is often the female member in such a couple who appears to be disadvantaged.

Further reading

Helen Thorne, *Journey to Priesthood*, Centre for Comparative Studies in Religion and Gender, Department of Theology and Religious Studies, University of Bristol, 1999

Monica Furlong (ed.), *Act of Synod, Act of Folly*, SCM, London, 1998

Statistics of Licensed Ministers: some facts and figures as at 31 December 2000 (GS Misc 638)

Knocking at Heaven's Door, Diocese of London, 1996

Gordon Kuhrt, *Clergy Security*, Ministry Division, 1997

38

The Episcopal Ministry Act of Synod

Edwin Barnes

When the Church of England began its legal path towards the ordination of women to the priesthood in 1992, it also said that those who did not accept this new step were as much part of the Church as those who did. The Eames Commission, set up by the Archbishop of Canterbury primarily to look at the ordination of women as bishops in different parts of the Anglican Communion, reached the same conclusion. In 1998, the Lambeth Conference, attended by bishops from the worldwide Anglican Communion, endorsed this.

The Church of England set about finding a mechanism for giving members of the Church opposed to women's ordination the space to remain in the Church. This was because although women were ordained, the Church still recognized that such ordinations might come to be rejected after a process of 'reception'. In the 1993 debate leading up to this mechanism, the Archbishop of York (John Habgood) proposed the word 'discernment' for this process of testing. It was a word he preferred to the technical theological word 'reception', since people misunderstood the idea of 'receiving' a doctrine. 'Reception' sounded as though there was no alternative; eventually everyone would come round. But in fact, the word includes the idea of 'non-reception' as a possibility. In other words, in time it might become clear that this new practice of ordaining women was *not* in line with the will of God for his Church.

In 1993, the General Synod accepted the Act of Synod by which those opposed to women's ordination could honourably remain members of the Church of England. Synod did this because the ordination of women to the priesthood was something entirely new in the life of any Church which maintained the threefold ministry of bishops, priests and deacons, and because those who opposed it must be allowed to continue to disagree with the majority. They must be given space because in the end they might prove to be right – and 'the end' would only be when not just the Anglican Communion, but the entire Church, Catholic, Reformed, Anglican and Orthodox, had reached a common mind.

The original Measure passed by the General Synod and Parliament involved parishes being able to vote not to accept a woman incumbent and not to permit a woman to celebrate Holy Communion. The Act of Synod allowed parishes to petition their diocesan bishop to provide them with some other bishop who was opposed to women as priests to give them 'extended episcopal care'. If the church council voted for such a petition, the bishop would have to consider it. If they voted overwhelmingly for it (by a two thirds majority) then he *must* make such care available to them. He could do this by putting them under the pastoral and sacramental care of his suffragan bishop, provided that bishop was himself opposed to women's ordination and did not take part in their ordinations. If there was no such suffragan in the diocese, then he might make an arrangement with a neighbouring diocese so that an 'opposed' bishop from there would take on the task. But if no such bishop were available anywhere near, he must use the ministry of a provincial episcopal visitor (PEV) whom the archbishop would appoint for this task. The Archbishop of Canterbury has ordained two such suffragans as full-time PEVs in southern England: Ebbsfleet, who covers the west side of Canterbury Province; and Richborough, who covers the east side. The Bishop of Beverley covers the whole northern province on behalf of the Archbishop of York.

When diocesan bishops behave generously towards the PEVs, inviting them to their staff meetings from time to time, involving them in appointments to parishes, sometimes making them honorary assistant bishops in their dioceses, then the system works pretty well. Difficulties arise when, instead of interpreting the Act of Synod generously (and Archbishop Habgood said this need for flexibility was why there was an Act of Synod, rather than the more legally constraining Measure), diocesans insist that the PEV shall *only* be involved in parishes which have successfully petitioned for his care. That leaves out of account many who are in teams or groups, where it is more difficult to petition; and all who are in chaplaincies, whether service, school or college, hospital or prison. The PEVs have a responsibility still to be their 'spokesmen', as indeed they have even in dioceses with local or regional arrangements; but the people themselves, priests and laity, can feel very marginalized by the Church at large. And the PEV has always to remember that it is the diocesan bishop who is the 'ordinary', who has the rights and responsibilities, while the PEV only has delegated responsibility, and few rights.

Soon after the ordination of women became possible, many people left the Church of England. Priests retired early, some went through medical retirement (for many became ill at this time), others availed themselves of the ability to retire 'under the Measure'. It is thought that something like 500 priests,[1] and many thousands of lay people, simply left the Church of England, some to join other churches, others to abandon the Faith altogether. The Act of Synod exists to try to ensure that no more people leave us than absolutely must. If the Church were to proceed to ordain women to the episcopate, then the Act would have to be replaced with something quite different. No longer would the PEVs, or indeed some of the diocesan and suffragan bishops, be able to continue as part of the 'college of bishops' of the Church of England. Of course, if the Church became convinced that it was utterly right in what it was doing, and everyone who disagreed must leave, the matter would be resolved. That has happened in some Anglican provinces overseas, and has resulted in great loss to those provinces. While we have time, we should all work to ensure that what our Church has said is acted upon. That is to say, that all of us, whether we believe women's ordination is right or wrong, are loyal Anglicans, all hold our beliefs with integrity, and all have and must continue to have an honoured place within our tolerant and inclusive church.

Further reading

The Episcopal Ministry Act of Synod, 1994

The Role of Provincial Episcopal Visitors (House of Bishops Paper HB(96)8 and annex)

Report of Proceedings of the General Synod, November 1993: Act of Synod Debate, pp. 718–82 and 982–1017

The Ordination of Women to the Priesthood Code of Practice, DC(94)1

The report of the Eames Commission on Women in the Episcopate, printed in *Women in the Anglican Episcopate*, published for the Anglican Consultative Council, Anglican Book Centre, Ontario, Canada, 1998

The Official Report of the Lambeth Conference 1998: Morehouse Publishing, Harrisburg, PA, USA. Specifically, Resolution III 4 in which the conference 'accepts and endorses' the report of the Eames Commission, recognizing 'the ongoing, open process of reception'

The Report of the Episcopal Ministry Act of Synod Review Group (GS 1395), 2000

39

The financial situation

Shaun Farrell

Key points

- Dioceses and parishes successfully taking on the bulk of the cost of ministry support.

- Three years to go before pensions transition completed.

- Giving has increased well ahead of inflation. Can the pace be maintained?

- Church as a whole projected to be in surplus but dioceses feeling the pinch as pension contributions bite.

- Outcome of stipends review and review of pension contribution rate are crucial factors.

Church finances – an overview

In order to put the various issues into context it is necessary to understand how the Church is currently financed. In 1998 (the latest year for which full data is available) the total cost of running the Church of England was nearly £740m (i.e. over £2m per day). Inevitably the largest proportion (46 per cent) was spent on the stipendiary ordained ministry (training, stipends, pensions and housing), with a further 30 per cent spent on worship and buildings.

On the income side, 61 per cent of the money required comes from the parishes in the form of giving, collections, donations and legacies and 34 per cent comes from investment in all forms.

It is interesting to note that over the last five years overall expenditure has

Diagram 13: Church finances: income and expenditure

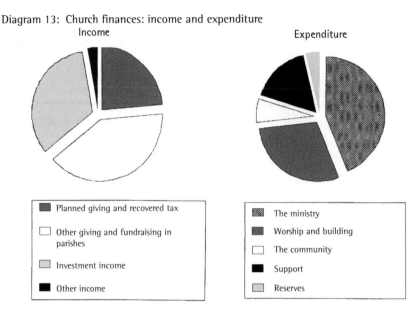

increased on average by 3.3 per cent p.a. and income by an average of 4.3 per cent p.a. On the basis of these figures, total Church income in 1998 exceeded expenditure by around £40m.

Future projections, presented recently to the Inter-Diocesan Finance Forum, suggest that expenditure could rise from £738m in 1998 to £944m in 2005 (an annual increase of 3.4 per cent). Projections of Church income show the figures rising from £778m in 1998 to £956m in 2005 (an annual increase of 3.1 per cent). Clearly, any projections are only as good as the data and assumptions that underpin them, and one must allow a certain margin for error. The assumption for future giving levels is particularly important. However, the projections probably give a reasonable indication of how the finances of the Church are likely to develop over the next few years. Obviously this overall national picture will conceal quite wide variations in the financial health of individual dioceses, and in policy setting these variations cannot be ignored.

The projections suggest that the *average* increase in parish quota will be around 4.9 per cent p.a., i.e. considerably in excess of the rate of price inflation. This is significant because we know that some dioceses have already given their parishes undertakings that quota increases will not exceed a certain percentage (often inflation + 1 or 2 per cent). Two thirds of dioceses reported annual budget *surpluses* over the period 1993–7, but the trend since then has been moving towards more dioceses declaring deficits. The major factor here is the introduction in 1998 of a funded scheme for future service pensions.

The issues

I now turn to the specific issues currently being addressed and how they may influence the overall picture described above. The amount of detail covered in this report is designed only to give a broad outline of the issues concerned, many of which will be the subject of more comprehensive reports to the Archbishops' Council and/or General Synod in due course.

Expenditure

Clergy stipends

As at 31 December 1999[1] there were 8,941 full-time parochial clergy serving 13,041 parishes and 16,225 churches. There were in addition 392 dignitaries (bishops, archdeacons, deans and provosts and other cathedral clergy) and 325 non-parochial diocesan clergy (mainly sector ministers), bringing the overall number of stipendiary clergy to 9,762 (8,773 men and 989 women).

Although the number of people recommended for training for ordination to the stipendiary ministry has been rising for the last six years, this increase is still not sufficient to offset the overall decline in the total number of stipendiary ministers, primarily the result of the high number of retirements of people ordained in the early 1960s. Future projections clearly need to be treated with caution but on the basis of current assumptions the total number of stipendiary clergy is expected to decline by over 6 per cent, to 9,180, by 2004.

By contrast, the total number of non-stipendiary ministers (1,796), ordained local ministers (274) and Readers (9,972) has continued to grow. These trends suggest that the role for stipendiary clergy is changing and becoming one of encouraging all baptized people to develop their ministries. However, the decline in the number of stipendiary clergy remains a concern financially if it has the effect of discouraging local giving.

The diagram on the next page shows how the cost of stipends in 1999 was met, with the lion's share once again coming from parish giving.

The stipends support for parish clergy provided by the Church Commissioners (currently £20m p.a.) represents approximately 11 per cent of the total stipends bill. The overall quantum of this support has reduced from £66m p.a. in 1991 to its current level in 1997 and dioceses/parishes have responded magnificently to the challenge in funding that that has represented. The latest actuarial valuation of the Commissioners' funds indicates that their assets and their total liabilities are now in balance. It is also pleasing to note that the

Diagram 14: How the cost of stipends was met in 1999

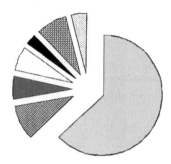

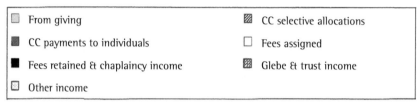

From giving	CC selective allocations
CC payments to individuals	Fees assigned
Fees retained & chaplaincy income	Glebe & trust income
Other income	

investment returns from their assets have exceeded their benchmark in each of the last six years. At the end of 2000, which brought to an end a decade of very strong investment markets, their assets were valued at £4,380m (compared with the figure of £2,126m at the end of 1992). The increase in their actuarial value, which is used to assess the Commissioners' distribution capacity, was much less dramatic.

The general improvement in the Commissioners' financial position now means that they can offer a modest £3m p.a. increase in the amount they make available, via the Council, for parish ministry support in 2002, and discussions about the distribution of this sum are ongoing at the time of writing.

Stipend support

Of the £20m p.a. referred to above approximately £15m p.a. is distributed in the form of *selective* stipend support to dioceses, the balance being made up of £4.7m p.a. of non-selective support (mainly guaranteed annuities of around £1,000 p.a. paid direct to most parochial clergy) and £0.3m p.a. in other grants. Responsibility for the distribution of selective stipend support passed from the Church Commissioners to the Archbishops' Council with effect from 1 January 1999 under the provisions of the National Institutions Measure 1998. However, the distribution arrangements must continue to honour the Commissioners' historic trust, as set out in Section 67 of the Ecclesiastical Commissioner Act 1840, to assist parish ministry in the most needy parts of the Church. This assistance need not actually be limited to supporting clergy stipends but it has been in recent years and at present the Council is continuing to use the broad concept and methodology that it inherited from the Commissioners.

The current methodology, which has been in use since the early 1990s (subject to some modification in 1996), uses the five factors listed below converted into a point score to produce a table of need on which the distributions are based:

- historic resources income (mainly income from diocesan investments);
- potential income (giving by church members if all gave in accordance with the General Synod target of 5 per cent);
- actual giving in relation to potential;
- OxLip (Oxford Low Income Predictor);
- unemployment rate.

A review group, chaired by Stewart Darlow (Chester DBF Chairman) is currently looking at possible revisions to the formulae used to distribute stipend support *and* to apportion between dioceses the cost of the Council's budget (£17.5m p.a.).

The amount of money available for distribution via the national bodies can, of course, only go a small way towards equalizing the resources available to each diocese to support its ministry, and General Synod has already endorsed the principle of interdependence within the Church (i.e. mutual support). The review group believes that its new proposals provide a ready means of distributing any additional funds made available through mutual support arrangements. For such arrangements to be put into operation in a meaningful way it would, however, require those dioceses at the wealthier end of the financial spectrum to raise additional money to support those dioceses with fewer resources. Even in the former category of dioceses there is an understandable backlash against a prolonged period of quota increases.

Pensions

In order to cap the Commissioners' liability for meeting the full cost of clergy pensions (which was threatening to absorb all their income) a new funded scheme was introduced to finance pension entitlements earned after January 1998. Contributions, currently at the rate of 21.9 per cent of the pensionable stipend (for incumbents the national minimum stipend in the previous year), are paid by the respective 'responsible bodies' (principally the dioceses) into the pension scheme managed by the Pensions Board. The Church Commissioners remain responsible for meeting the full cost of all pension rights earned *before* January 1998. This 'past service' pension liability will continue to dominate the Commissioners' expenditure patterns for many years to come and over the next 60 years or so they will need to expend approximately 46 per cent of their current asset base (as well as the income on it) to extinguish that liability.

The additional financial burden represented by the contributions into the new funded scheme (currently £35m p.a.) was too great for the dioceses and parishes to take on in one go and so the Commissioners originally agreed to provide transitional relief on a sliding scale over the period 1998–2002, amounting to approximately £65m. However, the first triennial review of the clergy pension scheme at the end of 2000 revealed the need to increase the contribution rate to 29.1 per cent of the pensionable stipend with effect from 1 April 2002 in order to meet the current benefits package. The main reasons for this sharp increase were:

- increased life expectancy;
- the likelihood that investment returns would be lower in the future;
- stipends (to which pensions are currently automatically linked) are rising faster than expected.

In response to this sharp increase in costs, the Church Commissioners have agreed to find an extra sum of £10m in the form of transitional support over the period 2002–4 to help offset the extra costs falling on the parishes. In parallel with this, work is currently underway to re-examine aspects of the current benefits package and to consider possible options for change.

Conclusion

I hope that in the course of this chapter I have been able to give a reasonable feel for the current financial picture and the issues that will need to be addressed in the short to medium term. It is obviously important to avoid too mechanistic an approach to these individual matters (because of the other non-financial factors involved), but decisions in one area will impact on others and cannot be taken in isolation. The Church clearly faces some difficult challenges ahead but there will also be exciting opportunities and these must be exploited to the full.[2]

See Appendix 12 for the 2001 budget.

Diagram 15: Diocesan pension contributions, 1992–2003

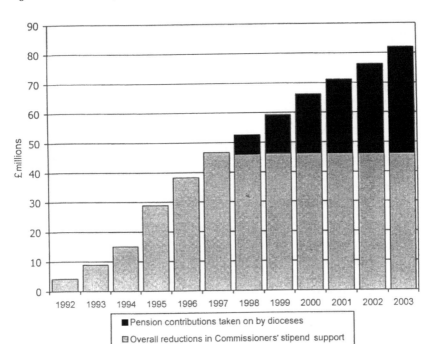

Diagram 16: Annual apportionment increases and reserves, 1994–2004

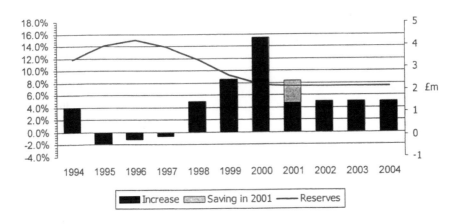

The financial outlook

Aggregate Church bodies

	1998 £m
EXPENDITURE	
THE MINISTRY	339
Training	13
Stipends	167
Pension contributions	31
Pensions paid by Commissioners	85
Housing	43
WORSHIP AND BUILDINGS	225
Building works and repairs	108
Running costs	83
Wages of organists, vergers, etc.	34
THE COMMUNITY	46
Education	8
Charities and mission	38
SUPPORT AND ADMINISTRATION	128
Dioceses	38
Parishes	58
Cathedrals	8
National Church excluding training	24
TOTAL EXPENDITURE	738
Pensions paid by clergy pension scheme	0
INCOME	
GIVING	474
Covenanted before tax	139
Tax recovered	42
Collections, donations and other giving	171
Gift days, fetes, special appeals, grants, etc.	93
Bequests	29
INVESTMENT INCOME	262
Dioceses	36
Parishes	55
Cathedrals	12
Church Commissioners – income	128
Church Commissioners – capital spent	31
OTHER INCOME	42
Grants	5
Fees and part-time chaplaincies	37
TOTAL INCOME	778

40

The Pastoral Measure

Martin Elengorn

Pastoral Measure review

Review of the Dioceses and Pastoral Measures (and related Measures) is under way and is due to report to the Archbishops' Council by summer 2003. The Pastoral Measure provides, *inter alia*, the legal process for reorganizing parishes and arrangements for staffing them. The review will seek 'to ensure flexible and cost effective procedures which fully meet changing pastoral and mission needs'. This will include examination of the scope for devolution and deregulation, within the context of enhancing flexibility for mission, and also facilitating creative experiment in ministry.

The review group will undertake wide consultations and will consider the impact of both the financial situation and of changing patterns of ministry, clergy numbers and deployment. Among the issues to consider is whether there should be, for example, central strategies in accordance with which dioceses produce local plans, or whether there should be a continuation of the current, essentially 'bottom up' approach.

The question of clergy freehold is not part of the review's remit, nor is the parish system itself under review. Amending legislation is likely to be brought forward in the quinquennium 2005–10.

Code of practice to the Pastoral Measure

A code of practice was first issued by the Commissioners in 1976. The current version, the third, was issued in 1999 after extensive consultation. Its aim is to provide practitioners with a distillation of best practice. It offers extensive guidance on procedures, and seeks to identify those areas where problems may occur.

Ministry issues include the following:

Patronage

In considering representations, the Commissioners take account of whether the diocesan proposals have regard to existing patronage interests, including giving fair and proper weight to the respective interest of each patron.

Dispossession

The consent of a priest who is to be dispossessed of a freehold office by virtue of a pastoral scheme is not required, but the code underlines that the bishop or his representative should contact him or her at an early stage and before knowledge of the proposal becomes public. Dispossession is very rare, and the Measure and the code incorporate detailed provisions for the payment of compensation.

The Gaulby Judgement

In 1999 the Judicial Committee of the Privy Council dismissed an appeal from the Revd A. F. B. Cheesman and others against a decision by the Commissioners to overrule representations against a pastoral scheme affecting the benefice of Gaulby in the diocese of Leicester. The issue before their Lordships was whether it was right to use the Pastoral Measure procedures to reduce the size of the benefice of Gaulby when pastoral breakdown procedures under the Incumbents (Vacation of Benefices) Measure that had been brought against the incumbent then discontinued. The Judicial Committee concluded that use of the Pastoral Measure was appropriate in this case.

The following points emerge from the Judgement:

- The need to have regard to the traditions, needs and characteristics of individual parishes in a proposed pastoral reorganization can include consideration of 'interpersonal factors'.
- Such consideration can include the relationships between parishes, between parishioners, between clergy as well as the ability of particular incumbents to contribute to the better cure of souls.
- The organization of the diocese into parishes is for the ease and benefit of the people and not the incumbent.
- The justification for a pastoral scheme must be the better cure of souls; if the sole or dominant purpose of a scheme was to punish an incumbent or deprive him or her of his or her benefice solely to remedy a breakdown in the relationship between him or her and his or her parishioners, it could not be upheld.

- There must be adequate evidence of any factors taken into consideration in a proposed reorganization; any bad faith would invalidate a proposed scheme.

Trends

There are currently in the region of 8,000 benefices and around 16,000 church buildings in use. The number of benefices has reduced by some 400 in the last five years, partly matching the reduction in stipendiary clergy numbers. The number of churches in use has reduced by a net figure of 70 during that same period. The number of pastoral proposals received by the Commissioners each year is slowing slightly and numbers around 200, some 10 per cent lower than during the early 1990s.

Further reading

The Pastoral Measure, HMSO (current version January 2001)
The Code of Recommended Practice to the Pastoral Measure 1983, Church House Publishing, 1999
The Code of Recommended Practice to the Team and Group Ministries Measure, Church House Publishing, 1995
A short leaflet about the Pastoral Measure entitled *Answers to Some Questions*, 1994

41

Chaplaincy

Giles Legood [1]

Context

Until the Industrial Revolution most people lived and worked in one place (parish) for most of their lives. Urbanization and new technology altered that forever: many now travelled in a way previously unknown and resided in a number of places during their lives. New generations were born in towns and cities and the link with a particular parish church and its priest was weakened. The nineteenth century saw the Church lose influence in a whole host of areas in people's lives. Responsibility for charity for the poor moved from the parish vestry to local government. Trades unions and employers' associations replaced Christian guilds of craftsmen. This all added to the growing secularization.

The experience of the First World War profoundly affected the religious mood of the country. Although many at home felt that God had either abandoned the troops or did not care, many soldiers' experience of the ministry of padres, who had been heavily recruited, was good. After the war there was considerable effort to build up the chaplaincies to the three services. After the Second World War the need for permanent provision was recognized. Many had become used to having chaplains involved in every aspect of military life and felt a similar experience might be replicated elsewhere. Clergy began visiting factories, and the pioneering industrial mission work of Bishop Ted Wickham soon became known.

While financially the Church has had to re-adjust in the task of serving nationwide, almost all of its deliberations have focused on parish ministry. Clergy working in chaplaincy, however, have much to contribute to the question of what roles the Church should adopt in the new century. Chaplains are paid to spend their working time with those who do not go to church (those the Church claims it most wants to reach).

Main chaplaincy groupings

In addition to such ministries, there has always been a tradition of clergy serving in non-parochial settings. Since the parochial system in England was first sketched out by Theodore (died c.690), full-time, stipendiary clergy have served as cathedral staff, archdeacons, bishops' chaplains, chantry priests and domestic chaplains to families, among others. Priests have also served for centuries as chaplains in three particular settings: hospitals; the army and navy; prisons. Clergy were intimately involved with setting up institutions which ministered to the sick and dying. Priests accompanied armies into battle as early as the Battle of Crecy (1346) and ships of the English fleet as early as Cadiz (1597). Chaplains were appointed to the newly built prisons of the late eighteenth century, where even today they exercise statutory functions. In addition, priests have served in Oxford and Cambridge colleges as dons (Holy Orders being a requirement of appointment).

The current position

Since the Second World War there has been a large expansion of chaplaincy provision. Today chaplains are to be found working in a wide variety of institutions and sectors. Chaplains serve in schools, armed forces, hospitals and hospices, prisons, universities, arts and recreation, legal services, police forces, airports, agriculture, retail trade and commercial seafaring. The largest provision is in the sectors of healthcare, universities, prisons and armed forces.

Healthcare chaplains have had an important role to play since the creation of the NHS in 1948 which made specific provision for 'spiritual care'. The more recent *Patients' Charter* has required NHS Trusts to make provision for the religious beliefs of 'patients and staff'. The last decade has consequently seen increase in chaplaincy numbers, though now numbers have reached a plateau. University chaplaincy has also expanded dramatically in the last 50 years. In 1952 there were eight chaplains in universities outside Oxbridge, and by 1985 chaplaincies (either full- or part-time) were established in every higher education institution. This expansion matched expansion in higher education: in 1954 there were 82,000 students in HE, by 1997 there were 1,750,000 (and the government plans for this figure to grow). *Crockford* lists approximately 90 prison chaplains, the majority of whom (though not all) are full-time. Chaplaincy provision in England and Wales, paid for by the Home Office, has remained relatively constant. Chaplains still have statutory duties to see every prisoner on the latter's entry to, and exit from, gaol. Armed Forces chaplains are approximately: Royal Navy 50; Army 100; Royal Air Force 50. In the last 30 years chaplaincy provision here has shrunk dramatically, perhaps by as much as 50 per cent. This is due, of course, to the dramatic reduction in armed service personnel and defence spending. Various Ministry of Defence reviews have had implications for chaplaincy, and chaplaincy numbers are now described as being in a 'steady state' and unlikely to change.

Issues of importance

It is hoped that just as it might be seen as problematic to talk about issues in parochial ministry as if this were a single, homogeneous whole, talking of 'chaplaincy' generically is even more complicated, given the wide range of provision. Nevertheless the following points might be made:

- Very often chaplains work in an ecumenical way which their colleagues in a parochial setting are not able to do. A range of paid chaplaincy provision may be made by institutions and this opens up exciting possibilities for ecumenical dialogue and practice.

- Similarly, many chaplains work in inter-faith situations. Where chaplaincy provision is small, Christian chaplains may carry the role of 'religious professional'. Where provision is greater, Christian chaplains will work alongside chaplains of other faiths.

- Because parishes are now larger than they once were (for instance George Herbert's benefice of Fugglestone and Bemerton had a population of 400 in the 1630s, today it is 8,000), parish priests inevitably have more people to minister to. Chaplains often minister in smaller situations and are given greater opportunity for intimacy with those around them (though this is not necessarily the case: the chaplain at Heathrow Airport ministers to 40,000 staff alone, quite aside from the millions of passengers).

- The realities of today's Church include a diminution in the number of clergy. With fewer assistant clergy and larger parishes, despite best intentions, some parish churches may become more congregational in feel. Chaplains are able to maintain the historic Anglican notion of caring for all, regardless of religious belief.

- Chaplaincies allow the Church to engage more easily with the challenges of the society it seeks to serve as they ensure that the Church is fully enmeshed in them. For instance, armed service chaplains are increasingly occupied with the complex moral questions faced by the Armed Forces, as are chaplains in regard to research in healthcare and university sectors.

- Through working with people in the context in which they spend the greater amount of their lives, the world of work, chaplains are able to represent the Church to the world and the world to the Church in a unique way.

- Chaplaincy provision is increasingly being paid for by the institutions in which chaplains work. This is a testimony not only to the chaplains themselves but also to the notion that there is an increasing recognition of pastoral and welfare issues in the workplace and religious provision as part of this.

- The existence of chaplains most often means that institutions have easy access to a person with religious knowledge and expertise. Chaplains in such places have long been familiar with concepts of annual appraisal and review. This means that not only are they paid by the institution but they are accountable to it also, as well as being accountable to the Church.

Further reading

Little has been published in this field, and what has mostly consists of papers and articles (almost all of which are from the USA). The few books that have been written about chaplaincy describe one particular area. In 1983 a working party of the National Society produced the report *Sector Ministries*, which was concerned only with terms and conditions of chaplains. One generic book and one sector-specific book have been recently published. Both have bibliographic references:

G. Legood (ed.), *Chaplaincy: The Church's Sector Ministries*, Cassell, London, 1999

H. Orchard, *Hospital Chaplaincy: Modern, Dependable?*, Sheffield Academic Press, 2000

42

The Church Army

Philip Johanson

Background information

Church Army is a society of 350 trained evangelists, both men and women, lay and ordained, reflecting all traditions within Anglicanism. They work in a variety of settings throughout the British Isles, Ireland and with the British Forces and their families in Germany. There are also 150 retired Church Army evangelists, many of whom are still very active within their own local churches and communities.

The society was founded in 1882 by Prebendary Wilson Carlile during his time on the staff of St Mary Abbots Church, Kensington, London. Carlile was committed to relevant and sensitive evangelism in the community and had a desire to enable and encourage Christian people to share their faith in Christ. This has remained a hallmark of Church Army ministry over the years.

There are now eight sister societies around the world, working in more than twelve different countries. Each society has its own board or council, with an appointed leader responsible for the work. Occasionally, Church Army evangelists have the opportunity to be seconded from one society to another for both short- and long-term appointments.

People to People

During the early 1990s the society undertook a major review of its work which led to the publication of *People to People*, a corporate strategy document. It has also produced a purpose, vision and values statement, which now underpins the development of all new work.

Arising out of the review, the board decided to focus the work of the society in five specific areas:

- Area evangelism
  Providing training and resources for groups of churches. Helping them to develop and implement relevant and effective strategies for outreach.

- Children and young people
  Working with local churches by providing trained and enthusiastic people to work in new and imaginative ways with the younger generation.

- Church planting
  Helping to establish new communities of faith among people and in areas where the church traditionally has made little or no impact.

- Homeless people
  Working with homeless people on the streets, in day centres and in hostels. Providing for material needs, offering friendship and helping them to discover a living faith in Christ.

- Older people
  Enabling older people to discover their own potential in evangelism as members of the Church. Reaching out to other older people in the community, through day centres and in residential/nursing homes.

To assist in supporting and developing new initiatives within the five areas of focus, the society has established five focus groups, each convened by a senior member of staff. The groups meet annually for a residential training and development conference. The convenor of each group has been chosen for their experience and knowledge in that particular focus area.

Recruitment and training for Church Army evangelists

In co-operation with the Ministry Division of the Archbishops' Council and diocesan advisers for ministry (diocesan directors of ordinands and lay ministry advisers), Church Army selects its own candidates for a three-year training course at its own purpose-built college in Sheffield, which was opened in 1992. It is also possible to train through the recently developed mixed mode training course. A shorter course may occasionally be agreed for certain candidates who have previous theological training and appropriate ministry experience.

The society employs its own full-time Vocations and Candidates Secretary. Selection conferences are held at the training college and the panel of selectors always includes a bishops' selector appointed by the Ministry Division, a counsellor in private practice and Church Army staff members.

There are no minimum academic requirements for entering training. Each individual needs to demonstrate that they are called by God to serve as an evangelist within the Church Army and that they are able to benefit from the training available. The three-year course contains several block field-training placements.

Evangelists in training work to attain the Diploma of Higher Education in Evangelism Studies, which is validated by Leeds University and offered through the University College of York St John. Several students work to attain the graduate diploma. The college syllabus is submitted to and approved by the Ministry Division of the Archbishops' Council. The college will have its first review (inspection) by the House of Bishops Inspectorate in 2002.

Employment/deployment

On the successful completion of initial training evangelists are admitted to the office of Evangelist in the Church (Canon E 7(2)) by the Archbishop of Canterbury or the Archbishop of York. They are also commissioned as Church Army evangelists by the Chief Secretary of the Church Army.

In consultation with the relevant diocesan bishop and his staff, the Church Army Area Co-ordinator is responsible for identifying an appropriate first 'training' post for the newly admitted and commissioned evangelist. It is the Area Co-ordinator's responsibility to maintain ongoing contact with the evangelist and with the relevant people in the diocese.

The Area Co-ordinator will consult with the Church Army evangelist and diocesan staff regarding subsequent appointments, although the individual concerned might apply for a post in another diocese. All Church Army evangelists are licensed by the bishop in whose diocese they work.

Church Army is committed to partnership in ministry. In financial terms this may mean sharing the cost of a post with parishes, diocese or other agencies. A number of Church Army evangelists are employed directly by the society and others are employed directly by a diocese.

Management

Church Army is governed by a board of which two members are nominated by the Appointments Committee of the Archbishops' Council. The board determines policy and delegates the day-to-day leadership of the society to the Chief Secretary. He shares that task with a senior team of four people: the Principal of the Wilson Carlile College of Evangelism has responsibility for all training, both initial and further training; the Operational Director is responsible for frontline work; the Central Services Director is responsible for all support functions; and the Corporate Planner works closely with the Chief Secretary on future direction and planning.

Church Army has divided the Church of England into eight areas, each with an area co-ordinator. It is the responsibility of the Area Co-ordinator in consultation with others, both within Church Army and the wider Church, to share in the development of Church Army evangelists, together with appropriate posts for them to fulfil their ministry.

Communication

Communication is important for Church Army both within the Church and the world at large. It therefore has a marketing department to assist in this task, with a small team of field staff responsible for promotion and fundraising. In addition, there is a specialist fundraising development officer with responsibility for raising financial support specifically for building-based initiatives.

The society publishes three times a year a magazine called *Share It*, complete with a prayer guide which is mailed to all supporters. It also produces a range of literature on various aspects of the society's work.

For the purposes of internal communication, the society publishes *Church Army News* four times a year. Area co-ordinators chair area business meetings (similar to clergy chapter meetings) in the spring and autumn for all staff in the area and regional day conferences are held in four locations each year. The society holds a residential conference for all staff every other year.

See Appendix 13 for a chart of the distribution of Church Army officers.

43

Strategies for deployment: ecumenical responses

Flora Winfield

In a number of dioceses in the Church of England, questions about strategies for the deployment of resources to meet the needs for mission and ministry into the future are being addressed with partner churches. A variety of ways of working ecumenically are being developed, in response to the differing needs of the particular places. Below are some examples of responses to the question – how can we, together, best serve the gospel in this place?

The Diocese of Norwich – mapping the churches

In Norfolk, the conversation about deployment has focused on identifying and locating the resources of the churches in terms of ministers and buildings, and mapping the boundaries of Anglican and Roman Catholic deaneries and Methodist circuits. This work began in 1989, and has developed as information about the congregations has been collated by grid square. An information pack for each grid square is available to resource discussions about deployment. In 2000, the information was further collated into a database of non-Anglican congregations, to complement the new diocesan database. This year, new mapping work has been undertaken to show the places of residence of stipendiary ministers from the Church of England, Roman Catholic Church, Methodist Church, URC, Baptist churches and Salvation Army officers, an exercise which has proved revelatory about location of the churches' existing resources. Recently more detailed work has been done to look at the resources of Anglicans and Methodists, dividing the county into five areas, with rural deans and superintendents meeting in each area.

The experience of the mapping exercise in Norfolk has been that good-quality information about the churches is essential for fruitful discussion about strategies for deployment.

The Diocese of Newcastle – clustering churches in rural areas

In June 1999, the Newcastle Church Relations Group (NCRG) held a consultation on ministerial resources in Northumberland. The consultation focused on the issues of the provision of pastoral care and training for lay ministries, and included those concerned with questions of strategy from the Church of England, Baptist churches, Methodist Church, Roman Catholic Church, Salvation Army and URC. Each Church gave an overview of its own situation, and the realities of issues were brought into focus through two case studies. The consultation reported to the NCRG that 'There were suggestions about how the churches could organize and manage their provision of pastoral care in partnership with each other. If the local churches organized themselves into Clusters, they could work together to enable a wider variety of ministries than any church could manage by itself. The pattern of staffing could be looked at in new ways.'

As a next step, it was agreed that pilot projects on the clusters idea would be undertaken in the areas bounded by the civil districts of Berwick and South West Tynedale. A database of all the churches and ministers in both areas was compiled, together with maps, which reveal, among other things, how far clergy are travelling to take services. In the autumn of 2000, consultations were held in both areas with ministers and lay representatives from each local church, who were asked to identify the particular characteristics of their area, to share information about what the churches are currently doing, together and separately, by way of mission, and to express their hopes for their communities. The report of this consultation process has now been circulated, and looks to the next stage, which is detailed follow-up work in the two areas on planning for clergy deployment.

The Diocese of Bradford – a Churches Action Zone

The area within the inner ring road of Bradford has been identified by the churches as in need of special action. Through the West Yorkshire Ecumenical Council, they have undertaken a survey of church activity in the area, which maps present patterns of practice and aspirations for future development in the inner city. A total of 69 churches were included in the survey, of whom about 50 per cent responded, from the Church of England, Baptist churches, Independent, Methodist, Roman Catholic and West Yorkshire African Caribbean Council of Churches. The purpose of the survey, together with other work, has been to provide evidence to enable informed decision-making. It identifies high levels of involvement in community ministry in a difficult area with a high level of social exclusion, and a complex multi-faith population, with demographic changes which mean that the congregations are diminishing as families move out of the area. Alongside the survey, over a period of a year, working groups were established to look at:

- new ways of being the Church;
- Christians and the public life of the city;
- training and education for Christians in these new circumstances;
- ways of working with children and young people.

In September 2000, a consultation was held to draw conclusions and chart the way forward. From this it was evident that radical measures were needed, to face together questions of evangelism and evangelization, the Christian–Muslim context and how the churches may be part of the social fragmentation of the area, rather than of its healing.

The churches agreed to establish an action zone, within which the usual working culture could be suspended, in response to the needs of the area. The inner ring now uses four quarters, created by the four major roads into the city centre, within which to organize work, putting aside their existing boundaries and working towards a goal of 'more tents, fewer buildings', a flexible and responsive way of being the Church. A task group has been set up to take this forward, and a Methodist deacon is working to co-ordinate the project and to 'develop effective means through which the lives of Christian communities can be strengthened'.

A variety of ways of working

As well as these examples, there are many other places where work on strategies for deployment is being undertaken ecumenically, for example:

- In the Diocese of Salisbury, Wiltshire Churches Together have been working in two of the County Council community areas to 'survey the Church's assets, in plant and personnel'.
- In the Diocese of Lincoln, the Church of England and the Methodist Church have established a mission partnership across two Methodist circuits and an Anglican feanery.
- In the Diocese of Guildford, the churches have undertaken work on strategies for ministry in Epsom offering 'leadership to provide a framework for risk taking'.

Appendix 1

Number of licensed Readers in the Church of England from 1969 to 1999 inclusive

Alan Wakely

- Reader ministry was first opened to women in 1969.

- From 1969 to 1982 inclusive the figures can be further broken down by province.

- From 1983 onwards figures are available for each diocese.

- PTO Readers (i.e. retired because over 70, but active and with permission to officiate) are *excluded* from these figures. This category existed from 1989 onwards. At the end of 1999, 1,081 men and 329 women were so registered, giving an active total of 9,934 – and allowing the '10,000 active Readers' claim to be made early in 2000.

- Some of the figures for earlier years in this list vary a little from one source to another. For figures up to 1984 I have used a return published for internal use in 1985.

Table 11: Number of licensed Readers, 1969–99

Year to 31 Dec	Men	Women	Total	% of women	Increase in % of women
1969	6515	9	6524	0.14	
1970			Not available		
1971	6556	120	6676	1.80	1.66
1972	6392	159	6551	2.43	0.63
1973	6370	223	6593	3.39	0.96
1974	6328	263	6591	3.99	0.60
1975	6215	322	6537	4.93	0.94
1976	6169	363	6532	5.56	0.63
1977	6094	432	6526	6.62	1.06
1978	6088	487	6575	7.41	0.79
1979	6078	560	6638	8.44	1.03

Year to 31 Dec	Men	Women	Total	% of women	Increase in % of women
1980	6129	662	6791	9.75	1.31
1981	5993	766	6759	11.33	1.58
1982	5934	856	6790	12.41	1.08
1983	6029	949	6978	13.60	1.19
1984	6038	1070	7108	15.05	1.45
1985	6028	1172	7200	16.28	1.23
1986	5935	1268	7203	17.60	1.32
1987	5864	1398	7262	19.25	1.65
1988	5864	1565	7429	21.07	1.82
1989	5820	1702	7522	22.63	1.56
1990	5659	1939	7598	25.51	2.88
1991	5510	2070	7580	27.31	1.80
1992	5463	2193	7656	28.64	1.33
1993	5309	2391	7700	31.05	2.41
1994	5376	2569	7945	30.90	−0.15
1995	5289	2775	7964	34.84	3.94
1996	5142	2955	8097	36.49	1.65
1997	5162	3110	8272	37.60	1.11
1998	5131	3258	8398	38.79	1.19
1999	5105	3419	8524	40.11	1.21

- The number of women Readers expressed as a percentage of the total complement of Readers has increased every year since it became possible for women to enter Reader ministry in 1969 – except for one year (1994).

- This year-on-year percentage increase has been surprisingly steady in the small range of +1.11–1.82 per cent – since 1980, with four exceptions (1990, 1993, 1994 and 1995). Since 1995, figures have again 'settled' within the pre-1990 parameters.

- This roughly static percentage increase hides a steady increase in absolute numbers of women – 1.5 per cent of 6,500 being less than 1.5 per cent of 8,500!

- This suggests that removal from the licensed lists (by death, or becoming PTO) still involves more men than women. This is no surprise, given that pre-1969 *all* Readers were male.

- Conversely, the numbers being admitted and licensed for the first time show greater equality among the sexes. Indeed in 1999 of the 43 dioceses, 25 had *more* women than men in training.

- The 'blip' in these statistics in the period from 1990 to 1995 might suggest that the ordination of women had an effect. However, this is probably fallacious given that all those women ordained to the priesthood in the first 'wave' in 1992 had been in the diaconate for some time, and had commenced their training well before 1990.

- However, there was considerable publicity about women's ministry in the period around 1992. Did this, perhaps, stimulate interest in ministry of all kinds among women, from which Readership benefited along with the ordained ministry?

- The two previous bullet points still do not explain the 'rogue' figures for 1994. However, there is a training period before Readers are licensed, so those who were licensed in 1994 started training when the furore about women priests was at its height. Perhaps there is, in the 1994 figures alone, a reflection of this – either because people were uncertain about the future course of the Church of England, or because they offered themselves for the priesthood instead. The very high percentage increase in the following year (1995) may be significant.

Appendix 2

The Canons that concern Readers[1]

E 4   Of Readers

1. A lay person, whether man or woman, who is baptized and confirmed and who satisfies the bishop that he is a regular communicant of the Church of England may be admitted by the bishop of the diocese to the office of Reader in the Church and licensed by him to perform the duties which may lawfully be performed by a reader according to the provisions of paragraph 2 of this Canon or which may from time to time be so determined by Act of Synod.

2. It shall be lawful for a Reader:

    (a) to visit the sick, to read and pray with them, to teach in Sunday school and elsewhere, and generally to undertake such pastoral and educational work and to give such assistance to any minister as the bishop may direct;

    (b) during the time of divine service to read Morning and Evening Prayer (save for the Absolution), to publish banns of marriage at Morning and Evening Prayer (on occasions on which a layman is permitted by statute law so to do, and in accordance with the requirements of that law), to read the word of God, to preach, to catechize the children, and to receive and present the offerings of the people;

    (c) to distribute the holy sacrament of the Lord's Supper to the people.

2A. The bishop may also authorize a Reader to bury the dead or to read the burial service before, at or after a cremation but only, in each case, with the goodwill of the persons responsible and at the invitation of the minister of a parish or an extra-parochial place within the meaning of section 1 of the Deaconesses and Lay Ministry Measure 1972.

When a cure is vacant the reference in this paragraph to the minister of a parish shall be construed as a reference to the rural dean.

3. The bishop of every diocese shall keep a register book wherein shall be

entered the names of every person whom he has either admitted to the office of Reader or licensed to exercise that office in any place.

E 5 *Of the nomination and admission of Readers*

1. A candidate for the office of Reader in a parish or district shall be nominated to the bishop by the minister of that parish or district; and a candidate for the said office in a wider area by one of the rural deans or archdeacons after consultation with the minister of his parish or district.

2. The nominator in making such a nomination shall also satisfy the bishop that the said person is of good life, sound in faith, a regular communicant, and well fitted for the work of a reader, and provide all such other information about the said person and the duties which it is desired that he should perform as the bishop may require.

3. No person shall be admitted to the office of Reader in the Church except it be found on examination, held by the bishop or by competent persons appointed by the bishop for this purpose, that he possesses a sufficient knowledge of Holy Scripture and of the doctrine and worship of the Church of England as set forth in *The Book of Common Prayer*, that he is able to read the services of the Church plainly, distinctly, audibly, and reverently, and that he is capable both of teaching and preaching.

4. Every person who is to be admitted to the office of Reader shall first, in the presence of the bishop by whom he is to be so admitted or of the bishop's commissary, make the declarations set out below, the preface which precedes the Declaration of Assent in paragraph 1(1) of Canon C 15 (with the appropriate adaptations) having first been spoken by the bishop or commissary:

> I, A, B, do so affirm, and accordingly declare my belief in the faith which is revealed in the Holy Scriptures and set forth in the catholic creeds and to which the historic formularies of the Church of England bear witness; and in public prayer I will use only the forms of service which are authorized or allowed by Canon.

> I, A, B, will give due obedience to the Lord Bishop of C and his successors in all things lawful and honest.

5. The bishop shall admit a person to the office of Reader by the delivery of the New Testament, but without imposition of hands.

6. The bishop shall give to the newly admitted Reader a certificate of his admission to the office; and the admission shall not be repeated if the Reader shall move to another diocese.

E 6   *Of the licensing of Readers*

1. No person who has been admitted to the office of Reader shall exercise his office in any diocese until he has been licensed so to do by the bishop thereof: Provided that, when any Reader is to exercise his office temporarily in any diocese, the written permission of the bishop shall suffice.

1A. A licence authorizing a Reader to serve in a benefice in respect of which a team ministry is established may be in a form which specifies the term of years for which the licence shall have effect.

2. Every Reader who is to be licensed to exercise his office in any diocese shall first, in the presence of the bishop by whom he is to be licensed, or of the commissary of such bishop, (a) make the declarations of assent and of obedience in the form and manner prescribed by paragraph 4 of Canon E 5; (b) make and subscribe the declaration following:

> I, A, B, about to be licensed to exercise the office of Reader in the parish (or diocese) of C, do hereby promise to endeavour, as far as in me lies, to promote peace and unity, and to conduct myself as becomes a worker for Christ, for the good of his Church, and for the spiritual welfare of [my] *all people. I will give due obedience to the Bishop of C and his successors and the minister in whose cure I may serve, in all things lawful and honest.

If the declarations of assent and of obedience have been made on the same occasion in pursuance of paragraph 4 of Canon E 5 it shall not be necessary to repeat them in pursuance of this paragraph and in the declaration set out above the words 'the Bishop of C and his successors and' may be omitted.

3. The bishop of a diocese may by notice in writing revoke summarily, and without further process, any licence granted to a Reader within his diocese for any cause which appears to him to be good and reasonable, after having given the Reader sufficient opportunity of showing reason to the contrary; and the notice shall notify the Reader that he may, within 28 days from the due date on which he receives the notice, appeal to the archbishop of the province in which that diocese is situated.

On such an appeal the archbishop may either hear the appeal himself or appoint a person holding the office of diocesan bishop or suffragan bishop in his province (otherwise than in the diocese concerned) to hear the appeal in his place; and, after hearing the appeal or, if he has appointed a bishop to hear the appeal in his place, after receiving a report in writing from that bishop, the archbishop may confirm, vary or cancel the revocation of the licence as he considers just and proper, and there shall be no appeal from the decision of the archbishop.

Where the see of the archbishop is vacant or the archbishop is also the bishop of the diocese concerned, any reference in the preceding provisions of this paragraph to the archbishop of the province shall be construed as a reference to the archbishop of the other province, but any bishop appointed by the archbishop of the other province by virtue of this paragraph shall be a bishop serving in the province which contains the diocese concerned.

Any appeal under this paragraph shall be conducted in accordance with rules approved by the Archbishops of Canterbury and York; and any such rules may provide for the appointment of one or more persons to advise the archbishop or bishop hearing such an appeal or any question of law arising in the course thereof.

3A. Where a bishop has granted a licence to a Reader to serve in his diocese for a term of years specified in the licence, the bishop may revoke that licence under paragraph 3 of this Canon before the expiration of that term, and where he does so that Reader shall have the like right of appeal as any other Reader whose licence is revoked under that paragraph.

4. No bishop shall license any Reader to be a stipendiary in any place until he has satisfied himself that adequate provision has been made for the stipend of the said Reader, for his insurance against sickness or accident, and for a pension on his retirement.

Note: The word 'my' should have been removed by Amending Canon No. 23. A future Amending Canon will correct this omission, but in the meantime, the word should be omitted as required by the sense.

Appendix 3

Terms of reference and membership of the Structure and Funding of Ordination Training Working Party

Terms of reference

1. Building on the work of the Vote 1 review group, to consider and advise on the wider issues identified in that report concerning the funding and structure of initial training for ordination.

2. To review the training needs of the Church in the light of developing patterns of ministry and the Church's future needs in ministry.

3. To comment on the specific areas listed by the Vote 1 report:

   - Diversification by colleges and courses – wider issues
   - Exploring the different types and length of training
   - Funding of research in colleges and courses
   - Impact of lay ministry and other authorized ministries on the number of stipendiary clergy needed
   - Incorporation of pooling costs within the apportionment
   - Possible economies of scale through fewer institutions
   - Sponsorship category for ordained ministry (stipendiary and non-stipendiary)
   - Ways of working with the wider church to reduce overheads.

Membership

The Rt Revd John Hind, Bishop of Europe
The Rt Revd Peter Forster, Bishop of Chester
The Revd Canon Keith Lamdin
The Revd Canon Dr Robin Greenwood
The Revd Dr Richard Burridge
The Revd Dr Judith Maltby
The Revd Barry Nichols

The Revd Dr Jeremy Sheehy
The Revd Dr David Hewlett
Mr Phil Hamyln Williams
Professor Dianne Willcocks
The Revd Donald Pickard
The Revd Canon Wendy Bracegirdle
The Revd Canon June Osborne
Mr Richard Finlinson
Mr Anthony Archer
Mr Richard Hopgood
The Ven. Dr Gordon Kuhrt

Appendix 4

Training for the ordained ministry: questions frequently asked[1]

When is some hard thinking going to be done on how many clergy the Church of England needs and can afford?

This question is key and continues to be given serious consideration by the Ministry Division. Work is being done on providing projections taking account of the age profile of both clergy in post and of those coming into the ministry. However it is already clear that even the current rise in the number of ordinands will not sustain the present number of stipendiary clergy. This will need to be followed by a dialogue with dioceses about needs in the light of costs.

Why is there no method of controlling the numbers of people who are trained, the date they start or the form of training they undertake?

The Church sees ordained ministry as a particular calling – from God and the Church. As a matter of House of Bishops policy everyone recommended by their Bishop for training is given a place on the form of training and time of commencement which the Bishop, advised by his Director of Ordinands, considers most appropriate. The House of Bishops continues to believe that the spiritual formation and depth of theological study which a theological college can offer is most appropriate for the younger candidates who will give many years of ministry.

Why were larger reserves not retained to fund the upturn in numbers?

In the mid-1990s dioceses were under financial pressure because of the reduction in the Church Commissioners' contribution to the stipends bill. The CBF responded to the pressure to hold down diocesan apportionment during this period of increasing demands on diocesan budgets by the use of reserves. In addition the reserves have been utilised to cushion the cost of pension contributions for clergy staff included in the fees of Colleges and Courses.

Why aren't the costs of supporting candidates and their families included in Vote 1 along with other training costs? There is concern over the pooling arrangements for candidates' support and the difference in the application of the guidance from diocese to diocese.

The management of support costs by dioceses is considered efficient in that the Diocesan Director of Ordinands will be in a better position to know the needs and situations of individual candidates than a Ministry Division Officer in Church House, Westminster. Nevertheless the concern over consistency of treatment and the possibility of inclusion of the total costs within Vote 1 merits further work.

Why is there a disparity between the fees charged by different colleges?

Nearly all the colleges charge broadly similar fees which are carefully scrutinised by the Finance Panel. The only scope for a significantly smaller fee is where a college subsidises the cost of training out of its own endowment income. In addition, the size of colleges varies from Mirfield with a total of 38 students to Trinity Bristol with capacity for 130. Also some colleges work in federations which gives scope for cost sharing whilst others are located far from other colleges without the possibility for such efficiency savings.

Why aren't more candidates trained through courses which are significantly cheaper than colleges?

As a matter of policy the House of Bishops believes that it is right to train in residential colleges younger stipendiary clergy who will offer many years' service in parishes. On the face of it Courses appear cheaper but some costs are hidden, particularly with the smaller courses. Here teaching staff will often be part-time and stipendiary clergy or others in full-time employment offer their services free of charge. Courses save on residents' costs but the residential life also has benefits for candidates in their formation. College fees are more expensive; yet total contact teaching time in three years part-time on a Course is probably not more than one year's contact teaching time at a College. Thus in terms of cost per teaching hour there is a much smaller disparity.

Could college training be made more cost effective: for example, could college terms be extended to make better use of the year?

The College year is fully utilised these days with vacation placements for candidates. This is seen as an essential part of their training and also provides the answer to why they are not encouraged to find paid employment in vacations to help finance the cost of their training. In addition, if training is to be of a good quality, staff need time for preparation, study and research. It is also the case that many Colleges use their premises during the vacation period for income-generating activities.

What about an Archbishops' appeal to set up a substantial training fund?

This is certainly a suggestion that needs to be considered. However, training clergy is part of the core activity of the Church and so should be seen as a core cost along with the stipend and housing.

Why are there unfilled places in some colleges when others take more than their share?

The variety of colleges largely reflects different church traditions. Normally candidates will gravitate to one of the colleges that reflect their tradition. Equally colleges will develop reputations which candidates will follow. It has been noticed over time that there is a natural ebb and flow of candidates between colleges. Numbers between the colleges are regulated and a financial restraint is being considered where colleges go over their allocated number.

Why have training costs risen over recent years?

The main reason for rising training costs is the increase in numbers being trained. Other factors include the rise in stipend levels and clergy pension contributions which impacts on the cost of teaching staff. In addition the reduction of LEA funding and increased Higher Education costs have driven up unit costs.

Why does the Church of England support 11 Theological Colleges with an average of 56 ordinands each? Do we have the most rational provision of training facilities? Is there sufficient focus on the unit cost of training?

The number of Colleges is a product of history and since they are all independent they cannot be closed by the Church. If they are closed the proceeds from any sale of premises reverts to the trustees of the college rather than being capable of redeployment to other Colleges. Nevertheless the House of Bishops can withdraw approval, in effect cease to use the College for ordination training. This has been done on occasions over the years and this has led to a more rational picture. A number of reports have been produced which considered this subject and put forward proposals but it has generally been recognised that there is limited scope and limited benefit in withdrawing approval. Clearly this subject needs to be reviewed periodically.

Should the cost of training be born locally in dioceses and parishes for the candidates they produce?

Training for ordination candidates benefits the Church of England as a whole and therefore it is right that the Church as a whole, through the dioceses, pays for the training. But certainly some parishes may see it as part of their mission to provide support to a candidate from their congregation.

Does the training given produce what parishes need when seeking a priest? How far is training in collaborative ministry given in colleges compared to courses?

Colleges and courses are required to review their training thoroughly every five years to ensure good standards and that the training they offer is appropriate to the future needs of the Church. These issues are checked by Bishops' Inspectors and by the Educational Validation framework process.

Why are not more funds made available to students for University-taught degrees?

Enabling more students to study for university-taught degrees would require further funding from the centre and the dioceses.

Appendix 5

Archbishops' Council Clergy Stipends Review Group: Consultation Document[1]

The Archbishops' Council has commissioned a major review of stipends paid to clergy and licensed layworkers. This is in response to concerns within the Church about whether stipends are adequate, and also about how stipends are to be funded, now that an increasing proportion of the stipends bill is being met from the current giving of lay people. The Group's terms of reference are set out on the last page. It is hoped that this document will be discussed widely throughout the Church by clergy, lay people, PCCs and other interested groups. The Group is also conducting a survey of all those people on the central payroll, held by the Church Commissioners, who are in receipt of stipends.[2]

Note: Chaplains to prisons and the armed forces are paid salaries by the Home Office and the Ministry of Defence. Most full-time hospital chaplains and some university chaplains are paid by NHS Trusts and universities respectively. Their remuneration levels do not form part of this review.

Comments are particularly invited on the following issues:

1. The concept of the stipend
2. The level of the stipend
3. The use of differentials
4. The setting of stipends
5. Other elements in the remuneration package
6. How any increases in stipends might be funded.

The concept of the stipend

1. The majority of clergy and licensed layworkers receive stipends. The stipend has been variously described as '... not a reward but rather a means of releasing someone to give all of their time to the ministry ...' and '...

an allowance or contribution designed to maintain a person who has chosen to follow a particular calling or vocation'. In 1943 the House of Bishops made the following statement about stipends:

> '... *The stipends of the clergy have always, we imagine, been rightly regarded not as pay in the sense in which that word is understood in the world of industry today, not as a reward for services rendered, so that the more valuable the service in somebody's judgement or the more hours worked the more should be the pay, but rather as a maintenance allowance to enable the priest to live without undue financial worry, to do his work effectively in the sphere to which he is called and if married to maintain his wife and bring up his family in accordance with a standard which might be described as that neither of poverty nor riches ...'*

2. This definition was framed at a time when all clergy were male, most clergy wives did not work outside the home and there were no clergy couples. A consultation on clergy conditions of service undertaken in 1994 indicated a large measure of support for the spirit of this definition, particularly as far as equal stipends for all incumbents are concerned. There is a debate in the Church about whether differentials should be paid to dignitaries. As recently as 1996 the General Synod voted against the abolition of such differentials. There is a view that they might be paid to other clergy as well.

The level of the stipend and how it is set

3. The stipends of parochial clergy and licensed layworkers are set by the dioceses, on the basis of recommendations from the Archbishops' Council in its role as Central Stipends Authority (CSA). Details of the CSA's recommendations for 2000/01 are shown at the end of this document. More details are contained in the CSA report for 1999, which is available on request from the Ministry Division.

4. Recommendations by the CSA for increases in stipends are made after detailed consultation with dioceses. One aim of the CSA is to encourage the maintenance of a nationally coherent stipends system. This reflects the self-understanding of the Church of England as being a national Church. Broad conformity of stipends between dioceses is also seen as important in enabling clergy mobility throughout the country.

5. Each year the CSA recommends a National Stipend Benchmark for clergy of incumbent status. This is then adjusted to take account of regional variations in the cost of living using data from the Reward Group on

comparative costs of a standard 'basket of goods' in nine different regions. The aim of such regional adjustment is to give clergy parity of purchasing power irrespective of their geographical location. Dioceses are encouraged to pay stipends not more than 2.5 per cent above and not less than 1.5 per cent below their Regional Stipend Benchmark. In all but a few dioceses, the greatest number of clergy of incumbent status in the diocese receive a stipend within this range.

6. The CSA also recommends a National Minimum Stipend for incumbents; no incumbent should be paid less than this for full-time ministry. This is increased each year by the same percentage as the National Stipend Benchmark and is used to calculate pension levels for clergy.

7. The CSA tracks the changes in clergy stipends against changes in the Retail Price Index and the Average Earnings Index. It also compares the purchasing power of clergy stipends with disposable incomes available to certain other professional groupings. This is done to provide a general indication of the adequacy of the stipend.

8. The CSA recommends a scale for assistant staff (including layworkers) with annual increases during the first four years of ministry, and additional payments for seniority or responsibility. Details are given at the end of the document.

9. The CSA also recommends to dioceses a stipend for archdeacons and makes recommendations to the Church Commissioners about the stipends paid to bishops, deans and provosts, and residentiary canons. Neither the stipends paid to dignitaries nor those paid to assistant staff nor pensions are adjusted regionally.

10. Dioceses employ a number of clergy in sector ministry posts such as directors of education or youth officers. They may be paid either a salary or a stipend. Accommodation may be provided for them or they may receive a housing allowance.

Other elements in the remuneration package

11. On retirement at or after the minimum normal pension age (65 for both women and men) clergy who have completed at least 37 years' pensionable service receive, in addition to their state pensions, a church pension of two-thirds of the previous year's National Minimum Stipend for incumbents plus a lump sum of three times the pension. The pension and lump sum for those with less than 37 years of qualifying service are proportionate.

12. The Church Commissioners are responsible for funding pensions arising from service before 1 January 1998. Under the new pension arrangements, the cost of pensions for service by parochial clergy after that date is funded by contributions from dioceses and parishes. Because of the link between the National Minimum Stipend and the pension (see paragraph 6), increases in the CSA's recommendations for stipends directly affect the cost of pensions for both past and future service.

13. Clergy make no direct contribution towards the cost of their pensions. If they were to make contributions, then stipends would need to rise to cover these payments and the National Insurance contributions that these increases would attract. The Church would also become liable for additional 'employer's contributions'.

14. Apart from the stipend and pension provision, the main element of the clergy remuneration package is the provision of housing (including the payment of Council tax, water charges, maintenance, external decorations and insurance). Although clergy do not have to pay these costs, it should be noted that clergy are generally required by virtue of their office to live in the accommodation provided for them, and thus have no choice about where they live. Clergy also have to provide accommodation for themselves and their families on retirement. The formula for calculating the pension and lump sum takes this into account, and additional help with buying or renting retirement housing is available on a discretionary basis. Approximately one third of retired clergy make use of this. Clergy are also eligible for removal grants, subsidised motor and household contents insurance in high-risk areas, and car loans at a concessionary rate of interest.

Terms of reference

i) To consider the concept and definition of the stipend;

ii) To examine the content of the clergy remuneration package (including retirement provision) and its comparability with remuneration for other groups;

iii) To ascertain, through a properly-conducted large-scale survey of clergy and consultations with dioceses and charities, the financial circumstances of clergy;

iv) To review the size of dignitaries' differentials;

v) In conjunction with the Finance Committee, to evaluate the affordability and long-term financial sustainability of the present arrangements and any proposals for change;

vi) To consider the implications of any proposals for:

clergy deployment and partnership between dioceses;

future numbers of stipendiary clergy and patterns of ministry;

vii) To consider whether the present structure for setting stipends should be retained and outline possible alternative structures;

viii) To consult with the Church Commissioners, the Pensions Board and dioceses;

ix) To consult with other national Church bodies through the Churches Main Committee and government agencies on matters of fiscal and taxation policy which affect stipends, in particular the treatment of benefits in kind;

x) To determine options for wide debate within the Church.

The CSA's recommendations for 2000–01

Recommendations to dioceses for incumbents and clergy of incumbent status

i) a National Stipend Benchmark of £16,420;

ii) Regional Stipend Benchmarks for each diocese at a level between £15,750 and £16,810;

iii) a National Minimum Stipend for incumbents of £15,570.

Assistant staff and licensed layworkers

A stipend between £14,680 and £15,820 according to length of service, responsibility or personal circumstances.

Archdeacons
A stipend of £24,630

Recommendations to the Church Commissioners

Residentiary Canons	£20,200
Deans and Provosts	£24,790
Suffragan Bishops	£24,790
Diocesan Bishops	£30,120
Bishop of London	£45,480
Archbishop of York	£48,770
Archbishop of Canterbury	£55,660

Appendix 6

Explanatory notes to the Employment Relations Act 1999[1]

Section 23: Power to confer rights on individuals

229. The employment rights legislation has developed piecemeal over a period of many years. While some aspects – such as the right not to have unauthorised deductions made from wages – extend to a relatively broad description of workers, most are currently restricted to employees as narrowly defined, i.e. to workers engaged under a contract of employment. Whether or not a worker is engaged under such a contract is not always an easy question to answer, however. This is because it is a common law question of mixed fact and law which in the event of a dispute can be definitively determined only by a court or tribunal. No single factor is conclusive; all relevant circumstances must be taken into account.

230. The Government considers it desirable to clarify the coverage of the legislation and to reflect better the considerable diversity of working relationships in the modern labour market. Currently, significant numbers of economically active individuals – including for example many home workers and agency workers – are either uncertain whether they qualify or else clearly fail to qualify, for most if not all employment rights. Some work providers offer jobs on the basis of contracts under which the workers, although acting in a capacity closely analogous to that of employees and not genuinely in business on their own account, are technically self-employed or of indeterminate status according to the established common law criteria, and are thus effectively deprived of the rights in question.

231. Certain descriptions of individuals are explicitly excluded from exercising some or all of the rights, although not on a consistent basis, and others – such as members of the clergy – are incapable of qualifying owing to the nature of their appointment.

232. Section 23(2) gives the Secretary of State the power, by order subject to the affirmative resolution procedure (under section 42), to extend to individuals who do not at present enjoy them employment rights under the 1992

and 1996 Acts, this Act and any instrument made under section 2(2) of the European Communities Act 1972. The Government envisages using this new power to ensure that all workers other than the genuinely self-employed enjoy the minimum standards of protection that the legislation is intended to provide, and that none are excluded simply because of technicalities relating to the type of contract or other arrangement under which they are engaged.

Appendix 7

Curacy appointments

Here are some factors that should be considered when you are either looking for a curacy or hoping to appoint a curate.

- Does the incumbent have a clear plan for training – making use of *Beginning Public Ministry* (ABM Ministry Paper No. 17)?

- Is there a job description? – with proposals for development of responsibility in years 2, 3 and 4?

- Do the incumbent and PCC have agreed objectives – with spiritual vision?

- Is there opportunity to meet other parochial church leaders, and attend Sunday worship?

- Is there a written understanding (and diocesan guidance) dealing with:

    Reimbursement of expenses

    Time off and holidays

    Study, Continuing Ministerial Education and retreat?

- What pattern is envisaged concerning

    Daily offices

    Staff meetings

    Supervision?

- Is the accommodation adequate? And approved by the Diocese? Who undertakes and pays for repairs, external and internal redecoration?

- Are there other expectations (from either side)? And/or expectations of (or from) the curate's spouse?

- Will you work together helpfully – in terms of theological and ministerial approach and personal style? Are the incumbent's/parish policies (e.g. on baptism and 're-marriage') fully understood?

Appendix 8

The parish system and localities: material from Diocese of Durham documents

1. From *Living in God's Reality* by the Bishop of Durham (July 2000)

   Long-term action – REDEFINING THE PARISH

   We need to

   1 Emphasise the value of *locality* but recognise that for most people this is not the parish as we have known it.

   2 Recognise people live in a locality which involves travel to amenities such as school, library, cinema, restaurants, playing fields, team sport activities, shopping, banking, post office, adult learning. Patterns will vary enormously – compare for instance the upper Weardale villages with an urban housing estate – but most people will travel beyond the *parish* for many amenities

   3 Look to establishing a *locality* ministry rather than *parish* ministry as currently. *Locality ministries* may include neighbourhood churches for worship, but wider learning activities and engagement with the community and church administration would be on the wider scale of *locality.*

   4 To service this, a group combining a number of stipendiary clergy, NSMs, Readers, OLMs, Lay Ministries, and sector ministries could be established.

2. From *Building Localities in the Diocese of Durham* (Sept. 2000)

   Guidelines

   - The process of determining effective localities in the deaneries should not be held back by the burden of having to change legal boundaries at this stage. The momentum can be established by agreeing that the localities can come into being in most cases through the readiness to work across current boundaries in partnership. Changing the boundaries where necessary can come later as a confirmation of the partnerships which have been built.

- Localities should be defined according to a locally agreed understanding of the Church's mission challenge in the area concerned.

- Localities should relate to real communities and their projected growth or change, even if this means suggesting alterations to current deanery boundaries.

- Localities need to be devised in the light of an assessment of the level of ministry – lay and ordained – which is necessary to sustain and extend the mission of the Church with fewer stipendiary clergy in each deanery.

- Localities need to be defined with local expectations clearly in mind.

- Locality arrangements need to take into account and develop the potential of Shared Ministry.

- Localities will need to relate to, support and sometimes supply the specialist ministries operating in the area.

- Localities once established will be responsible for the Church's key resources: people, financial giving and buildings. Time and talents will have been considered above. The devising of localities will also need to take into account the absolute commitment to stewardship and sustainability through co-operation.

3. From *Promised Feedback from the Task Force* (Dec. 2000)

The Consequences – for what we do in the Deanery Pastoral Committee.

The Committee will want to pay close attention to the outline characteristics of a locality which are listed below. Localities will have different geographical boundaries, cultural identities and economic profiles. These must genuinely be worked out locally. There will be, however, common characteristics some of which localities must share:

- A locality needs to create and reinforce pastoral units which can deliver effective mission, ministry and pastoral care.

- A locality should also be more than just a convenient ecclesiastical unit from an administrative point of view. It must relate to one or more communities which cohere sufficiently through culture and economy, distance and history to make a locality recognisable to people outside the Church.

- A locality must be financially viable overall, even if smaller units within the locality are struggling. Financial viability means the ability to pay the fair Share assessment now and the expectation to continue to meet these obligations in the future through a genuine commitment to Stewardship. Deaneries with the Diocese will continue to support locality ministries which require a largely subsidised stipendiary ministry where there is recognised social and economic need.

287

- A locality needs within it congregations sufficiently large and active in their working together to provide centres of celebration, active mission and Shared Ministry in teaching and preaching and pastoral care so as to attract and nurture new disciples as a natural development. This should apply in all areas and across all traditions.

- A locality also needs the size and vigour to be able to recruit and support the training of an active lay leadership which could, over time and with training, take on much of the administration of the locality. There could be an effective concentration of expert roles across a locality, with one trained Treasurer looking after the finances of the whole unit and, perhaps, with one 'locality office' from which lots of the day-to-day administration could be carried out by lay administrators.

- A locality is likely to have more than one stipendiary priest ministering in collaboration with other clergy and accredited ministers for mutual support and more effective working across existing boundaries. This means that priests and lay ministers might be able to play to their particular strengths, one person taking responsibility for education across the locality, while others concentrate on worship, leading in evangelism, etc.

- A locality may have a number of church buildings and congregations but they will share stipendiary ministers who will reside in different parts of the locality but close enough to each other and to other accredited ministers to meet regularly for prayer and mutual support.

- Buildings within the locality must be capable of being sustained by those who use them

- It is hoped that each locality which has sister churches within it will look to create an ecumenical dimension to the locality mission plan even if it has to remain only an aspiration until beyond March 2002.

- Currently running and well-developed Group Ministries and Team Ministries provide two existing models of co-operation between clergy and laity and different churches. It is conceivable that these groupings might become localities or be enlarged into them, although such decisions lie with the deanery.

Appendix 9

Local ministry: a key element in the Church's strategy for mission

The Report of a National Consultation on the Development of Local Ministry, 4th–6th October 1994, High Leigh, Hertfordshire

Representatives of more than 30 dioceses of the Church of England took part in a National Consultation on the Development of Local Ministry sponsored by the Edward King Institute for Ministry Development.

Conclusions and recommendations

1. Local ministry is a key element in the Church of England's strategy for mission and ministry over the next 20 years.

The growth in lay ministries of different kinds has been one of the 'success stories' of the Church of England over the past 20 years. There is evidence of rising expectations among lay people of active participation in the ministry of their local church. With the expected decline in the number of stipendiary clergy this is a critical factor in maintaining and developing the Church's mission.

2. There are very great differences in the way local ministry is developing between one diocese and another.

The variations in the character of the local communities in dioceses is a major factor in this, but theology is also a factor. Local ministry needs to be sensitive to the local context, and can therefore be expected to develop differently from one area to another. The Consultation considered that different models of local ministry need to be explored, and that at the present stage variety is a positive feature.

3. There is little evidence of dioceses learning from each other.

This is a serious weakness. There were numerous references at the Consultation to 're-inventing the wheel'. Lessons learned in one diocese seemed to be ignored by others. There is no mechanism in the Church of England by which dioceses can learn from each other.

4. A national focus for local ministry is needed.

Specific recommendations that emerged at the conference were:

    a. A national collection of resource material for local ministry training, put together in a way that shows different theological and educational approaches.

    b. A national project to identify and disseminate good practice in local ministry.

    c. Regional integration of theological and ministerial training resources, which brings together initial ministerial training, training for local ministry, continuing ministerial education and the continuing education of local ministerial teams.

5. To those outside it the Church of England appears to be inhibited by rules and regulations.

This point was made strongly by one of the representatives of the United Reformed Church in his reflections at the end of the Consultation. What is needed at the present stage of local ministry is not regulations but work on hammering out principles and establishing what constitutes good practice.

6. The dialogue between 'the local' (e.g. the parish or group of parishes) and 'the diocese' (e.g. the Bishop or the Board or Council) is a crucial element in the effective development of local ministry.

In this relationship both have something to contribute and something to learn from each other. How this can become an effective working relationship was a major area of discussion in the Consultation.

7. Institution services (of clergy starting their ministry in a parish) need to include an appropriate recognition of the existing ministry in the parish, e.g. Reader, non-stipendiary Minister, local ministry team.

An alternative to the term 'interregnum' needs to be found.

Appendix 10

A fair, open and welcoming selection process: arrangements for selection after the Synod decision on women priests[1]

Approved by the House of Bishops, June 1993

1. All of those involved in the selection of candidates for ordained and accredited lay ministry following the decision of the General Synod on the ordination of women to the priesthood should recognise the differing convictions which are held within the Church of England on the ordination of women. They should also acknowledge the range of perceptions and feelings which this decision has created, not only in candidates but also in those who work with candidates in parishes and dioceses as well as in their colleagues in the task of selection. For some the decision is a source of joy and fresh opportunity but for others it is a cause of great grief and anxiety. However, it means for all a measure of uncertainty and a testing period in which mutual respect and understanding will be vitally important.

2. In this context the Advisory Board of Ministry is resolved to ensure that:

   i confidence in the selection process is sustained across the whole range of opinion of the ordination of women which is represented in the Church of England

   ii there is no discrimination in selection between candidates on the ground of their views about the ordination of women to the priesthood

   iii the selection process remains fair, open and welcoming to different opinions on this question

   iv the selection system is maintained as a single and unitary system in which all candidates and selectors participate on an equal footing

   v all candidates and Bishops' Selectors who wish to participate in the selection process should, as far as possible, be enabled to do so.

Sponsorship of candidates

3. The sponsorship of candidates for selection and the decision on which candidates may enter training remains the responsibility of the sponsoring bishop. The ABM undertakes to arrange for all candidates sponsored by a bishop to be invited to a Bishops' Selection Conference irrespective of their views on the ordination of women.

Appendix 11

Budget 2001: the national picture[1]

The Archbishops' Council gratefully acknowledges the monetary support it receives from the parishes. This is evidence of the growing partnership between parishes and the national support functions. The national support functions in Church House, Westminster, are committed to provide the Church with a whole range of cost-effective services all the way from selecting and training new clergy to campaigning for a reduction on the ruinous VAT charged on church repairs.

Another aspect of our partnership is our interwoven budgets. The Archbishops' Council has responded to the very real concerns from parishes and dioceses for a lean national budget for 2001. The budget proposed here was put before General Synod in July.

Training for ministry (Vote 1)

The Archbishops' Council is committed to funding the growth of numbers selected for ordination training and that is reflected in the budget. In 2001 some 1,500 ordinands will be in training, producing some 500 new clergy annually. This budget also includes an additional provision to help smooth future cost increases as requested by many dioceses.

2001	2000	% increase
£8,806,303	£8,204,000	7.3

National support (Vote 2)

Includes all administration and support provided at national level. The particular focus is on work done more cheaply and better in one place than in 44 dioceses. This Vote accounts for less than 1 per cent of the Church's total budget and has held steady in real terms for the past eight years. This recommended budget is below inflation. Council hopes to hold increases in Vote 2 to no more than earnings inflation for the foreseeable future in exchange for a sustained funding commitment from dioceses and parishes. In 2001, Church House, Westminster, will also cut 13 posts and introduce other cost savings.

2001	2000	% increase
£7,342,868	£7,270,890	1.0

Grants and provisions (Vote 3)

Covers the Church of England's contributions to various Anglican Communion and ecumenical bodies. Most are being frozen at 2000 level.

2001	2000	% increase
£1,004,900	£998,300	0.7

Mission agencies' clergy pension liability (Vote 4)

This is a statutory obligation. General Synod voted in 1997 for the central Church to take on the mission agencies' liability for clergy pensions contributions. This is being phased into the budget over five years from 1999, accounting for the high percentage increase.

2001	2000	% increase
£299,000	£194,000	54.1

Getting the most from your money

Careful stewardship of resources has meant that no more was being spent in 2000 than was spent in 1994. In addition, the council is currently carrying out a thorough review of its activities to ensure that all are necessary, efficient and cost-effective. This is part of our commitment to ensuring that we provide services and support to the parishes and dioceses at the lowest reasonable cost.

Taking its work altogether, the Church of England has an annual expenditure of some £760m. The proposed General Synod expenditure for 2001 amounts to £17.5m (i.e. just over 2 per cent of the total). Half of that sum is spent on training new clergy.

Appendix 12

Church Army officers

Table 12: Church Army officers, 2001

Diocese	Men	Women
Birmingham	4	1
Blackburn	4	0
Bradford	4	1
Bristol	1	1
Bath & Wells	4	1
Canterbury	5	1
Carlisle	2	2
Chelmsford	12	5
Chichester	5	3
Coventry	4	2
Chester	3	1
Derby	3	4
Durham	2	0
Ely	9	0
Exeter	8	0
Gloucester	6	6
Guildford	4	1
Hereford	0	1
Leicester	4	1
Lichfield	9	4
Lincoln	3	2
Liverpool	6	3
London	10	3
Manchester	5	3
Newcastle	2	1
Norwich	4	2
Oxford	8	5
Peterborough	4	1
Portsmouth	2	0
Ripon & Leeds	3	3
Rochester	6	2
Salisbury	1	0
Sheffield	16	8
Sodor & Man	2	0
St Albans	3	3

Diocese	Men	Women
St Edmundsbury & Ipswich	3	1
Southwark	12	5
Southwell	3	3
Truro	2	1
Wakefield	3	0
Winchester	4	2
Worcester	5	3
York	11	0
Church in Wales	4	0
Episcopal Church of Scotland	3	1
Church of Ireland	13	6
Germany	2	1
Seconded to Canada	1	1
Seconded to New Zealand	1	1
Seconded to USA	2	1
Seconded to OMF	1	0
Seconded to Africa	1	0

Notes

Chapter 1

1.　See Elaine Storkey, *What's Right with Feminism?*; Rosie Nixson, *Liberating Women for the Gospel*; Elaine Storkey and Margaret Hebblethwaite, *Conversations on Christian Feminism*; and the extensive literature cited in them.

Chapter 3

1.　See Anthony Russell, *The Clerical Profession*, SPCK, 1980.
2.　This paper was originally prepared for an Archbishops' Council debate on Ministry Strategy in 2000.
3.　See also Chapter 36, on the diaconate.

Chapter 4

1.　From *The Ordained Ministry: Numbers, Cost, Recruitment and Deployment*, ABM Ministry Paper No. 2, 1992, pp. ii and iii.

Chapter 5

1.　See *To a Rebellious House? Report of the Church of England's Partners in Mission Consultation, 1981*, p. 31, para. 110; *The National Partners in Mission Consultation: Follow-up Report by the Standing Committee*, GS 547, p. 4, para. 10.

Chapter 8

1.　From *Common Worship: Services and Prayers for the Church of England*, Church House Publishing, 2000.

Chapter 10

1.　The Stephen Lawrence Inquiry report, p. 20, para 6.4.
2.　*Ibid.*, p. 28, para. 6.34.
3.　*How We Stand, Called to Serve.*

Chapter 12

1.　Taken from *A Summary of the Criteria for Selection for Ministry in the Church of England*, Ministry Division of the Archbishops' Council, 2001.

Chapter 18

1.　*Theological Training, A Way Ahead: A Report to the House of Bishops on the General Synod of the Church of England*, Church House Publishing, 1992.
　　Theological Colleges, The Next Steps: Report of the Assessment Group on Theological Colleges, Church House Publishing, 1993.

Chapter 20

1.　Out of print.
2–4.　Out of print but widely available in diocesan libraries.

Chapter 22

1.　The text on pages 164–9 was provided by Patrick Shorrock, and Roger Radford provided the section on pensions (pp. 169–71).

Chapter 23

1. The text on pages 172–7 was provided by Margaret Jeffery, the section on the Employment Relations Act (pp. 177–80) by Gordon W. Kuhrt, and the text on pages 180–82 by Bryan Pettifer.

Chapter 24

1. David Parrott provided the text on pages 183–7 and John Lee provided the text on pages 187–9.
2. Benefices Act 1898 (Amendment) Measure 1923; Benefices (Transfer of Rights of Patronage) Measure 1930; Benefices (Exercise of Rights of Patronage) Measure 1931; Benefices (Purchase of Rights of Patronage) Measure 1933.
3. Benefices Measure 1972.
4. Benefices (Exercise of Rights of Patronage) Measure 1931 had introduced the right for churchwardens to be consulted.
5. Canons C 13, C 14 and C 15 respectively.
6. Canon C 11.

Chapter 26

1. Tony Chesterman provided the text on pages 192–4, Gordon W. Kuhrt provided the text on pages 194–6 and Neil Evans provided the text on pages 196–9.

Chapter 29

1. Tony Sparham first coined the term dual role ministries in an article in *Expository Times*, vol. 103, no. 5, February 1992.
2. Nigel Peyton, 'Dual Role Ministries – Two for the Price of One?', in *Ministry: The Journal of the Edward King Institute for Ministry Development*, no. 27, winter 1996.
3. Nigel Peyton, *Dual Role Ministry: First Choice or Mixed Blessing?*, Grove Pastoral Series no. 73, 1998.

Chapter 32

This chapter was originally prepared for the Archbishops' Council debate on Ministry Strategy issues in 2000.

Chapter 34

1. Mark Hodge provided the text on pages 219–21 and John Mantle the text on pages 221–3.

Chapter 35

1. John Tiller, *A Strategy for the Church's Ministry*, 1983.
2. July 2001.
3. 1991.
4. 1998.
5. 1987 (but see Chapter 17).
6. ABM Policy Paper No. 1.
7. 1 Peter 2.9; Revelation 5.10.
8. Ephesians 4.4–16.
9. Robin Greenwood, *Practising Community*, 1996.
10. 1 Corinthians 12.27f; Romans 12.5–8.
11. John Nightingale, *A Time for Sharing*.
12. ABM Policy Paper No. 1.
13. *Stranger in the Wings*, 1998.
14. Tiller, *op. cit.*

Chapter 36

1. Gordon W. Kuhrt provided the text on pages 229–30 and Paul Avis the text on pages 230–32.

Chapter 37

1. Gordon W. Kuhrt provided the text on pages 234–6 and Lesley Bentley the text on pages 236–9.

2. As at 31 December 1999. Figures taken from *Statistics of Licensed Ministers*, GS Misc 638.
3. Figure taken from *Episcopal Ministry Act of Synod: Report of a Working Party of the House of Bishops*, GS 1395.
4. See *Knocking at Heaven's Door*, Diocese of London, 1996, and Gordon Kuhrt, *Clergy Security*, Ministry Division, 1997.

Chapter 38

1. At 31 December 2000, 61 clergy had 're-entered' Church of England ministry [Editor].

Chapter 39

1. *Statistics of Licensed Ministers* 31 Dec 1999, GS Misc 616.
2. This chapter was abstracted from General Synod, *Forthcoming Financial Issues*, GS Misc 627, October 2000.

Chapter 41

1. The author of this chapter consulted with the Revd Ron Hesketh, Director (Policy and Plans) of the Chaplaincy Services RAF, and the Revd Mark Cobb, Senior Chaplain at the Royal Hallamshire Hospital, when writing this text.

Appendix 2

1. From *The Canons of the Church of England*, 6th edition, Church House Publishing, 2000.

Appendix 4

1. Published by the Ministry Division of the Archbishops' Council, 2000.

Appendix 5

1. Produced by the Ministry Division of the Archbishops' Council, 2000.
2. The categories for membership of the review group were agreed by the council as follows:

    Four clergy, including at least one archdeacon and at least two members of the parochial clergy
    Two chairmen of Diocesan Boards of Finance
    An expert in Human Resources
    An expert on remuneration issues.
3. The following people have been appointed by the Appointments Committee to fill these places:

    The Ven. Dr John Marsh, Archdeacon of Blackburn (Chairman until May 2001)
    The Revd Lesley Bentley (Liverpool)
    The Ven. Robert Reiss (Guildford)
    The Revd Dr Richard Turnbull (Winchester; Chairman from May 2001)
    Mr Alan King (Bath and Wells)
    Mr Bryan Sandford (York)
    Mr David Phillips (Chelmsford)
    Mr Keith Stevens (St Albans)

Appendix 6

1. Reproduced under Licence Number C01W0000297.

Appendix 7

1. Agreed by the Bishops' Committee for Ministry, March 1999.

Appendix 10

1. Produced by the Advisory Board of Ministry, 1993.

Appendix 11

1. Extracts taken from *Budget 2001* leaflet, The Finance Division of the Church of England, 2000.

Bibliography

ABM   *Ordination and the Church's Ministry* (ABM Ministry Paper 1), London, 1991

ABM   *Local NSM* (Policy Paper 1), London, 1991

ABM   *The Ordained Ministry: Numbers, Cost, Recruitment and Deployment* (ABM Ministry Paper 2), London, 1992

ABM   *Order in Diversity* (ABM Ministry Paper 5, GS 1084), London, 1993

ABM   *Criteria for Selection for Ministry in the Church of England* (ABM Policy Paper 3A), London, 1993

ABM   *Regulations for Non-Stipendiary Ministry* (Policy Paper 5), London, 1994

ABM   *Ministerial Review: Its Purpose and Practice* (ABM Ministry Paper 6), London, 1994

ABM   *The Training of Readers* (ABM Ministry Paper 9), 1994

ABM   *Moving Out of Full-time Ministry* (ABM Policy Paper 4), London, 1994

ABM   *Our Common Calling* (Report on Vocations Strategy Group), London, 1995

ABM   *Partners in Marriage and Ministry* (ABM Ministry Paper 11), London, 1995

ABM   *A Review of Selection Procedures in the Church of England* (ABM Policy Paper 6), London, 1995

ABM   *Recovering Confidence: The Call to Ordained Ministry in a Changing World*, London, 1996

ABM   *Steering Group for Theological Colleges and Courses: Final Report* (ABM Ministry Paper 12), 1996

ABM   *The Care of Candidates before and after Selection Conferences* (Ministry Paper 16), London, 1997

ABM   *The Church among Deaf People* (ABM Ministry Paper 14, GS 1247), CHP, London, 1997

ABM   *Shaping Ministry for a Missionary Church* (Ministry Paper 18), CHP, London, 1998

ABM   *Stranger in the Wings* – report on LNSM (Policy Paper 8), CHP, London, 1998

ABM   *Selection for Reader Ministry* (ABM Policy Paper 7), 1998

ABM   *The Deployment of Readers* (ABM Ministry Paper 20), 1998

ABM   *Beginning Public Ministry: Guidelines for Ministerial Formation and Development for the First Four Years after Ordination* (ABM Ministry Paper 17), London, 1998

ABM   *Servants and Shepherds* (ABM Ministry Paper 19), London, 1998

ABM   *Welcome to Pre-Theological Education*, London, 1999 (annual)

ACCM   *The Continuing Education of the Church's Ministers* (GS Misc 122), ACCM, London, 1980

ACCM   *Education for the Church's Ministry* (ACCM Paper 22), London, 1987

ACCM   *Call to Order: Vocation and Ministry*, London, 1989

ACCM   *Ordination Training on Courses* (ACCM Occasional Paper 30), 1989

Anglican–Lutheran International Commission   *The Diaconate as Ecumenical Opportunity*, Anglican Communion Publications, London, 1996

Anglican–Reformed International Commission   *God's Reign and Our Unity*, SPCK, London, 1984

Anglican–Roman Catholic International Commission   *The Final Report*, CTS/SPCK, London, 1982

Archbishops' Commission on Rural Areas   *Faith in the Countryside*, Churchman, London, 1990

Archbishops' Commission on the Organization of the Church of England   *Working as One Body*, CHP, London, 1995

Archbishops' Council   *Theological Training in the Church of England*, London, 2000

Archbishops' Council Church Schools Review Group   *Consultation Report*, Archbishops' Council, London, 2000

Archbishops' Council   *Called to Lead: A Challenge to include Minority Ethnic People* (GS Misc 625), AC, London, 2000

Archbishops' Group on the Episcopate   *Episcopal Ministry*, CHP, London, 1990

Bibliography

Archbishop of Canterbury's Commission on Urban Priority Areas	*Faith in the City*, CHP, London, 1985
Archbishop of Canterbury's Advisory Group on Urban Priority Areas	*Living Faith in the City* (GS 902), General Synod, London, 1990
Avis, Paul	*Authority, Leadership and Conflict in the Church*, Mowbray, London, 1992
Baelz, Peter and Jacob, William (eds)	*Ministers of the Kingdom: Explorations in Non-stipendiary Ministry*, CIO, London, 1985
Bishops' Advisory Group on Urban Priority Areas	*Staying in the City: 'Faith in the City' Ten Years On* (GS 1181), CHP, London, 1995
Board of Education	*All are Called: Towards a Theology of the Laity*, CHP, London, 1985
Board of Education	*Christian Education and Training for the 21st Century*, CHP, London, n.d.
Board of Education	*Called to be Adult Disciples*, CHP, London, 1987
Board of Education	*Children in the Way*, NS, CHP, London, 1988
Board of Education and Board of Mission	*All God's Children?: Children's Evangelism in Crisis*, NS/CHP, London, 1991
Board of Education	*An Excellent Enterprise: The Church of England and Its Colleges of Higher Education* (GS 1134), London, 1994
Board of Education	*Tomorrow is Another Country: Education in a Post-modern World* (GS Misc 467), CHP, London, 1996
Board of Education	*Youth A Part: Young People and the Church* (GS 1203), NS/CHP, London, 1996
Board of Education	*Taking the Credit: NVQs*, CHP, London, 1996
Board of Education	*Called to New Life: The World of Discipleship*, CHP, London, 1999
Board of Education	*Formal Lay Ministry*, London, 1999
Board of Education	*A Learning Church for a Learning Age*, CHP, London, 1999
Board of Education	*Investors in People in the Church*, CHP, London, 1999
Board of Education	*Investors in People in the Church: Progress Report*, CHP, London, 2000
Board of Mission	*Good News in our Times: The Gospel and Contemporary Cultures* (GS 980), CHP, London, 1991
Board of Mission	*A Time for Sharing – Collaborative Ministry in Mission* (GS Misc 465), CHP, London, 1995

Board of Mission *The Search for Faith and the Witness of the Church* (GS 1218), CHP, London, 1996

Board of Mission *The Way of Renewal* (GS Misc 533), CHP, London, 1998

Board of Mission *Setting the Agenda: Report of the 1999 Conference on Evangelism*, CHP, London, 1999

Board of Mission and Unity *Priesthood of the Ordained Ministry*, London, 1986

Bourne, C. *The Discrimination Acts Explained*, HMSO, London, 2000

Bowering, Michael (ed.) *Priesthood Here and Now*, Diocese of Newcastle, 1994

Brierley, Peter *Christian England*, Marc Europe, London, 1991

Brierley, Peter *The Tide is Running Out*, Christian Research, London, 2000

Buchanan, Colin *Is the Church of England Biblical? An Anglican Ecclesiology*, DLT, London, 1998

Bunting, Ian *Models of Ministry: Managing the Church Today*, Grove Books Pastoral 54, Cambridge, 1993/96

CACTM *Partners in Ministry*, CIO, London, 1967

Cavender, Martin *Springboard Newsletter*, London, 2001

Chubb, Richard *Lifting Holy Hands: A Dictionary of Signs used in Church Service* (ABM Paper 7), London, 1994

Church Assembly *The Pastoral Measure*, CC, London, 1969

Church Commissioners *Parsonages: A Design Guide*, London, 6th edn, 1998

Church Commissioners *The Pastoral Measure*, HMSO, London, 2001

Church of England *The Church of England Yearbook*, CHP, London (annual)

Church of England's Partners in Mission Consultation *To a Rebellious House*, London, 1981

Coates, Mary Ann *Clergy Stress*, SPCK, London, 1989

Collins, John N. *Diakonia: Reinterpreting the Ancient Sources*, OUP, Oxford, 1990

Committee for Minority Ethnic Anglican Concerns *The Passing Winter* (GS 1220), CHP, London, 1996

Committee for Minority Ethnic Anglican Concerns *Serving God in Church and Community: Vocations for Minority Ethnic Anglicans*, CHP, London, 2000

Committee for Minority Ethnic Anglican Concerns *Simply Value Us: Meeting the Needs of Young Minority Ethnic Anglicans* (GS Misc 601), CHP, London, 2000

Cray, Graham *From Here to Where? The Culture of the Nineties*, Board of Mission, London, 1992

Cray, Graham — *The Gospel and Tomorrow's Culture*, CPAS, Warwick, 1994

Croft, Steven — *Ministry in Three Dimensions: Ordination and Leadership in the Local Church*, DLT, London, 1999

Davies, Gaius — *Stress: The Challenge to Christian Caring*, Kingsway, 1988

Department of Trade and Industry — *Fairness at Work*, HMSO, London, 1998

Dow, Graham et al. — *Whose Hand on the Tiller?*, Grove Books Pastoral 16, Bramcote, 1983 (response to Tiller Report)

Dulles, Avery — *Models of the Church*, Gill and Macmillan, 1988

Farrell, Shaun — *General Synod: Forthcoming Financial Issues* (GS Misc 627), London, CHP, 2000

Finney, John — *Finding Faith Today – How Does It Happen?*, Swindon, BFBS, 1992

France, R. T. — *Women in the Church's Ministry: A Test-Case for Biblical Hermeneutics*, Paternoster, Carlisle, 1995

Francis, I. M. and Francis, L. F. — *Tentmaking: Perspectives on Self-Supporting Ministry*, Gracewing, 1998

Fuller, John and Vaughan, Patrick (eds) — *Working for the Kingdom: The Story of Ministers in Secular Employment*, SPCK, London, 1986

Furlong, Monica (ed.) — *Act of Synod, Act of Folly*, SCM, London, 1998

General Synod of the Church of England — *Improving Clergy Conditions of Service* (GS 1173), 1995

General Synod of the Church of England — *Under Authority: Report on Clergy Discipline*, CHP, London, 1996

General Synod of the Church of England — *The Canons of the Church of England*, CHP, London, 6th edn, 2000

Green, David and Green, Maxine — *Taking A Part: Young People's Participation in the Church*, NS/CHP, London, 2000

Green, Maxine and Christian, Chandu — *Accompanying Young People on their Spiritual Quest* (GS Misc 523), NS/CHP, London, 1998

Green, Michael — *Freed to Serve*, Hodder and Stoughton, London, 3rd edn, 1996

Greenwood, Robin — *Transforming Priesthood*, SPCK, London, 1994

Greenwood, Robin — *Practising Community*, SPCK, London, 1996

Greenwood, Robin — *The Ministry Team Handbook*, SPCK, London, 2000

Grubb, Kenneth — *A Layman looks at the Church*, Hodder and Stoughton, London, 1964

Hall, Christine (ed.) — *The Deacon's Ministry*, Gracewing, Leominster, 1992

Hall, Christine and Hannaford, Robert (eds)	*Order and Ministry*, Gracewing, Leominster, 1996
Hart, Colin	*On Being Not Recommended for Training*, CPAS, Warwick, 1992
Headley, Carolyn	*Readers and Worship in the Church of England*, Grove Worship No. 115, Cambridge, 2000
Higginson, Richard	*Transforming Leadership*, SPCK, London, 1996
Hiscox, Rhoda	*Celebrating Reader Ministry*, Mowbray, Oxford, 1991
Hodge, Mark	*Non-stipendiary Ministry in the Church of England*, CIO, London, 1983
House of Bishops of the Church of England	*Deployment of the Clergy* (GS 205), General Synod, London, 1974
House of Bishops	*The Ordination of Women to the Priesthood: A Second Report*, CHP, London, 1988
House of Bishops	*The Ordination of Women to the Priesthood: A Digest*, CHP, London, 1990
House of Bishops	*Issues in Human Sexuality*, CHP, London, 1991
House of Bishops	*Theological Training: A Way Ahead*, CHP, London, 1992
House of Bishops	*Theological Colleges – The Next Steps*, CHP, London, 1993
House of Bishops	*Breaking New Ground: Church Planting in the Church of England* (GS 1099), CHP, London, 1994
House of Bishops of the Church of England	*Ministry: A Pastoral Letter*, London, 1994
House of Bishops of the Church of England	*On The Way: Towards an Integrated Approach to Christian Initiation* (GS Misc 444), CHP, London, 1995
House of Bishops of the Church of England	*Eucharistic Presidency: A Theological Statement* (GS 1248), CHP, London, 1997
House of Bishops of the Church of England	*Good News People: Recognizing Diocesan Evangelists* (GS Misc 565), CHP, London, 1999
House of Bishops of the Church of England	*Bishops in Communion: Collegiality in the Service of the Koinonia of the Church*, CHP, London, 2000
Hull, J. M.	*Touching the Rock: An Experience of Blindness*, SPCK, London, 1990
Hurley, James B.	*Man and Woman in Biblical Perspective*, IVP, Leicester, 1981
International Ecumenical Working Group	*The Place of Deaf People in the Church* (1994 Canterbury Conference Papers), Visible Communications, Northampton, 1996
Irvine, Andrew	*Between Two Worlds*, Mowbray, Oxford, 1997

Jarrett, Martin and Kuhrt, Gordon	*What Do the Bishops' Selectors Look for?*, CPAS, Warwick, 1991
King, Philip	*Good News for a Suffering World*, Monarch, Crowborough, 1996
King, T. G.	*Readers: A Pioneer Ministry*, Central Readers' Board, London, 1973
Kuhrt, Gordon	*Believing in Baptism*, Mowbray, Oxford, 1987
Kuhrt, Gordon	*Issues in Theological Education and Training* (ABM Ministry Paper 15), CHP, London, 1997
Kuhrt, Gordon	*Clergy Security: A Discussion Paper, Ministry Division*, London, 1998
Kuhrt, Gordon	*An Introduction to Christian Ministry*, CHP, London, 2000
Legood, G. (ed.)	*Chaplaincy: The Church's Sector Ministries*, Cassell, 1999
MacDonald, Gordon	*Ordering your Private World*, Highland, 1984
Mantle, John	*Britain's First Worker-Priests*, SCM, London, 2000
Marriage, Alwyn	*The People of God: A Royal Priesthood*, DLT, London, 1995
Martin, B.	*A Sociology of Contemporary Social Change*, Oxford, Blackwell, 1981
Martineau, Robert	*The Office and Work of a Reader*, Mowbray, Oxford, 1980
Mason, Kenneth	*Priesthood and Society*, Canterbury Press, Norwich, 1992
Melinsky, Hugh	*Patterns of Ministry* (GS 202), CIO, London, 1974
Melinsky, M. A. H.	*The Shape of the Ministry*, Canterbury Press, Norwich, 1992
Ministry Co-ordinating Group	*The Church's Ministry: A Survey* (GS 459), CIO, London, 1980
Ministry Co-ordinating Group	*The Ordained Ministry: Numbers, Cost and Deployment* (GS 858), General Synod, London, 1988
Ministry Division	*Mission and Ministry: The Churches' Validation Framework for Theological Education*, CHP, London, 1999
Ministry Division	*Moderation of Reader Training 1994–1999*, London, 1999
Ministry Division	*Ministry Guidelines*, London, 2000
Ministry Division	*Bishops' Regulations for Reader Training*, London, 2000
Ministry Division	*Reader Ministry and Training 2000 and Beyond*, London, 2000

Ministry Division	*Managing Planned Growth: A Report by the Vote 1 Working Party* (GS Misc 597), London, 2000
Ministry Division	*Mind the Gap: Integrated Ministry for the Church's Ministers*, CHP, London, 2001
Ministry Division	*Statistics of Licensed Ministers*, London (annual)
Ministry Division	*A Climate of Encouragement*, London, forthcoming
Moberley, R. C.	*Ministerial Priesthood*, John Murray, London, 1897
Moody, Christopher	*Eccentric Ministry*, DLT, London, 1992
National Centre for Social Research	*British Social Attitudes*, Sage, 2000
Nixson, Rosie	*Liberating Women for the Gospel*, Hodder & Stoughton, London, 1997
Nelson, John (ed.)	*Management and Ministry*, published for Modem, Canterbury Press, Norwich, 1996
Nelson, John	*Leading, Managing, Ministering*, published for Modem, Canterbury Press, Norwich, 1999
Open University	*Constructing Deafness*
Orchard, H.	*Hospital Chaplaincy: Modern, Dependable?*, Academic Press, Sheffield, 2000
Parrott, David and Field, David	*Situations Vacant: A Guide to the Appointment Process in the Church of England*, Grove Pastoral 65, Cambridge, 1999
Paul, Leslie	*The Deployment and Payment of the Clergy*, CIO, London, 1964
Peyton, Nigel	*Dual-Role Ministry: First Choice or Mixed Blessing?*, Grove Pastoral 73, Cambridge, 1998
Price, Janice	*Telling our Faith Story* (GS Misc 550), CHP, London, 1999
Ramsey, Michael	*The Christian Priest Today*, SPCK, London, 1972 (revd 1985)
Redfern, Alistair	*Ministry and Priesthood*, DLT, London, 1999
Russell, Anthony	*The Clerical Profession*, SPCK, London, 1980
Shirras, Eddie and Walton, Steve	*Church of England: Obstacle or Opportunity?*, CPAS, Warwick, 1992
Spence, H.	*Decently and In Order: Practical Hints for Readers*, RSCM, 1995
Statistics Unit	*Statistics: A Tool for Mission*, London, CHP, 2000
Statistics Unit	*Church Statistics* (annual)
Stevens, Paul R.	*The Abolition of the Laity*, Paternoster, Carlisle, 1999
Storkey, Elaine	*What's Right with Feminism?*, London, SPCK, 1985

Storkey, Elaine and Hebblethwaite, Margaret	*Conversations on Christian Feminism*, London, 1999
Stott, John R. W.	*One People: Clergy and Laity in God's Church*, Falcon, London, 1969
Stott, John R. W.	*I Believe in Preaching*, Hodder and Stoughton, London, 1982
Thorne, Helen	*Journey to Priesthood*, University of Bristol, 1999
Tidball, Derek	*Skilful Shepherds*, Apollos, Leicester, 1986, 1997
Tillard, Jean	*What Priesthood has the Ministry?*, Grove Booklist on Ministry and Worship, Bramcote, 1973
Tiller, John	*A Strategy for the Church's Ministry*, CIO, London 1983
Tiller, John	*Tiller Ten Years On: Changing Prospects for the Church's Ministry*, Grove Books Pastoral 55, Bramcote, 1993
Walker, Andrew	*Restoring the Kingdom*, Hodder and Stoughton, London, 1998 (revd edn)
Walrond-Skinner, Sue	*Double Blessing*, Mowbray, London, 1998
Walton, Steve	*A Call to Live: Vocation for Everyone*, SPCK Triangle, London, 1994
Warren, Robert	*Being Human, Being Church*, Marshall Pickering, London, 1995
Warren, Robert	*Building Missionary Congregations*, CHP, London, 1995
Warren, Robert	*Signs of Life: How goes the Decade of Evangelism?* (GS 1182), CHP, London, 1996
World Council of Churches	*Baptism, Eucharist and Ministry*, WCC, Geneva, 1982

Index